WOMEN EMBRACING ISLAM

Women
Embracing
Islam

GENDER AND CONVERSION IN THE WEST

Edited by Karin van Nieuwkerk

UNIVERSITY OF TEXAS PRESS ⬥ AUSTIN

All photographs are by Kevin van der Brug,
who received the Gold Award in the
category "People and Portraits" from the
PANL (Photographers Association of the
Netherlands) for his series on Dutch Muslimas.

Requests for permission to reproduce material
from this work should be sent to:
  Permissions
  University of Texas Press
  P.O. Box 7819
  Austin, TX 78713-7819
  www.utexas.edu/utpress/about/
     bpermission.html

♾ The paper used in this book meets the mini-
mum requirements of ANSI/NISO Z39.48-1992
(R1997) (Permanence of Paper).

Library of Congress Cataloging-in-Publication Data

Women embracing Islam : gender and conversion in
the West / edited by Karin van Nieuwkerk.   1st ed.
        p.   cm.
    Includes bibliographical references and index.
    ISBN-13: 978-0-292-71273-7 (cloth : alk. paper)
    ISBN-10: 0-292-71273-1 (cloth : alk. paper)
    ISBN-13: 978-0-292-71302-4 (pbk. : alk. paper)
    ISBN-10: 0-292-71302-9 (pbk. : alk. paper)
  1. Muslim converts from Christianity—
Europe.   2. Muslim women—Europe.   3. Women
in Islam—Europe.   4. Gender identity—Europe.
5. Sex role—Religious aspects—Islam.
I. Nieuwkerk, Karin van, 1960–

BP170.5.W66   2006
297.082'091821—dc22

2005037096

Contents

Acknowledgments

I wish to thank several people who advised, criticized, and helped during the process of finishing this book. First of all I would like to thank ISIM (the International Institute for the Study of Islam in the Modern World, Leiden) for helping to organize and financing the symposium Gender and Conversion to Islam. Second, I would like to express my appreciation for the peer reviewers and editors of the University of Texas Press for their helpful comments. Third, I would like to thank Kevin van der Brug for generously providing his photo series on Dutch Muslimas for publication in this book, as well as the Dutch Muslimas for their permission to be represented in this book. Last but not least, I would like to express my gratitude to my partner Hans Stukart for his help in editing the manuscript.

Conversion and Gender, Two Contested Concepts

Willy Jansen

This book is the outcome of a conference, Gender and Conversion to Islam, held at Nijmegen, the Netherlands, in May 2003. It tackles a topic that is highly relevant at the moment. The two main concepts, conversion and gender, are in themselves and in their combination highly contested.

The past decades have seen a shift toward an increased interest in religion. The processes of conversion toward Islam have apparently accelerated significantly after September 11, 2001, as has the expression of suspicion and hostility among the Western Christian or agnostic population toward such converts. These religious shifts are increasingly given political weight. Conversion, in particular conversion to Islam, has a political dimension, whether intended by the convert or not. Understanding the effects this brings about, both in the convert and in the surrounding society, is of crucial importance and the subject of several of the following studies.

A discussion of conversion is not only socially but also theoretically relevant. The concept of conversion has been found difficult to define. The common definition of conversion as an act of free will, as an authentic experience, or, in the Christian Pauline sense, as an inward transformation after a thorough search and/or divine inspiration, has been criticized before. Conversion takes on a wide variety of forms and meanings, which can only be understood in the specific contexts and specific power relations of the individuals and groups involved. The individual's free choice of religion is more an ideal, abstract notion than an observable fact. The level of freedom varies according to the rules set by the available religions or the accessibility of information, as well as to the historical context. The scholars in this volume have applied themselves to the task of uncovering the level of freedom within the context of restraints and opportunities, and indicated in which cases the concept of conversion is appropriate and what it exactly means. They have shown how personal conversion narratives form part of several wider discourses. Conversion is analyzed as a complex social phenomenon rather than only as an individual spiritual transition.

Conversion, beyond being a personal experience and an expression of personal religious preference, has a much wider impact and meaning. It nearly always is a confrontation between two religions, the receiving and the deserted religion. All religions, including world religions like Christianity and Islam, have at certain points in their history tried to attract believers, whether by reason, by offering privileges, or through the sword. While the receiving religion attracts and respects new believers, and may openly target potential converts by missionary action or give rewards to newcomers in the community of believers, the deserted religion will reject and punish any apostates, and denounce the calls made by other religions. Punishments for apostasy may range from calling names—with negative connotations such as renegade, apostate, backslider, or turncoat—to ostracism, forfeiture of inheritance rights, loss of guardianship of children, loss of conjugal rights, or even death. Conversion therefore always has a double face, from the perspective of the receiving and of the departed religious group.

Religious boundaries are often vigilantly guarded, opened up for eligible newcomers, but quickly closed for people who want to leave. Religions differ over time and place in the level of control they are able or willing to exert over their boundaries. Conversion can therefore only be discussed in historical contexts and by taking the power relations between the particular religions into account.

The concept of gender is, like that of conversion, highly contested as well. Here it is most interesting in its combination with conversion. The two are connected on different levels. First, gender figures in the different participation levels of women and men in processes of conversion. When women convert more often to Islam, why would that be so? How is this connected to different positions of women and men or to notions about them? These are some of the questions answered in this volume.

Relevant in this context is the notion of the person who decides on an inward transformation. In many cultures, notions of the person are not applied in the same way for women as for men. Due to their social position, women often have less power of agency in many fields, including religion. For example, in my research I found that in Jordanian history, both the Christian minority and the Muslim population adhered to the rule that "a woman will follow the man," indicating that upon marriage a woman was supposed to take on a man's religious denomination (Jansen 2004). This custom implies that autonomy of the person in accepting religious beliefs is less recognized for women than for men. The level of sincerity or authenticity normally requested of converts is as a result less strictly imposed on women. More than men, women are seen as passive and obedient. Many life decisions are made for them by the family, including the choice of religion. This happens in spite of general views that women and men are equally responsible for their own salvation and that conversion needs to be based on authenticity. There are cases in which women refuse to follow their husband's religious choices, but this often has severe consequences ranging from nonacceptance by their in-laws to loss of legal rights to their children, pension, and inheritance.

Gender also impinges on the protection of religious boundaries. The different Christian churches in Jordan had agreed in a covenant to solve the problem of mixed marriages by letting the wife follow the husband. Mixed marriage among the Christian denominations was quite common, and it was expected that the losses and gains in female church members would in the end be balanced. Crossings between Christianity and Islam were far more difficult. In Islam certain rules developed in order to avoid the effects of such submission of women to men and the resulting loss of female believers. A Christian woman was therefore allowed to marry a Muslim man, as it was thought that she would follow his religion and thus increase the community of believers, and even if she did not, the children would still be Muslim. The reverse, a Muslim woman marrying a Christian man, was not possible; it would mean the loss of a Muslim and was therefore forbidden. Such marriages can still not be legally contracted in Jordan. In such a context, not only are women given less voice and autonomy in deciding about their religion, but also the protection of religious boundaries takes on a specific gendered character.

The association of women's religious choices with their role in the family is repeated in theories that attribute the greater frequency of conversion of women to their family relations. The narratives in the following articles indeed show that quite a few women converted to Islam because they wanted to "follow their husband and his family" when they married a Muslim migrant. This social pattern does not necessarily exclude a "genuine inward transformation." Yet, the emic conviction of genuineness in the conversion narratives can well be combined with the etic positioning of the convert's actions and convictions in this wider context. The understanding of the larger impact of social ties for women's conversions, compared to men's, is seldom a sufficient explanation for the gender differences.

The articles in this volume repeatedly show a theoretical shift toward a focus on the agency of women. They uncover women's own views and actions toward conversion, their agency both in freely choosing a new path and in spreading the Call. New religions tend to target women and to be particularly attractive to women. The first Muslim convert was a woman, Khadija, Muhammad's first wife, who supported her husband morally and financially. The first Christian, that is, the first person who was asked to believe in Jesus' resurrection, was also a woman, Mary Magdalene. Young religions or new offshoots of established religions (like Sufism in Islam and Protestantism in Christianity) tend to target women. Unfortunately, many do so only in the beginning. Once established and grown, many a religion has ousted women from religious leadership. This raises questions on women's activism in both expanding religions and in contributing to the development of their doctrines.

In the focus on women's agency, not only the reasons why women convert, but also their role in actively spreading the faith, will be discussed. Spiritual reasons are likely to take center stage, but social, material, or political aspects need to be taken into account as well. They do not necessarily exclude each other.

Second, gender not only intersects with the freedom and reasons to convert, but also with the effects of conversion. It affects the ways in which the person expresses and incorporates his or her new beliefs, and how others react to that. One example is the adoption of the symbols used to express the new faith. For instance, a beard or male circumcision evokes far less reaction than taking on the veil. Western society has made the *hijab* and the subordinated position of women into symbols of the "Otherness" of Islam, which raises the question of how female converts deal with this and give meaning to it. Another example of the gendered consequences is that female converts to Islam are confronted with a larger gap than men in the gender positions in the respective religious cultures. A Christian woman converting to Islam has to give up more freedoms (as defined by her culture of birth) than a man. Following Anne Sofie Roald's line of thought, it can moreover be expected that women need a longer period of time to accommodate and familiarize themselves with the new paradigm. The suggestion by Margot Badran and Gwendolyn Zoharah Simmons to see whether this leads to feminist activity by converted women is therefore very exciting.

As this book will show, there are many points of connection between gender and conversion. It is a rich and fascinating field to explore.

Reference

Jansen, W. 2004. "Conversion, Marriage and Gender: Jordanians and the Christian Mission." *SMT Swedish Missiological Themes/Svenksk Missions Tidskrift* 92 (1): 99–122.

WOMEN EMBRACING ISLAM

Gender and Conversion to Islam in the West

Karin van Nieuwkerk

Conversion to Islam by women in the West may evoke a range of sensitive issues. Crossing religious and ethnic boundaries generally disturbs conventions and can engender hostility. Female conversions may raise even stronger reactions because traditions have often constructed women as symbols of ethnic and religious boundaries. Female conversion to Islam summons up particularly fierce battles because gender issues have been pivotal in the construction of Otherness between "Islam" and the "West." Female converts are thus regularly treated with hostility. A Dutch convert said, "People stare at you because they see that you are white. Maybe that is the cause of the aggression; you are a traitor to the race." By some Muslims, however, conversion by Western women is proclaimed and promoted. "Despite all the negative propaganda regarding Muslim women, female converts to Islam outnumber their male counterparts by an estimated ratio of 4:1!" Thus we are informed by "The True Religion," a Web site with a clear missionary goal.[1]

One contentious issue is the extent of the phenomenon. Is the number of converts increasing? Are more women attracted to Islam than men? In a videotape, Osama Bin Laden told his Saudi visitor that after the 9/11 "operation" more Dutch people had converted to Islam than in the previous eleven years.[2] Similar rumors regarding Americans were spreading in the United States.[3] These claims, as well as the statement that women converts outnumber men "by an estimated ratio of 4:1," are clearly part of an ideological struggle (see also Allievi 1998, 241). Some academic research indicates, however, that maybe not four-fifths, but still two-thirds, of converts to Islam are female (Wohlrab-Sahr 1999b; Wagtendonk 1994; Haleem 2003). Whether this is generally valid is not clear. At this point we must simply state that we do not know exactly, since for most countries no statistics are available or the statistics do not distinguish between second-generation-born Muslims and native converts. What is clear, though, is that gender issues are focal in the discussions of conversion to Islam, whether statistically, ideologically, or symbolically.

This book intends to go beyond the claims, competitions, and statistics, and to investigate why women are attracted to Islam. What are their motives and backgrounds and to what kind of Islam are they converting? To which messages are they attracted and in which ways? It will show the wealth of experiences behind conversion, as well as analyze the narratives that express this experience. Conversion is not only a momentary experience but an ongoing process of religious, social, and cultural transformation. How do converts create, embody, and transmit their new identity? What are the reactions and responses of society toward converts? What is the role converts play in society at large? What is their contribution to discourses on gender and Islam? This book will address these issues and provide empirical and comparative materials from Europe, the United States, and South Africa.

Despite the importance of conversion and gender to Islam, these topics have hardly been studied. The literature on conversion particularly deals with new religious movements in the United States (Bruce 1999; Aldridge 2000)[4] and does not include conversion to Islam. Although the spread of Islam in historical perspective has received attention (Bulliet 1979; Dutton 1999), conversions in present-day Western countries are not widely covered. Within the existing literature on contemporary conversion to Islam, a gender focus is not yet well developed. Gender issues are crucial, however, for our understanding of conversion to Islam, a task this volume intends to undertake.

In this introduction, I will give an overview of the current state of research concerning gender and conversion to Islam. I will start with an examination of the conversion literature, followed by a discussion on what Islam has to "offer" converts. Next, I will examine what the literature has thus far mentioned about gender and conversion to Islam. Lastly, I will propose a tentative approach to the study of gender and conversion to Islam.

Conversion

There is a huge body of literature on conversion that is also relevant for the study of conversion to Islam. Historical developments noted by sociologists of religion, such as pluralism, secularization, and privatization of religion, are vital preconditions for the state of religion in general. As such, they are also important for conversion, including conversion to Islam (Luckmann 1999; Allievi 1998). In addition, the general process of modernization and individualization, which makes the individual agent the center of his or her biography, has a direct bearing on conversion (Hofmann 1997). The changed place of religion and the process of individualization transformed religion and religious goods into matters of individual choice. Actors choose among several religious options the worldview that suits them best. Ideas of religion as a commodity on the expanding market of religious goods, picked and chosen by religious agents, are particularly applied to new religious movements (Bruce 1999; Iannaccone 1990; Finke and Stark 2000). Yet ideas of the religious market and rational choice can also be applied to Islam (Allievi 1998; Wohlrab-Sahr this volume). Islam has become one of the players on the religious market in the West, and its message makes sense to individual converts.

Besides analyses of these general sociohistorical developments, conversion theories developed within the body of anthropological, sociological, and religious studies clarify aspects of conversion to Islam. Poston (1992) deals with different forms of da'wa, calling to Islam, in the West. He applies Lofland and Stark's "predisposing factors" for conversion and Starbuck's list of "motivational factors" to his sample of seventy-two American and European converts to Islam and tries to present a profile of the "typical" convert to Islam. The material in the present volume, however, shows that it is difficult to assume any typicality among converts. They are a far too heterogeneous group. Köse (1996) studies native British Muslims and applies several psychological and religious theories to his sample of seventy converts. He critically assesses "crises" theories with regard to the preconversion life histories. He finds that commonly held ideas on conversion as being induced by moral and religious crises of adolescence or failed socialization do not apply in the case of Islam.

In addition to typologies of converts, diverse routes to conversion are analyzed (Rambo 1993). Allievi (1998, 1999, and 2002) develops a useful typology of conversion itineraries to Islam. He distinguishes relational from rational conversions. Relational conversions are further subdivided into instrumental and noninstrumental forms. Noninstrumental relational conversions are induced by relationships with Muslims either by way of marriage, family, meeting immigrants, or traveling. Instrumental conversions are usually related to marriage of a European male with a Muslim woman and do not necessarily entail a religious transformation. The rational conversions, in contrast, are not induced by personal contacts but rather by an intellectual search. This form is therefore more specifically Islamic in its discourse and rationalizations. Allievi further subdivides the rational itinerary according to intellectual, political, or mystically oriented paths.

Besides theories on the background and trajectories of converts to Islam, some analyses of testimonies and conversion narratives are available. A few books have been published that contain conversion stories or are descriptive in nature (Anway 1995; Crijnen 1999; Haleem 2003). Several Web sites have been created offering a great amount of testimonies. Hermansen has studied conversion narratives of European and Euro-American Muslims written between 1900 and 1980. Insights from postcolonial theory are applied to understanding the historical shifts that occur in converts' views of Islam and the Muslim world, as well as in their self-presentation (1999). Conversion testimonies are a specific genre with a particular narrative structure (Beckford 1978; Stromberg 1993; Luckmann 1986; Snow and Machalek 1983, 1984; Ulmer 1988). Conversion narratives are created backwards; that is, they are told after the conversion, and thus past events are reinterpreted in light of current convictions. This reconstructing process takes place not only at the individual level but also at the group level. In the process of telling and retelling conversion experiences, a common model is created (Hofmann 1997; van Nieuwkerk this volume). Converts do not simply reproduce a rehearsed script but include elements of the new religion's ideological rationale into their narratives. It is thus important to analyze the goals and ideologies that are promoted by Islamic organizations and Web sites and the specific *da'wah* functions they perform (Haddad this volume).

Conversion is increasingly analyzed as an ongoing process. Rambo (1993) developed a dynamic and processual conversion theory, integrating research within various disciplines. Conversion takes place in several stages and is usually experienced as a substantial transformation of religious, social, and cultural aspects of daily life. Conversion to Islam is embodied through taking up new bodily practices pertaining to praying, fasting, and food. In addition, important markers of identity are often changed, such as the name and appearance, including *hijab* or occasionally *niqab*. Moreover, converting frequently leads to changing social and cultural practices, for instance, those related to celebrations or contacts with the opposite sex. These transformations regularly create problems with the family of origin (Bourque this volume; Allievi this volume; van Nieuwkerk 2004).

Whereas for some new Muslims conversion is radical, others slowly transform aspects of their identity and practice. Roald (this volume) describes a three-stage process for most European converts, the stages being "love," "disappointment," and "maturity." In the initial phase many converts tend to be emotionally obsessed with the new religion and want to practice every detail of the Islamic precepts. The second stage is strongly linked to a disappointment with born-Muslim behavior and ideas, and here some converts tend to turn away from Islam. During the third stage many new Muslims search for new understandings of Islamic ideas and attitudes according to the particular cultural context they live in. Sultán (1999) observes that, paradoxically, the features that originally attracted the converts, in particular gender issues, are later seen as sources of conflict.

Converts play an important role in society and often function as cultural and political mediators between the state and Muslim communities. Some of them are engaged in the interpretation of the Islamic sources and developing new discourses (Allievi 1998; Wagtendonk 1994; Gerholm 1988; El Houari Setta 1999; Roald this volume). Allievi further maintains that converts are crucial in three fields. Converted intellectuals, in particular, offer legitimatization in the eyes of society. Besides, converts can provide confirmation for immigrants of the rightness of their faith. Moreover, converts form an element of guarantee, since they are citizens who cannot, even if they act as militant Islamic leaders, be expelled from the country (1998, 2002). Female converts also play a role in the development of new discourses on gender and Islam (Roald this volume). Converts such as Amina Wadud (1999) are important in the Islamic feminist production of knowledge. Recent research indicates that Islamic feminism is also gaining ground among female converts in the Netherlands, England, and South Africa (Badran this volume).

Islam

Whereas the push factors have been reasonably studied, the pull factors have received less attention. With regard to the question of why people turn to Islam, that is, what is the specific appeal of Islam, less material is available. This raises immediately the question "which Islam?" There are many converts to Sufism, which has "religious goods" to offer that contrast with those of modernist or Islamist versions of Islam. Also the large differences within the group of converts with regard to gender and ethnicity, as for instance the differences between Euro-American or African American converts, make it difficult to assume a single appeal of Islam.

Several authors indicate that Sufism is the main agent for conversion to Islam in the West. A considerable number of people first convert to Sufism and then to Islam. While in the 1960s, Sufism was part of the "hippie" movement and divorced from its Islamic roots, in the 1990s, it was increasingly known as Islamic mysticism (Jawad this volume; Köse 1996; Hofmann 1997; Allievi 1998). Jawad (this volume) highlights the Sufi appeal for women. She outlines how the Sufi emphasis upon feminine values pertaining to the family and the feminine element in spiritual life can be attractive to women in the West.

Alternatively, a modernist interpretation of Islam, with a message of rationality, is spreading and resonates in conversion stories on the Internet (van Nieuwkerk this volume). Köse shows that his informants interpret their conversion as a journey from the secular to the sacred. Islam offers them a practical way to direct the everyday life toward God. Since Islam is an encompassing religious worldview and does not compartmentalize religion, choosing Islam enables the converts to connect their daily life to their beliefs (1999). The religious discourse of converts on the attraction of Islam over Christianity converges at certain points. For instance, the absence of the concept of the Trinity and Jesus' prophethood is deemed more logical. Also, the encompassing ritual praxis and the direct accessibility of God without mediators make Islam seem a rational and undeniable truth (Allievi 1998; Anway 1995; Daynes 1999; Hofmann 1997; Van Nieuwkerk this volume).

Dannin (1996) investigates the appeal of Islam for a specific group of converts, the incarcerated African Americans in a New York prison. Using a Foucauldian approach, he analyzes Islam's attractiveness as a counterdisciplinary force in resistance to the prison's own stringent discipline. Islam offers the prisoners an activity structure including such features as prayers and lessons, and an alternative social space within the confinement of the walls. The new Islamic identity also means a fresh start. The Islamic counterculture is attractive because, according to Dannin, it has the power to transcend the material and often brutally inhuman conditions of the prison (1996, 144). McCloud understands the conversion of African Americans to Islam as a response to American racism (1991, 1995). Islam promises a new identity, a feeling of "somebodiness," denied by the dominant culture. Conversion brought liberation from Christian domination, perceived as the root of their oppression for its glorification of suffering and promise of redemption in the hereafter. The "somebodiness" partially achieved by conversion to Islam also results, however, in new forms of oppression. Simmons, for instance, shows that the Nation of Islam attracts women, while at the same time promoting a subordinated role for women (this volume).

Despite the different Islamic "offers," a common observation is that Islam appeals because it gives the convert the greatest possible contrast with the culture he or she comes from (Allievi 1998; Hofmann 1997; Wohlrab-Sahr 1999b). In particular, converts who are critical of Western society are fascinated by and attracted to the Otherness of Islam. It becomes an ideological and political framework from which they criticize Western society. According to Wohlrab-Sahr conversion becomes "a means of articulating within one's own social context one's distance from this context and one's conflictive relationship towards it" (1999a, 352). This conflictive relationship can be the result of a (politically) critical stance or the result of a sense of marginalization. Hofmann also relates Islam's attraction to the converts' possibility of provoking society at large (1997, 121). Yet, on the other hand, it is observed by Hofmann (1997) as well as Allievi (this volume) that many of Islam's offers, particularly relating to gender issues, are close to what former generations in the West found self-evident. Islam can also appeal because it restores familiar notions on gender and the family (see below).

Allievi distinguishes different "offers" for the various conversion itineraries. Whereas the "relational converts" are attracted to general aspects such as belonging to a different culture and having a sense of community, "rational converts" adopt a more specific Islamic discourse. In their formulations Islam is perceived as clear, simple, and rational. It has sources that everyone can consult, without mediators. For the politically inclined converts, Islam provides a "spiritualization" of politics. For the mystically inclined the Sufi tradition in Islam has a wide appeal as well. It is precisely Islam's broad spectrum of offers, religiously, ideologically, and in orthopraxy, that constitute its appeal to many converts. This warns us not to essentialize Islam, but to systematically analyze whatever elements of Islam have to offer diverse groups of converts at different times.

Gender

Gender is a crucial issue in conversion to Islam. Sultán (1999) mentions that female converts in Sweden are particularly attracted to Islamic conceptions of manhood and womanhood and to its clear moral boundaries and rules, an observation I can confirm for Dutch converts. Hofmann (1997) also theorizes the plausibility of Islamic notions of the family and construction of masculinity and femininity for German converts. Wohlrab-Sahr (1999a, 1999b, and this volume) did a comparative study of German and American male and female converts. I will summarize some ideas of the last two authors, as they provide important insights for the study of gender and conversion to Islam.

Wohlrab-Sahr connects conversion to biographical experiences. She defines conversion as the symbolic transformation of crisis experiences. In her research she found three different realms of problems that were transformed by conversion to Islam. The first type of conversion is related to issues of sexuality and gender relations. Converts report previously experiencing feelings of personal devaluation with regard to sexuality and gender norms. Female converts mention such problems as broken marriages, promiscuity, and sexual relationships with men from marginal groups. Male converts have often experienced problems with regard to transgression of the male gender identity, for example, loss of the dominant position in the family and shame inflicted by sexual conduct of female members of the family. Converts seek new boundaries, rules, and interpretations. Islam offers a clear model that articulates and solves the experience of transgressed sexual norms and uncertain relationships between the sexes. The second type of problems Wohlrab-Sahr distinguishes is related to social mobility. In case of a failed attempt at upward social mobility, e.g., due to drug addiction or criminality, conversion to Islam can provide an alternative and new career. Thirdly, she mentions problems related to nationality and ethnicity or problems of "belonging." Converting to Islam brings a new kind of belonging and community into existence. Islam thus offers converts the possibility of transforming experiences of devaluation, degradation, and disintegration.

Hofmann (1997) focuses on female converts and issues of gender in Germany. She illuminates female conversion against the background of the process of individualization. Individuals' possibilities to create their own biographies invoke feelings of freedom as well as risk. Failed life histories are experienced as personal failures. Hofmann argues that the process of female individualization shows ruptures and contradictions. Women are strongly connected to the family, which is associated with such values as belonging and connectedness. These community values contrast with dominant "modern" values such as rationality, individual performance, and personal perseverance. Women are confronted with conflicting expectations in different stages of their lives. They are brought up with ideals of individual autonomy but are expected to put these ideals aside at the moment they raise a family. If they decide to stay at home when they have small children, they experience the lack of esteem for this decision in society at large and as a result of their own socialization. According to Hofmann, the German-Islamic discourse offers a solution to these conflicting demands. The issues of family, marriage, and relationship between the sexes are given primacy in the

Islamic discourse. This articulation of Muslim values offers clear concepts of marriage and motherhood. The different and distinct natures of males and females, and particularly ideas on women's capacity as mothers and caretakers, are not only Islamically defined but also plausible in light of a deeply anchored German "cultural knowledge." This cultural knowledge about essential manhood and womanhood, however, is no longer uncontested. Today's German-Islamic discourse restores these ideas to their original position of "truth." Thus, women regain the possibility of living according to their "feminine nature." Contrary to Western socialization, Islam highly values motherhood and the nurturing qualities of women. Motherhood is not merely valued in Islam, but acknowledged as an important performance equal to labor and is also supported by men.

For converts in this society, German-Islamic discourse thus enables a critical stance toward German society. It uses aspects of feminist discourse, for example, in criticizing the prevalence of male norms and the devaluation of female norms. It also attacks the "Western exploitation of female sexuality and the marketing of the female body." These critiques hinge on ideas derived from radical feminism or differential feminism. Yet, whereas radical feminism tries to change patriarchal relationships, the German-Islamic discourse tries to restore the original "natural" order. In particular, the fact that German-Islamic discourse refers to a stock of common cultural knowledge that is contested and disparaged gives the Islamic reformulation an innovative and critical content. These critical yet familiar views on gender and sexuality make the Islamic discourse attractive and plausible to German female converts.

Hofmann's ideas are valuable in understanding Dutch female converts (van Nieuwkerk 2004) as well as Scandinavian converts (Roald this volume). The latter embrace the concept of "equity" because it includes the ideal of equal opportunities, but rejects the definition of women and men as "equal." Dutch female converts use a syncretic differential feminist discourse combining essentialist notions of womanhood and manhood with critical views on the prevalence of male norms and sexual exploitation of the female body. Yet I observed more variety of voices and also critical stances toward the essentialist discourse on women, gender, and Islam than Hofmann shows in the German case. It is therefore important to assess critically the "feminist" content of the gender discourses as developed by converts. In her contribution to this volume Badran analyzes the contribution of female converts to Islamic feminist discourses, which differs from the equity approach. Converts can

also shift position over time from an equity approach to a feminist understanding and critical reading of the Qur'an.

Discourses and Identities

Whereas Wohlrab-Sahr concentrates on functions of conversion in solv-
ing biographical problems, Hofmann focuses on the plausibility of Islamic
discourse for individual converts. They represent two main approaches to
gender and conversion to Islam. The first approach deals with conversion as
creating or gaining a new identity. It analyzes biographies, the factors that
can explain people's propensities to convert, and the experiences of crisis
they have had. It focuses on the problems converts have encountered and
how conversion has given them a new sense of self and helped them to create a new identity or a new form of belonging. It analyzes motives, routes,
and themes in converts' life stories that make them susceptible to conversion. Whereas this approach highlights the meaningfulness of conversion
in a person's life, the reason why individuals have opted for this particular
solution, that is, conversion to Islam, is not always clear. What is meaningful
in the message of Islam? Why Islam and which Islam? Which discourses are
they themselves creating? This approach thus underestimates the different
kinds of Islamic discourses that converts refer to.

The second approach deals with the diverse discourses and narratives produced in the communities of converts. It aims to critically deconstruct the
discourse and warns us not to confuse conversion narratives with conversion motives. This approach focuses on how discourses and stories are created and re-created in converts' communities and how they become meaningful in communicating conversion experiences. It analyzes the message
of Islam and how this can be attractive for individuals or groups. Whereas
this approach analyzes how discourses of Islam are created and spread and
become significant, the biographical aspects of the receivers are not clearly
included in the perspective. How individuals come to be attracted to these
discourses, how they make sense in converts' unfolding life stories, and how
the discourses are turned into lived experiences are questions beyond the
scope of this approach.

Both approaches are therefore important and valid in themselves. Yet,
combining insights from both identity studies and discourse analyses gen-
erates a more complex understanding. We need to understand both the receivers and the messages. Conversion is a multilayered, continuous process

in which new identities and discourses are produced and reproduced. Some individuals can become susceptible to conversion through personal trajectories and biographical experiences. Yet the new message must be plausible. In my study on Dutch female converts it became clear that their biographies and chosen modes of Islamic discourse were intimately connected. Whereas for some women a psychological crisis and addiction to medications convinced them of the natural and healthy character of Islam, for others sexual harassment or divorced parents made them realize the importance of maintaining a certain distance between the sexes. What Islam meant to them and the discourse they constructed were directly connected to their life stories.

Islam and Islamic discourse can be plausible to individuals for different reasons, and individuals can be addressed by Islamic discourse in manifold aspects of their identities. People convert to Islam as persons with specific professional, religious, racial, or ethnic identities. Converts not only convert as individuals but also as males or females or as Europeans or African Americans. Various aspects of a person's identity inform discourses, and discourses appeal to different aspects of identities. Islam not only offers various religious discourses, it also offers a discourse on race and ethnicity and a gender discourse that can appeal to people.

In an approach that analyzes conversion as a continuous process of embodying social practice, it is particularly important to investigate both discourses and identities. Conversion does not stop at the moment of embracing Islam, and it is not solely a mental activity of accepting a new belief. It requires embodiment of new social and religious practices. Within this process of embodiment and learning new practices, new ideas and insights are created that can generate new discourses and receptivity to other voices of Islamic discourse. In different periods of converts' lives, a revised or novel discourse can make sense. The approach to studying conversion as a process of embodying new practices brings to the fore the realization that identities and discourses are implicated in each other. Converts live religious practices related to discourses that are meaningful to them in specific contexts. Experiences with the new practices will lead to renewed understandings, interpretations, and negotiations of existing discourses. It is a continuous interplay. While their biographies unfold, converts remake and negotiate discourses, and these in turn inform the process of identity construction.

We thus need a multilayered approach to conversion. It is important to understand the personal trajectories and biographies as well as the diverse Islamic discourses on gender, race, and ethnicity in order to understand the plausibility of conversion to Islam for male and female converts in the West. We thus avoid an essentialist approach toward Islam and are able to investigate the diverse itineraries and discourses of various groups of converts in different countries. Inevitably this approach will not lead to any firm conclusions. The question of why women convert to Islam will not lead to a single and definite answer, but rather invoke a complex contextual picture of identities and discourses. It will sensitize us to the many ways in which these women make sensible choices, choices that can change over time.

On the Contributions

The essays in this collection are the outcome of a symposium, Gender and Conversion to Islam, which was organized by the Institute for the Study of Islam in the Modern World (ISIM), the Netherlands, on the 16th and 17th of May 2003. Our purpose in this collection of essays is to further our understanding of gender and conversion to Islam. As the authors are historians, sociologists, anthropologists, and theologians, the outcome is an interdisciplinary volume. The contributions add to our theoretical as well as empirical understanding. This book provides case studies of the manifold convert trajectories and narratives, and of discourses of and about them. It covers different forms of Islam, such as Sunni, Salafi, and Sufi Islam, as well as the Nation of Islam. It deals with the creation, maintenance, and transmission of Muslim identities. Despite the diversity of the research materials, the focus on gender allows for many connections to emerge as well.

In the first section gender and conversion to Islam are contextualized. Yvonne Haddad provides an overview of the phenomenon of conversion of American women. She outlines the diverse Muslim missionary groups and their specific *da'wa* discourses and activities in the West. She tries to answer why white American women convert to Islam and what it is they convert to. She also deals with the relations between immigrants and white converts. She concludes that conversion serves the multiple ends of spiritual fulfillment, community belonging, a husband and family, and often a new sense of self-assurance.

Anne Sofie Roald shows the development of a transcultural Islam. She understands the transformations from the late 1990s onward as the latest stage in the development of a Scandinavian Islam. She observes a growing acceptance of cultural diversity in the Muslim community on both a global and local scale. Within a creolization of practice and discourse new converts first tend to defend traditional gender systems. However, as they go through various stages in the conversion process they tend to incorporate Scandinavian ideals of gender relations into the Islamic framework. The new Muslims nonetheless diverge from the majority society in embracing concepts of gender equity rather than gender equality.

Monika Wohlrab-Sahr critically assesses the theoretical debates on rational-choice theory and concepts of the market that have been centrally important in the field of sociology of religion during the last years. She argues that we need to consider conversions as religious choices within a pluralistic market. Nevertheless we need to transcend the limitations of rational-choice theory. She introduces an approach that combines biographical analysis with a functional approach, illustrating her arguments with comparative material from Germany and the United States.

The second section focuses on conversion discourses and narratives. Karin van Nieuwkerk compares online and offline conversion narratives. She aims at understanding the different discourses that could help to explain why Islam can be attractive for women in the West. Besides the biographical narratives, the ethnic, religious, and gender discourses of new Muslimas are analyzed. Not only the content, but also the different contexts in which the narratives are produced—that is, fieldwork in the Netherlands versus self-written testimonies on the Internet—are compared.

Stefano Allievi discusses the shifting significance of boundary definitions, which he terms the *haram/halal* frontiers. He particularly focuses on narratives about wearing the *hijab,* an issue that is symbolically important both inside and outside the community of converts. He also suggests de-Islamizing approaches to conversion to Islam. The so-called "Islamic" discourses pertaining to gender that are attractive to converts are not distinctively Islamic, but very close to familiar European gender discourses of former generations.

In the third section, Islamic paradigms and trajectories are central. Haifaa Jawad brings forward the Sufi paradigm. Sufism has been and continues to be an important agent for conversion to Islam. She outlines how the Sufis' theological emphasis upon feminine values pertaining to the family and the feminine element in spiritual life can be attractive to women in the West.

Gwendolyn Zoharah Simmons uses her own experiences to contextualize conversion to Islam in the United States amongst African Americans. She particularly focuses on the Nation of Islam (NOI). She traces the attraction of the NOI to black-nationalist sensibilities on the part of the converts,

14

WOMEN EMBRACING ISLAM

which are a product of their exclusion from mainstream American life. She analyzes the gender discourse in the NOI and the subordination of women in the organization.

Margot Badran compares life stories of female converts from the Netherlands, England, and South Africa. During her research on Islamic feminism it became clear that converts are particularly important in articulating Islamic feminist discourses. She details women's trajectories toward a feminist understanding of Islam.

In the final section, transmission and creation of Islamic identities are examined. Nicole Bourque focuses on Scottish female converts to Islam and the way they re-create and renegotiate religious, national, and gender identities. She demonstrates that the creation of a new Muslim identity also entails the embodiment of this new identity by taking up new bodily practices.

Marcia Hermansen addresses the transmission of female Muslim identity by converts in the West. She focuses on mothers who converted between 1967 and 1980 and analyzes how they have tried to raise their daughters as Muslims. Her interviews with converted mothers suggest that despite the challenges of transmitting an identity that the mothers chose with great conviction but that daughters inherit, many, but not all, daughters absorb and retain a Muslim identity. The presence of a community of Muslims and a Muslim peer group, as well as a committed Muslim father, is influential in the converts' successful transmission of Muslim identities to the next generation.

Notes

1. http://www.thetruereligion.org.
2. *NRC Handelsblad,* December 14, 2001.
3. See Haddad this volume and articles at the Web site "The True Religion."
4. At the conference Cultures of Conversion: Paradigms, Poetics and Politics (held at Groningen University May 21–24, 2003, the Netherlands) it was concluded that the theme of conversion has generally been neglected. Only the theory of rational choice has made theoretical contributions to the theme of conversion in religious studies or the sociology of religion. This paradigm is critically assessed by Bruce (1999) and Wohlrab-Sahr (this volume).

References

Aldridge, A. 2000. *Religion in the Contemporary World: A Sociological Introduction.* Cambridge: Polity Press.

Allievi, St. 1998. *Les convertis à l'islam. Les nouveaux musulmans d'Europe.* Paris: L'Harmattan.

———. 1999. "Pour une sociologie des conversions: lorsque des Européens deviennent musulmans." *Social Compass* 46 (3): 283–300.

———. 2002. "Converts and the Making of European Islam." *ISIM Newsletter* 11: 1, 26.

Anway, C. L. 1991. "American Women Choosing Islam." In *Muslims on the Americanization Path?* ed. Y. Yazbeck Haddad and John L. Esposito, pp. 145–160. Oxford: Oxford University Press.

———. 1995. *Daughters of Another Path: Experiences of American Women Choosing Islam.* Lee's Summit, Mo.: Yawna Publications.

Beckford, J. A. 1978. "Accounting for Conversion." *British Journal of Sociology* 29 (2): 249–262.

Bruce, St. 1999. *Choice and Religion: A Critique of Rational Choice Theory.* Oxford: Oxford University Press.

Bulliet, R. W. 1979. *Conversion to Islam in the Medieval Period.* Cambridge, Mass.: Harvard University Press.

Crijnen, T. 1999. *Veertien portretten van Nieuwe Nederlandse en Vlaamse Moslims.* Amsterdam: Bulaaq.

Dannin, R. 1996. "Island in a Sea of Ignorance: Dimensions of the Prison Mosque." In *Making Muslim Space in North America and Europe,* ed. B. Daly Metcalf, pp. 131–147. Berkeley: University of California Press.

Daynes, S. 1999. "Processus de conversion et modes d'identification à l'islam. L'exemple de la France et des Etats-Unis." *Social Compass* 46 (3): 313–323.

Dutton, Y. 1999. "Conversion to Islam: Qur'anic Paradigm." In *Religious Conversion, Contemporary Practices and Controversies,* ed. C. Lamb and M. Bryant, pp. 151–166. London and New York: Cassell.

Finke, R., and R. Stark. 2000. *Acts of Faith: Explaining the Human Side of Religion.* Berkeley: University of California Press.

Gerholm, T. 1988. "Three European Intellectuals as Converts to Islam: Cultural Mediators or Social Critics?" In *The New Islamic Presence in Western Europe,* ed. T. Gerholm and Y. G. Lithman, pp. 263–278. London: Mansell.

Haleem, H. A. 2003. "Experiences, Needs and Potentials of New Muslim Women in Britain." In *Muslim Women in the United Kingdom and Beyond: Experiences and Images,* ed. H. Jawad and T. Benn, pp. 91–105. Leiden: Brill.

Hermansen, M. 1999. "Roads to Mecca: Conversion Narratives of European and Euro-American Muslims." In *Muslim World* 89 (1): 56–90.

Hofmann, G. 1997. *Muslimin werden. Frauen in Deutschland konvertieren zum Islam.* Frankfurt: Universität Frankfurt.

Houari Setta, El. 1999. "Le Suisse converti à l'islam: émergence d'un nouvel acteur social." *Social Compass* 46 (3): 337–349.

Iannaccone, L. R. 1990. "Religious Practice: A Human Capital Approach." *Journal for the Scientific Study of Religion* 29 (3): 297–314.

Köse, A. 1996. *Conversion to Islam: A Study of Native British Converts.* London and New York: Kegan Paul International.

———. 1999. "The Journey from the Secular to the Sacred: Experiences of Native British Converts to Islam." *Social Compass* 46 (3): 301–312.

Luckmann, Th. 1986. "Grundformen der gesellschaftlichen Vermittlung des Wissens: Kommunikative Gattungen." In *Kultur und Gesellschaft,* Special Volume 27, Kölner Zeitschrift für Soziologie und Sozialpsychologie, ed. F. Neidhardt,

M. R. Lepsius, and J. Weiss, pp. 191–211. Opladen: Westdeutscher Verlag.

———. 1999. "The Religious Situation in Europe: The Background to Contemporary Conversions." *Social Compass* 46 (3): 251–258.

McCloud, B. Th. 1991. "African-American Muslim Women." In *The Muslims of America,* ed. Y. Yazbeck Haddad, pp. 177–188. Oxford: Oxford University Press.

———. 1995. *African American Islam.* New York and London: Routledge.

Poston, L. 1992. *Islamic Da'wah in the West: Muslim Missionary Activity and the Dynamics of Conversion to Islam.* Oxford: Oxford University Press.

Rambo, L. R. 1993. *Understanding Religious Conversion.* New Haven and London: Yale University Press.

Snow, D. A., and R. Machalek. 1983. "The Convert as a Social Type." *Sociological Theory* 1: 259–289.

———. 1984. "The Sociology of Conversion." *Annual Review of Sociology* 10: 167–190.

Speelman, G. M. 1993. "Mixed Marriages." In *Muslims and Christians in Europe: Essays in Honour of Jan Slomp,* ed. G. Speelman, J. van Lin, and D. Mulder, pp. 138–150. Kampen, the Netherlands: Kok.

Stromberg, P. G. 1993. *Language and Self-transformation: A Study of the Christian Conversion Narrative.* Cambridge: Cambridge University Press.

Sultán, M. 1999. "Choosing Islam: A Study of Swedish Converts." *Social Compass* 46 (3): 325–337.

Ulmer, B. 1988. "Konversionserzählung als rekonstruktive Gattung. Erzählerische Mittel und Strategien bei der Rekonstruktion eines Bekehrungserlebnisses." *Zeitschrift für Soziologie* 17: 19–33.

Van Nieuwkerk, K. 2003. "Multiculturaliteit, islam en gender. Visies van Nederlandse nieuwe moslima's." *Tijdschrift voor Genderstudies* 3 (2003): 6–21.

———. 2004. "Veils and Wooden Clogs Do Not Go Together." *Ethnos* 69 (2): 229–246.

Wadud, A. 1999. *Qur'an and Woman.* New York: Oxford University Press.

Wagtendonk, K. 1994. *Islam, godsdienstwetenschappen en de ideeën van al-Nisa.* Amsterdam: Universiteit van Amsterdam.

Wohlrab-Sahr, M. 1999a. "Conversion to Islam: Between Syncretism and Symbolic Battle." *Social Compass* 46 (3): 351–362.

———. 1999b. *Konversion zum Islam in Deutschland und den USA.* Frankfurt: Campus Verlag.

PART ONE. CONTEXTUALIZING CONVERSION

CHAPTER 1

The Quest for Peace in Submission

Reflections on the Journey of American Women Converts to Islam

Yvonne Yazbeck Haddad

In the aftermath of the attacks on New York and Washington on September 11, 2001, the United States government declared a war on terrorism: on al-Qaeda for carrying out the attacks and on the Taliban for harboring terrorists. The war was justified as a defense against those who have chosen to be the enemies of American values and civilization, of democracy and freedom. At the same time, the war propaganda focused on the Taliban's mistreatment of women and cast the war effort as a means of liberating and empowering the oppressed women of Afghanistan. The noble goal of championing democracy and confronting Muslim societies deemed as mistreating their women harked back to the founding of the American Republic two centuries earlier. The Founding Fathers of the United States declared their first foreign war against the Barbary States, a war justified as targeting despotism and fostering an attitude of civility toward Muslim women. Islam and Muslims were cast as the "Other," the counterimage of what it means to be American.

The immediate response to the shock of the September attacks was the question posed by the media: "Why? Why do they hate us?" and the consequent attempt by the American public to learn more about the religion of Islam. As Qur'ans and books about Islam disappeared from bookstores, and Christians and Jews visited mosques and invited Muslims to explain the teachings of Islam, Muslims were awed by the number of people who were being exposed to the teachings of their faith. One leader is reported to have said, "Not even a billion dollars to support da'wa [propagation] would have made it possible to reach as many Americans with the message of Islam."[1] A few leaders have cited this fact as an assurance that God moves in mysterious ways, that he has not abandoned the Muslims but rather is testing them. And in the aftermath of 9/11 there were several reports that there was a palpable growth in the number of converts to Islam, especially among women,[2] leading some Muslims overseas to believe that there is a massive tide of conversion taking place. Despite the media focus on "the oppression" of Muslim women and the violence inherent in Islam, the process of conversion of

Americans to Islam has not abated, with one report estimating that thirty thousand are converting per year.[3]

Conversion to Islam has recently surfaced as an issue in the public discourse that aims at restricting the political and missionary activity of Muslims in the United States. Since 9/11 several converts, including those the media have dubbed the "jihadist" John Walker Lindt, the "dirty bomber" Jose Padilla, and "military chaplain" James J. Yee, have been accused of collaboration with the enemy and featured prominently in the press. This has led Senator Charles Schumer of New York to call for an investigation of educational institutions that prepare Muslims for chaplaincy positions in the United States. Others have sought the monitoring of Islamic organizations that work for conversion of Americans. Daniel Pipes, who was appointed by President Bush to the United States Institute for Peace and has appointed himself as the chief arbiter of moderate Islam, has called for a public inquisition of Muslim leaders. One of the defining questions that he believes would ferret out who is a moderate and who is an extremist terrorist is whether a Muslim is willing to renounce the Qur'anic commission to propagate Islam. From his viewpoint, the goal of converting others to Islam may be construed as concealing questionable motives and even promoting terrorism, and in the final analysis must be deemed as an anti-American activity.

For some, the conversion of American women to Islam has been very puzzling. Muslim women seem always to have been intriguing to Americans. Their perceived exploitation and suppression by Muslim men have driven the main plot line of many a novel and movie.[4] The concept of Muslim womanhood conjures up images of harems, sensuality, and abuse. For over a century American missionaries have sought to fashion Muslim women in their image, which has amounted to liberating them from an Islam that the missionaries perceived as relegating women to subservience, second-class status, a polygamous environment, and physical and sexual abuse. They saw this as a way to gain for Muslim women the right to equal status, equal treatment, and equal inheritance.[5] Coming out of this heritage, many Americans today find the conversion of American women to Islam bewildering. "How could they find anything attractive in that religion!"

Converts to Islam, whether male or female and especially if they are white, have proven to be very important to immigrant Muslims. The fact of conversion signals the claim of Islam to be relevant in all times and places, even in the West. High-visibility converts are often featured speakers at Muslim gatherings. Their presence offers an assurance of the viability of Islam in the

American context and is a source of pride for Muslim parents, who are eager to show their children that such well-known figures have opted for Islam over the temptations of popular American culture. This essay, which is based on a variety of sources—published reports, Web site postings, and extensive interviews held over the last twenty years—is an attempt to provide an overview of the phenomenon of conversion of American women to Islam. While a growing number of newspaper articles deal with women converts to Islam since 9/11, very little academic study of this phenomenon has been done. I will try to answer such questions as why these women convert and what it is that they convert to, dealing also with the relations between immigrants and white converts.

Da'wa in the West

The first Muslim missionary to the United States belonged to the Ahmadiyya Movement in Islam (Haddad and Smith 1993, 49–78), which had developed as a counter to intensive Christian missionary activity in India during the nineteenth century. Its missionary outreach in the United States dates back to the Centennial Exhibition. The initial goal of the Ahmadiyya missionaries in the United States was to create an environment hospitable to Muslim immigrants by engaging in outreach and trying to convert white Americans. While they were able to convert a few individuals, they were rejected by the immigrants, who deemed their message heretical. They soon realized that their efforts would bear more fruit if they concentrated on African Americans. The message they preached aimed at offering African Americans an alternative identity and a way to bracket the problems of race in America. It raised the consciousness of African Americans about their history, including the fact that many of them were descendants of Muslims who had been forcibly converted to Christianity. Ahmadis reminded them that their ancestors had forged one of the greatest civilizations in world history. They preached that only Islam contains an inherently egalitarian creed that did not discriminate against believers of different races. Only Islam provided a means to unite African Americans with African Muslims and all Muslim peoples abroad, a potent source of strength and community. The work of the Ahmadiyya influenced the emergence of several heterodox Islamic groups, including the Moorish Science Temple (Haddad and Smith 1993, 79–104; Allen 2000), the Nation of Islam (Gardell 1994), the Five Percenters (Haddad and Smith 1993, 109–132), and Ansaru Allah (Haddad and Smith 1993, 105–136). Since

1975, Warith Deen Muhammad has led the Nation of Islam into the Sunni movement. More recently, although there has been a growth in the number of Hispanic converts to Islam in the United States, the largest number of U.S. converts continues to be African American males. The second-largest convert cohort is white women.

"Da'wa" emerged, in the United States during the twentieth century, as the word of choice to delineate preaching and propagation of the message of Islam. With the growth of labor emigration from Muslim nations to the West, the question was raised concerning the legitimacy of Muslims living in non-Muslim nations (Abou El Fadl 2000).[6] Commitment to da'wa has in some Muslim circles become the condition that sanctions emigration and settlement in a nation not governed by the laws of Islam. The initial warning by Muslim leaders was from the Jamaati Islami of the Indian subcontinent such as Mawlana Abu al A'la al-Mawdudi and Sayyid Ali Nadvi that Muslims should not live in the West lest they be led astray. This warning was later reassessed by Mawdudi, who reportedly told his followers that since the West guarantees freedom of religion and freedom of propagation, Muslims were to justify their sojourn by engaging in witnessing to the truth of Islam.[7] This task is not to be restricted to a specially trained cadre of missionaries; rather, it is a commandment to all believers, an idea that became dominant during the latter part of the twentieth century.

Khurram Murad of the Jamaati Islami of Pakistan expounded on this theme when he was at the Islamic Foundation of Leicester in Great Britain (1978–1986). His publications on the topic became must reading for young Muslims seeking to understand their role in the United States. Several of his books, including *Da'wa among Non-Muslims* (1986) and *Islamic Movements in the West* (1983), set out the guidelines for da'wa, its method and content. For Murad, the message of Islam is neither progressive nor liberal; rather, it is eternal and unchanging. Conversion is to the ultimate truth, a "reversion" to the original nature of man, since all humans are born Muslim. He advocated a global agenda. Muslims must emphasize the fact that the Islamic ummah (worldwide community of Muslims) is not one among other nations, a mere other; rather, it is for all humanity, the universal community of believers. He warned against disputations and debates. Most importantly, the goal of da'wa is to win the individual to the truth, not to win the argument (Murad 1986, 16–17).

Da'wa among white Americans was assumed by Muslim foreign students on American campuses and the immigrants who settled after the revocation of the Asia Exclusion Act in 1965. The Muslim Student Association (MSA), formed by a small group of students in 1963, became the most effective instrument of propagation of the faith in North America. It was conceived as a project to fashion a core group of dedicated young Muslims committed to the vision of creating Islamic states that would act as a firewall to the spread of communism. These young people were expected upon their return to their homelands to become the vanguard of the Islamic future, in the process transforming the world by promoting and concretizing an ideal Islamic system. Its alumni who decided to settle in the United States formed the Islamic Society of North America (ISNA), a decision they justified by engaging in an effort to promote da'wa. While the primary goal of da'wa was to maintain the immigrants and their children in the faith and provide a shield from the seductive American environment, Society members did take on the challenge of witnessing to the American people.

The Islamic Society of North America, as well as several other umbrella organizations such as the Tableeghi Jamaat and the Islamic Circle of North America, has become enthusiastically engaged in da'wa activity. Their members take seriously the individual duty of inviting others to the faith. Their primary outreach, however, is to Muslim immigrants to engage them in their mosque organizations, given the fact that the majority of Muslim immigrants are secular and unmosqued. Several foreign da'wa organizations that flourished in the 1970s, such as the Muslim World League, Dar al-Iftah of Saudi Arabia, the World Organization of Islamic Services of Iran, and the Islamic Heritage Society of Kuwait, as well as the World Assembly of Muslim Youth, began to support da'wa activity in the United States.

Influencing the MSA and ISNA was the work of Temple University professor Isma'il al-Faruqi, who promoted a vision of da'wa in the United States with the hope of converting its population to Islam. He also hoped to wean Muslim students from feelings of gratitude and subservience to America, hence his three-pronged program: education, propagation, and community building. Al-Faruqi's message was contextualized in the American milieu. He pointed to American discourse in the media and school textbooks that presents Islam as the religion of the sword and one that is devoid of culture and civilization, a discourse that depicts Muslims as "barbarians, religious fanatics, and uncivilized people" bent on subjugating the world. He developed a program that presented Islam as a total way of life. With his convert wife Lamya he taught the students to recognize and appreciate the Islamic contribution to world civilization, to appreciate the distinctive role of women in Islam, to rid themselves of all vestiges of colonial subservience, and to become engaged in transforming the Muslim world (Shafiq 1994, 36–38).

Al-Faruqi believed that for da'wa to succeed, it had to be grounded in education and rational thought. He urged his students to begin with student unity and create a worldwide ummah converted to the faith, bound by commitment to the goal of redeeming the world through Islam. He created the Da'wa Movement of North America (also known as al-'Urwa al-Wuthqa). The model to be striven for is an Islamic community of all colors, races, and nationalities. He initiated a program of instruction for members of the Nation of Islam to help them understand the true teachings of Islam. He recruited fifteen students to operate the da'wa program. They organized classes of twenty-five to thirty students and provided intensive instruction in the true faith, avoiding argumentation and controversy. He also instituted a biweekly imam training program (Shafiq 1994, 46–48) and urged his students to do outreach to prisons and mosques and to lecture at schools and churches.

Al-Faruqi's project was universal in scope. Its outreach effort was aimed at "born-Muslims"[8] and people of other faiths, as well as agnostics and atheists. He established the International Institute of Islamic Thought (IIIT) to produce Islamic knowledge for the modern world, with branches in Bangladesh, Belgium, Cyprus, Egypt, England, India, Jordan, Lebanon, Malaysia, Morocco, Nigeria, Pakistan, Palestine, Qatar, Saudi Arabia, and Turkey (Shafiq 1994, xi). In the United States, the IIIT focused on both immigrant Muslims engaged in the mosque movement, in order to ground them in the proper interpretation of the faith, and converts, both Anglo and African American.

The Message of Islam to North America

Al-Faruqi depicted the West as suffering from a deep void that could only be filled by the teachings of Islam. Muslims could teach the West a sense of human dignity, as well as the importance and centrality of the family and the equality of men and women. They were to strive to become a living example, a model of the ideal family, a witness to the West. The family was central to the regeneration of American society, which was in dire need of Muslim values to help reduce the divorce rate, to teach sexual abstinence before marriage, to care for children, and to provide a support system. He believed that Americans suffered from spiritual bankruptcy, and that Muslims could help heal the pain and suffering of a society gone astray. Islam would cure the United States of Hellenized Christianity, which focused on the incarnation, the Trinity, and the crucifixion (Shafiq 1994, 48). The goal was to redeem America from its waywardness and return it to the worship of God, to provide Americans with a better option for a life of devotion and dedication to the service of humanity. Islam would offer a wholesome alternative to young Americans who appeared to be turned off by American values and culture, young people who were engaged in self-destructive activities, hippies adopting Hindu religious traditions or overdosing on drugs. For al-Faruqi, the only justification for living in the West was to promote Islam.

One of the basic texts that al-Faruqi encouraged his students to use in their da'wa is Hammudah Abd al-Ati's *Islam in Focus* (1978), a book that continues to be widely distributed as part of a da'wa package by various missionary organizations in the United States.[9] The text engages Christian missionary diatribes about Islam head-on and attempts to refute their denigration of the faith, in its place providing a calm and rational argument. For example, Abd al-Ati is among the first Muslims in North America to refute the accusations that Islam is a violent religion that demands conversion by the sword. He argued that the word "Islam" is derived from the Arabic root word "slm," peace, and that

Islam is the religion of peace in the fullest sense of the term; that unjust war was never among its teachings; that aggression was never in its tenets or tolerated by it; that force was never employed to impose it on anyone; that the expansion of Islam was never due to compulsion or oppression; that misappropriation was never forgivable by God or acceptable to Islam; and that whoever distorts or misrepresents the Islamic teachings will do more harm to his own self and his associates than to Islam. (Abd al-Ati 1978, 152)

For Abd al-Ati, "Contrary to popular misconceptions, Islam or submission to the will of God, together with obedience to His Law, does not mean in any way loss of individual freedom or surrender to fatalism" (Abd al-Ati 1978, 7). Islam provides freedom from worship of false deities, freedom from superstition and sin; it frees the self from greed, vanity, envy, insecurity, and tension. He provides a simple, convincing description of a reified Islamic faith that provides a compelling argument for its veracity, its ability to solve many of the social problems that afflict North Americans, such as racism and gender issues, while at the same time offering an alternate image of women and the family (Abd al-Ati 1978, 8–9; Abd al-Ati 1977).

Bearing this in mind, the Islamic concept maintains that religion is not only a spiritual and intellectual necessity but also a social and universal need. Its purpose is not to bewilder man but to guide him; not to debase him but to elevate his moral nature; not to deprive him of anything useful, or to burden him, or to oppress his qualities, but to open for him inexhaustible treasures of sound thinking and right action; not to confine him to narrow limits but to launch him into wide horizons of truth and goodness (Abd al-Ati 1978, 30).

Another theme, according to Abd al-Ati, in the message of Islam to North Americans is the similarity between Islam and the other monotheistic faiths. From this perspective, Jews and Christians converting to Islam are not opting for an exotic religion, nor are they becoming apostate from their inherited faith. Rather, Islam is the fulfillment of the promise of both Judaism and Christianity, a return to the simplicity of the divine, purified, authentic message. Islam supersedes both religions and offers a more pluralistic and universal vision.

Abd al-Ati devoted ten pages out of his two-hundred-page book to discussing Jesus in Islam. Increasingly, it is apparent that Muslims find Jesus and Mary to be useful points for contact, for dialogue, and for engaging Christians.[10] The emphasis is on the veneration and respect of Jesus as a prophet of God who was not crucified, because God would not abandon his prophet. It is not that Islam denies that a crucifixion took place; rather, that Jesus was not crucified, but the Romans believed that they had killed him (Abd al-Ati 1978, 163).

Abd al-Ati's book addresses other perennial topics, such as the role of women, polygamy, and easy divorce, that Europeans and North Americans have raised in criticizing Islam.[11] He also refutes other Muslims who have argued that marriage in Islam "is a business deal negotiated by two partners," and that there is a consensus among Islamic jurists that the marriage contract is a mere contract sanctioning the man's having sex with a partner. Rather, for Abd al-Ati, "It is something solemn, something sacred, and it would be erroneous to define it in simply physical or material and secular terms" (Abd al-Ati 1978, 179).

Abd al-Ati also addressed the role and status of women in Islam. He argued that males and females have equal rights and responsibilities, but not identical roles. "Equality is desirable, just, fair; but sameness is not. People are not created identical but they are created equal. With this distinction in mind, there is no room to imagine that woman is inferior to man. There is no ground to assume that she is less important than he just because her rights are not identically the same as his. Had her status been identical with his, she would have been simply a duplicate of him, which she is not" (Abd al-Ati 1978, 185). He went on to describe how women in other systems have fought hard to gain rights given to them begrudgingly because of shortage of man-power, economic needs, or wars. He questioned whether the rights granted to women in the West were what women really wanted. Regardless, what Islam has endowed is perfect and right. "Whether all women were pleased with these circumstances being on their side, and whether they are happy and satisfied with the results of this course is a different matter. But the fact remains that whatever rights modern woman enjoys fall short of those of her Muslim counterpart. What Islam has established for woman is that which suits her nature, gives her full security and protects her against disgraceful circumstances and uncertain channels of life" (Abd al-Ati 1978, 186).

The kind of da'wa material provided by Faruqi and Abd al-Ati affirms that Islam is beautiful. It is attractive to all who are able to see it in all its mag-nificence. In this literature, Muslims are assured that people will convert "upon seeing true Muslims and their lifestyle."[12] They are thus urged to live up to the ideal, since their lifestyle is a witness not only to the faith, but more importantly, to its serenity and peace. It is convincing through its simplic-ity and rationality and enticing when lived according to its tenets. Islam is reified as an ideal, a total way of life whose rituals involve the minutiae of daily life, providing for happiness in this world and felicity in the hereafter. Its guidelines govern this life, a haven from the hedonistic society where one can find rest from a troubled life and regain human dignity and worth.

The Conversion Experience[13]

While the articulation of Islam and its teaching for Westerners is important in appealing to seekers, crucial for many of the converts were their initial en-counters with Muslims—friends, classmates, boyfriends, spouses, acquain-tances, and neighbors who took the time and had the patience to explain, to mentor and guide. Converts often write that they were impressed by the inner peace, serenity, and strength of belief they witnessed in these Muslims. For many, their investigation of Islam was initiated by curiosity, a quest for knowledge or spiritual fulfillment. Many report that they began to look into Islam and to learn more without any intent to convert.

Some of the women who have related their stories are "serial converts," those who have set out on a spiritual journey, studied numerous religious traditions, converted to a variety of faiths before looking into Islam. Their encounter with Islam was often described as a part of their ongoing spiritual journey. "As you see I did not choose it at first sight and without thinking at all; on the contrary, I became a Muslim after examining Islam minutely, looking for the possible faults in it and finding their answers, and reaching the conclusion that it is an immaculate religion. Now I boast about being a Muslim."[14]

Some of the women emphasized their intellectual connection to Islam. Though they said that they had been fairly content and secure in themselves, they had genuine intellectual issues with Christianity. These individuals tended to begin their study of Islam out of curiosity. "When I first started to study Islam, I did not expect to find anything that I needed or wanted in my personal life. Little did I know that Islam would change my life."[15] Many wrote that the evidence in Islam's favor was too compelling to deny. These individuals did not deny the spiritual aspect of Islam, but claimed that they were able to use the intellect along with the heart in Islam (generally this was mentioned as a contrast to their experiences with Christianity). Many claimed that once they had encountered the intellectual evidence of Islam they had "no choice" but to convert. Some were impressed by the "inner logic" of Islam and referred to the wisdom of Islam as "common sense." As one convert wrote: "It was the wonderful logic, the pure commonsense in all Islamic teachings which attracted me so much."[16]

Some apparently stumbled on the faith while shopping around for something that made sense in America's supermarket of religions. "I joined the Christian and Islamic societies and all three political parties. I wanted to explore all the possibilities in order to dismiss them."[17]

Others report that they have been "captured by the Qur'an." In several of the testimonials, reading the text is often described as an integral part of an individual's conversion to Islam. Some recount an emotional response to their first encounter with the text. "The reading of the Qur'an and the hadith of the Prophet is what captured me. I went through a very odd experience whereby for a whole week it took me to read the Qur'an I couldn't sleep and seemed to toss and turn all night in a feverish sweat. I had strange and vivid dreams about religious topics, and when I would get up all I wanted to do was continue reading the Qur'an. I didn't even study for my final exams which were happening at the same time!" (Anway 1995, 34).

Some report having been impressed by the scientific aspects of the Qur'an. "I was amazed at the scientific knowledge in the Qur'an, which is not taken from the Bible as some would have you believe. I was getting my degree in microbiology at that time, and was particularly impressed with the description of the embryological process, and so much more."[18] As another convert put it, "The Qur'an speaks of embryonic development, cloud formation, and other recent scientific knowledge. It made sense."[19]

Others tended to focus on the intellectual appeal of the Qur'an. They often explained that the clarity and logic of the Qur'an are what influenced them most. Many experts on the Qur'an are confounded by the converts' contention that the Qur'an is easier to read and understand than the Bible, or that it does not have anything in it that a person cannot understand. The majority have read the Qur'an in Yusuf Ali's translation and exposition (1989), a fact that led a professor of the Qur'an to dismiss them as converting to "Yusuf Ali Islam." Its commentary provides tightly scripted information that smoothes over controversial sections and provides reinterpretations as a defense of the Qur'an and its message which had been developed over a century of encounter and debates with evangelical Christian missionaries.

Another important theme in conversion narratives relates to the negative experiences the converts had had with Christianity. Many converts witnessed hypocrisy among Christians or did not approve of the new "trends" in various denominations. They accused religious leaders of causing the crisis within the Christian church that has rendered it unprepared for the challenges young women face in today's world. For some, the Judaism and Christianity of their parents need revamping in order to provide a spiritual home where all are welcome, where chosenness and election are not a barrier that requires coercion or exclusion.

A couple years after college I began learning about Islam. I remember being utterly shocked when I first began reading, as I discovered the universal theory I had been looking for, the rejection of moral relativism, the explicit rejection of racism and sexism, the rejection of nationalism, and a strong emphasis on personal responsibility and social justice. It is important to make very clear that I converted to Islam because I wanted a sincere connection to God. The main reason for my conversion was a spiritual emptiness that I felt, an emptiness that Islam filled. What was so shocking to me was that Islam fulfilled me both spiritually and spoke to me politically and intellectually as well. It is a holistic philosophy in the truest sense.[20]

A large number of the women converts discussed, to varying degrees, the theological superiority of Islam over Christianity as an important reason for their conversion. Problems with Christian theology they identified included the perennial doctrines that have set the two faiths apart: the concepts of incarnation and Trinity, the divinity of Jesus, crucifixion, and the doctrine of original sin. Many said that they had been troubled by confusing and complicated theological notions in Christianity. Some described the appeal of the pure monotheism of Islam, presented not as a polemic, but in a rational, scientific exposition. Others insisted that they always "knew" that there could only be one God and that Jesus could not possibly be God. Still others wrote that when they encountered Islam, they found that its teachings matched their own beliefs. They had finally arrived home. Or "This is what I had always felt in my heart."[21] Or "I found a religion that fit what I already believed."[22] Or "Everything I read was exactly how I felt inside me" (in Anway 1995, 38). Or "I found that all along I shared the beliefs taught through Islam but never had a name for it" (Anway 1995, 42).

Other testimonials focused on the fact that their questions and doubts about Christianity as young people had not been acknowledged, or were avoided, by the adults. They reported that religious leaders had no answers but told them to "have faith" or to believe blindly in what they could not understand. "Throughout my childhood, I always felt like things were not right and when I began questioning people that actually took the time to listen they told me many times to 'just have faith.'"[23] Another reported that "As a young girl born in the Northwest of the USA, my dream was to become a nun. It was then I started having misgivings about Catholic doctrine, so I gravitated towards the Protestant faiths. The trinity was a lingering concern for me. I often just tried 'to have faith' but my own logic overruled this."[24] Another wrote: "I had studied very deeply, but I always felt that the hard questions went unanswered."[25]

There appears to be little awareness among the converts who have posted or published their conversion narratives of the development of Islamic thought and its rich history of intellectual debates. The conversion narratives lack any reference to intellectual challenges that Islam has not been able to resolve or questions that have not been answered. The texts they read are self-assured and persuasive. Many remarked that Islam was more pure than Christianity and less influenced by humans. "Muslims don't keep shifting their goal-posts. Christianity changes; it seems so wishy-washy."[26] Others focused on the fact that the message of Islam is simple and universal, in contrast to what they considered to be the convoluted and diluted message of Christianity. Christian doctrines did not make sense, they claimed, whereas in Islam everything can be answered with no requirement for a leap of faith. (In reality, while the term "leap of faith" comes from Christian theological writings, the Qur'an and centuries of Muslim theological interpretation have drawn a clear distinction between *islam* as simple submission and *iman* as the full response to God in faith.) A persistent theme was the notion that all theological answers could be found in Islam. "Islam for me gives me peace of mind because I don't have to understand the trinity and how God is 'three in one' or that God died on the cross. For me Islam supplies the answers" (in Anway 1995, 37). Another wrote, "Islam cooled me out. It helped me to find God without all of the hang-ups and guilt I felt as a Christian" (Anway 1995, 33).

Virtually all convert testimony describes the difficulties the women had in explaining their decision to their families. Their encounters ranged from complete acceptance to dramatic stories of rejection. In one extreme example a woman recounted her loss of her husband, children, and job. Others lost custody of their children or their marriages broke apart. Some families saw the conversion of their daughter as betrayal of their values and culture. Some converts report that their parents refused to see them after their conversion; others said that their mothers were ashamed to be seen with them wearing "shabby clothes." Some were told that they were going to hell. Many of the converts experienced some sense of alienation from families and friends.

On the other hand, some report that their decision to convert was accepted and even welcomed. Some described parents who were "just happy they were following a path to God."[27] Others report families that were initially very upset, but became more accepting. In a few instances, converts were able to convert other members of their family. One woman reported converting her entire family, as well as at least thirty other friends.[28] One interviewee reported that upon conversion, she divided the bedroom with a sheet and told her Christian husband that he was now a forbidden stranger and refused to relate to him until he finally converted in order to save the marriage. The families of some converts saw conversion to Islam as a sign of support for terrorism. One woman reported that her mother asked her, "What's the matter with you, do you love Osama bin Laden? Do you want to be his wife?"[29] Many wrote that their families considered this to be a temporary "phase." Consistently the *hijab* seemed to be a bigger issue for families and friends than the conversion itself. This visible display of Islam was seen as too radical. Family members were often concerned about what neighbors and other people would think about the change in wardrobe.

While some of the women interviewed report that the acceptance of Islam led to the conversion of their friends and acquaintances and to their making wonderful, accepting new friends, others described the painful loss of lifelong friends. Still others described the difficulty of explaining to people how they could be a Muslim, since Islam is generally identified with a foreign ethnicity. Many wrote about the frustration of constantly having to combat the assumption that women only converted to Islam for marriage. Many of the testimonials emphasized that a romantic relationship was not the main reason for conversion, even if they had married a Muslim man. Their critics said that their conversion was due simply to the fact that they wanted to get married. It is the case that despite the fact that Islamic law allows a Muslim man to marry a Christian or a Jewish woman, in most instances the Muslim men refrain from marrying women who do not convert.

Why Do They Convert?

Some converts identify the daily discipline and specific requirements of Islam as a crucial reason for their conversion. Islamic guidelines provide reasoned answers to their quest for a structured life, for boundaries and proscriptions, as well as demands for scrupulous adherence to prescriptions. Many reported that they have enjoyed having a "guide for life" that is precise and all-encompassing, clear and unambiguous, and that provides protection from sedition and a haven from a depraved society. Some converts described their satisfaction in living their lives according to specific rules, regular responsibilities, and a tightly regimented way of life. The daily prayers, emphasis on personal responsibility, and the clear moral message of Islam were also appealing to many converts. "I thought it was genius to pray five times a day. It is more comprehensive than Christianity. It's a total package."[30]

Others felt that their lifestyle had much in common with that prescribed by Islam. "For a number of years, I had been living a Muslim life without knowing it" (in Anway 1995, 42). They discover that their preference for modesty and chastity is not strange or defiant but is confirmed as a model way of life. It is the highest attainment of living in accordance with divine prescriptions.

A fundamental appeal of Islam evident in the testimonials is the strong community bonds and kinship that converts feel with other Muslim women. A large number of converts report that they were attracted to Islam because of the supportive community it provides, support they lacked prior to their conversion. Many report that they had sensed that they did not "fit in" socially and were aware and concerned about how they were perceived by others. Some discussed their experiences with dark periods of depression.

Conversion provided them not only with a ready-made accepting community, but a community that revered them as special and worthy of respect. Some report that while formerly they had been greatly concerned about the perceptions of their colleagues, of how they looked, how overweight they were, what values they held, what lifestyle choices they made, with conversion they were able to shed this burden and appear comfortable with who they had become. "I was looking for peace. I'd had a rough past. My teenage years weren't great; I was bullied at school, people called me fat and ugly, and I was looking for something to make me happy.... When you walk into a mosque you feel really peaceful. Praying five times a day is really focused. It gives you a purpose in your life. The Koran is like a guide to help you; when you read it, it makes you feel better."[31] For others, it was the attainment of a spiritual awakening after conversion: "Islam made me realize that there is more to life than our physical bodies."[32] Those who describe themselves as social misfits prior to their conversion, not belonging in any social or religious group, deeply appreciate the closeness they feel to their new Muslim sisters. "I was not very happy. I felt lost, I was drifting. I didn't feel like I belonged in my society," said one.[33] "If you come from a cold, WASP New England culture," wrote another, "the hugging and hospitality you get from Arab sisters is just wonderful."[34] What would appear at first to be a radical choice, a flouting of difference, can be seen as a means of finding confidence in the rightness of their choice and the superiority of their faith commitment.

A family-centered lifestyle appears to be greatly appreciated by convert women, since it provides for automatic inclusiveness and participation in shared activities and celebrations, as well as genuine mutual caring. "I fell in love with the Muslims whose actual biological family members I could not distinguish because all children were regarded the same and all parents were truly like brothers and sisters in one huge family."[35] The emphasis on family seems especially important to those who view Western society as devaluing traditional family relations. Included in the understanding of family for some converts is the focus on motherhood and the conservative values embodied in home-schooling children and trying to be a good wife.

Many appear to welcome the concept of the distinct responsibilities and duties within male/female relationships expressed in Islam. They commented on the importance of the fact that the equality granted to men and women in the Qur'an provided for different roles and functions for each gender. Some like the idea of a division of labor where it is a man's duty to provide for his wife and family, while the duty of a woman is to raise the children. "My husband has been kind and generous to me and allowed me to make decisions in our home. When I wanted to leave my teacher/counselor position before our first child was born, he willingly accepted my decision to stay at home and never asked me to keep working to help pay our expenses" (in Anway 1995, 87). Others feel that true liberation of women comes in being liberated from having to work. "The one right I have that's very important to me is not having to work and getting the chance to be with my daughter! It also is nice to have my husband provide for me at my standards and above without [my] really asking. I feel the home is for the wife and mother, and I love it" (in Anway 1995, 89).

One immigrant described the converts as "the collateral damage" of American feminism. Most have rejected the dominant contemporary paradigms of American womanhood and tend to view feminists as selfish and self-centered. Some feel more comfortable in an environment that is not constructed on female competition for male attention. "I like the fact that there are rules in place, the segregation of the sexes, more respect for women." Converts are impressed by the Muslim emphasis on equality of the sexes. They are also impressed with the teaching that there are different roles for men and women and want the respect that they believe Muslim men have for women. They find the price of freedom promised by American feminism to be too steep and dehumanizing. Feminists, they believe, are complicit in freeing men from a sense of responsibility toward women and the family and have revolutionized society to the end that it has brought about the breakdown of family values. They believe that American feminism is a distortion of nature, and condemn it as degrading to women. "Feminism has not liberated women; rather, it has liberated men from responsibility. In the process it has enslaved women. They have become imitators of men, not free to be themselves, always in the process of measuring up to the men."[36]

Others rejected American feminism as a way of life that is based on selfishness and egotism. "Why are American women converting to Islam? How did Islam answer to the role of feminism in my life? Islam liberates women by providing a connection to Divinity and a comprehensive way of life for all people within society. It provides balance for men, women, and children. It balances personal liberty with commitment to the community. It removes the emphasis on the ego and focuses attention on Divinity, the centrifugal force that unites all life. Feminism on the other hand focuses attention on one ego, de-contextualized from the needs and desires of everyone around her. Her desires deserve to be met as she sees fit, regardless of the repercussion on the family, children, the men in her family, or society as a whole. Feminism is one of many theories that worships the ego."[37]

Some specifically discussed their concern about patterns of sexuality in Western society and the emphasis on the packaging of the female body and its appearance. These women described themselves as having always been modest, prudish, and uncomfortable with Western notions of sexuality. Specific issues such as having a negative image of their body and concern about being overweight appear to be a factor in their sexual discomfort. They are deeply impressed by the modesty and conservative values of Islam. "Like most American females, I grew up in a slave market, comprised not only of the sexual sickness of my family, but the constant negative judging of my appearance by peers beginning at ages younger than seven. I was taught from a very early age by American society that my human worth consisted solely of my attractiveness (or, in my case, lack of it) to others."[38]

Many of the Internet testimonials reflect a rejection of the dominant paradigm of American womanhood that is depicted as empowerment through subservience to males by becoming sex objects available for men's pleasure. Converts appear to associate flirtatious advances by young men as demeaning and disrespectful rather than a compliment or appreciation of their physical attractiveness. "When I developed in the sixth grade, I got unwanted attention from guys. With Islam, I felt I got respect as a young woman."[39]

Other converts see their conversion as a cultural critique of Western materialism. These women argued that Islam is the answer to the moral decay of the West. Still others are uncomfortable with many aspects of the dominant culture that focus on drinking alcohol and dating.[40] They feel that freedom and the responsibility of choosing and accepting the consequences are actually a burden whose loss is more than rewarded by the respect they receive for willingly foregoing the many temptations of American culture. By relinquishing freedom, one gains respect.

Female converts to Islam voluntarily appropriate new concepts of space, as well as of proper dress and behavior in the company of men. They readily shed freedoms they have taken for granted and concepts of worth and value that are embedded in American society. They abandon models of proper beauty of dress, of women's attractiveness, that are part of the American cultural milieu. They are looking rather for a clearly defined role of womanhood and welcome the gender distinctions and roles of Islam. They are comfortable in the traditional roles of wife and mother and uncomfortable in trying to emulate men.

A preliminary attempt to analyze whether religious upbringing was instrumental in the proclivity to convert led to no clear results. The convert population appears to come from the whole spectrum of religious denominations in the United States. Some have had little or no religious upbringing, while others were raised in various Christian or Jewish denominations but found themselves looking for something else. The majority reflect in their backgrounds the dominant American ethos of pluralism and inclusivity. Common in the narratives of many of the converts was the search for a community of belonging. There is no question that for many women the possibility of marrying a Muslim man influenced their decision to convert.

Several Web sites have been created to facilitate Muslim marriages. Converts appreciate the fact that the individual not only can initiate the search for a marriage partner, but can also embark on getting married without the possibility of premarital intimacy and exploration. The Web sites include testimonials by individuals who have successfully found a partner through the search engine. One Web site provides information on Islamic marriage and family life, claiming that it has 2,500 individuals registered.[41] Another affirms its Islamic legitimacy by reiterating that dating is *haram*, forbidden in Islam, and that since it upholds this doctrine, the pairing of individuals seeking acceptable marriage can be done through the Internet.[42]

Many contended that they found relief in wearing *hijab* and felt that people were forced to judge them as an individual person, rather than on their looks. "Modesty, mostly. When you're covered, you're treating each other as human beings without being distracted."[43] "You seem to be really looked after, as a Muslim woman. Muslim men really respect you; they do everything for you. You're highly thought of and protected."[44] The donning of Islamic dress becomes the symbol of regeneration, where one is cleansed from doubt and a multiplicity of options is purged from life. The *hijab* connotes a dramatic decision to operate within a certain sphere of constraints, a public declaration, not only that one has opted to reject American culture because it was found wanting, but more importantly, because simplicity and modesty are superior choices for life. What others may see as exotic, converts affirm as comfortable and freeing: "Since I adopted the hijab, my sense of self-esteem has gone through the roof, even though I've sometimes gotten harassed. Young girls here feel their bodies need to be exposed—that's how the culture values them. . . . I feel I'm truly living my values and don't need to sell myself to the world."[45]

Spiritual/Sufi Appeal

A large number of the testimonials were from women who expressed disillusionment with the religion in which they were raised, and said that they were more "spiritual" than accepting of one particular religious system. Some had been active in a church but had harbored doubts about Christian theological affirmations and problems with Christian exclusivism. Others had never been tied to any particular religious tradition and wrote that they had never truly acknowledged the spiritual aspect of their lives. "I am a product of the end of the baby-boomer generation who experienced the spiritual and moral bankruptcy of American society. I found only material vacuity in Judaism and Christianity.... The mystical tradition of Islam appeals to me. What appealed to me about the *turuq* [Sufi orders] is that it provided lineage, method and doctrine that can be practiced, grounding you in a long tradition of human spirituality that stretches for generations, where thousands have found their mooring and their ability to be centered in humanity. Islam provides a powerful centering in spiritual consciousness."[46]

Throughout history Christians have generally found Sufism to be one of the most appealing expressions of Islam. This appeal is evident to those women who choose to be part of the more than fifty transplanted Sufi groups in the United States. The Bawa Muhaiyaddeen Fellowship, for example, established in the 1960s in Philadelphia by a Sri Lankan Sufi, has over two thousand adherents. Many were what might be called "serial converts," who had experimented with a variety of Eastern religions and cults. Sufism seemed to provide them with a structured life and a close and supportive community. Although Bawa himself is no longer alive, the Fellowship continues to flourish and to attract converts, many of them women.

Sufism appears to have a special appeal to women because it offers opportunities for full participation in its rituals and its communities. This is particularly true in some of the less traditional American Sufi groups. Women enjoy the music and the dance provided in some Sufi ceremonies, as well as the philosophy of openness and inclusivity that they feel they find inherent in Sufi teachings and practices. Involvement in Sufi communities also provides a haven from what they see as materialist American society, as well as a coed support system. One convert professes that as a Muslim she finds openness and acceptance in the Sufi movement that are a welcome relief from what she experienced as the constraints of the mosque. One can participate in Sufi practices anywhere, she says. "I do not need a priest. I have direct access to God. I do not need a church; I can carry my own carpet."[47]

For many converts Sufism provides a model of pluralism in which all humanity is bound in unity, captured by the love of God. It requires no denial of physical pleasure, but offers a disciplined celebration of life enjoyed in community. "The Sufism I favor does not require stringent adherence to the law. Orthodoxy did not appeal to me because it places restrictions on human choice and freedom. I do not have to take up the coloring of other cultures. I do not have to wear a headscarf. I would not be able to develop to my full potential."[48]

Immigrant-Convert Relations

Attitudes among immigrant Muslim women toward the converts vary. While many of the American-born children of immigrants are carefully attempting to steer between the constraints of their parents' values and culture and those that are propagated at the mosque, they are constantly challenged by the dominant culture of the United States. They tend to view the converts as not only converting to the religion of Islam, but in many cases also to the cultural trappings that their parents associate with the faith, trappings they themselves gingerly attempt to discard. They tend to see white converts as adapting themselves to various Islamic cultures that are imported and/or constructed by the immigrants in the United States. As one person put it, "They have on their own volition taken on the customs and mannerisms of different Muslim cultures that surround them."[49]

One American-born college student of Pakistani background, who identified herself as a Muslima [female Muslim] and "not very practicing," said that while she was impressed with the converts' extensive knowledge of Islam and their defense of its teachings, "My initial reaction to most of white converts I know is the same reaction I have to most overzealous Muslims—discomfort. Just as the 'native' Muslims who have been trained by their parents to quote certain hadith and create the gender tensions at MSA [Muslim Student Association] gatherings."[50]

Some of the women converts appear to be empowered by the act of conversion. As with the "born-again" in other faiths, they appear to gain resolution and clarity of purpose, and are transformed from a "bundle of doubt" to a "rock of assurance." Many assume leadership roles or have these roles conferred on them, inasmuch as they are considered experts who could guide immigrants through the intricacies of American society. They organize social events, Sunday school instruction, scout troops, and Qur'an study groups. Converts are featured as spokespersons for Islam and an embodiment of its power to transform lives and provide meaning and purpose. One second-generation Muslim agreed that most of the time converts take on roles of authority or become spokespersons because "converts know a lot more about Islam than those that are 'raised-Muslims'; having a convert to Islam speak on behalf of Muslims might give the side a little more credibility in some cases."[51]

As one immigrant informant put it, "Women may have more to gain from conversion than men because they tend to convert knowing that they are also fighting major stereotypes of Islam being anti-female. As converts, they are more moved by the religion and they seek to assert themselves within it. If their conversion is taken as a rejection of the culture and society that they were raised in, then it is fair to say that gaining a leadership role within the Muslim community would help to achieve personal fulfillment and purpose. But in general, I think that with the religion fresh in their hearts, they are more motivated and standing up for it and lead within it than pursuing other roles in a society that they find lacking."[52]

Younger women converts appear to have an easier time making friends with their peers among the second generation, although some of the latter at times grumble that the converts are marrying the most eligible men, hence depleting the pool of potential husbands. This may have the effect of relegating the immigrant Muslim women to spinsterhood, since Islamic jurisprudence does not allow a Muslim woman to marry outside the faith. Some older converts report that the Muslim community is not as friendly as it is purported to be in the testimonials. At times, especially in some of the traditional or ethnic mosques, the older generation of immigrant women tend to perceive their role as maintainers of the norms. They hold the converts accountable to the ideals and values of Islam, the cultural standards of Arab and/or Pakistani society. Some of the converts have reported that they feel monitored for every minor infraction of cultural or ritual expectation. There appears to be no reluctance on the part of the older generation to remind them to adhere to proper decorum such as lowering their gaze or maintaining the proper distance between the sexes, or covering every strand of hair. In interviews, several complained that some of the immigrants are too "cliquey." The converts feel ostracized. They never measure up. They are expected to live up to the model of the veiled, modest, demure person who at no time should compete for attention. Thus the convert may adopt the

projected model of the perfect Muslima and attempt to conform to its minutiae not only out of deep commitment to an ideal she has become convinced
is salvific, but in order to avoid criticism.

At the same time, members of the second immigrant generation have to
maneuver carefully in order to fit into the intricate cultural ties that bind
the immigrants together in an American culture that is discriminatory if not
outright hostile to Muslims. Some even grumble that the converts are pushy,
urging the Muslims to get out of their shell and open themselves up to the
community. Some single converts are known to become activists, prodding
and coaxing reluctant second-generation Muslim women to get involved,
sometimes urging them to do more to promote the faith, to expand their
closed circle of friends in order to promote knowledge of Islam, or at least to
court the goodwill of the American population toward Islam and Muslims.
The converts at times chastise the immigrants for not living up to the values
of Islam that they pronounce. While some immigrants appear to welcome the
energy and activism of the converts, others are more reserved in judgment.

African American converts in several interviews expressed their feeling
that immigrants tend to seek "Anglo" converts to Islam and regard them as
more important; they seem to prefer to associate with whites and pay more
attention to their speeches. African Americans accuse the immigrants of
valuing white converts as "special trophies." One African American interviewee ascribed this reality to racism among immigrants that makes them
want to marry white converts so as to "whiten the race." She also noted that
white women like to date immigrant men because "they pay when on a date,
and unlike American men, they marry."[53]

While many narratives provide a very positive description of postconversion acceptance, of being celebrated, of community support, of the experience of finally belonging and being at home, others revealed the profound
sense of loneliness and alienation experienced by converts in the Muslim
community. Converts contended that it is hard to fit in, especially as an unmarried, white female. Several wrote that it is hard to stay in the community
if a family does not adopt you or you get married to a Muslim. "Although
many Muslims welcomed me, I have come to realize there is an inherent
hatred among Muslims for Americans, and especially for single, white, female Americans."[54] This convert also described unwanted advances from
Muslim men who assumed she was promiscuous and "easy" since she was
an American. A few have recounted that they have been taken advantage of
by unscrupulous mosque leaders who ask them to become a second wife,

marrying according to Islamic law, only to discard them when a new convert appears on the scene.

One convert described the pain she felt, on the day she took *shahada* at the mosque, when she overheard a conversation among several Muslims about white women converting and then marrying "their" Muslim men. This convert also described the difficulty she had making friends with Muslim women and her struggle to find a Muslim roommate.[55] Others described how they were rejected by Muslim men once it was discovered that they were converts. One convert described her in-laws' fear that their son's marriage to a convert would give the family a bad name; she felt that she was her new family's "biggest enemy."[56]

Others described significant cultural and linguistic barriers they felt hindered them. One convert named Caroline contrasted the reactions she encountered among different generations. "Young Muslims are very accepting. They are really happy that you have chosen to become Muslim. The older generation is not so accepting. For them, Islam is part of their cultural background, it's about the country they came from, and it's what binds their communities together."[57]

The linguistic barrier of not being able to speak or read Arabic or Urdu was often mentioned as a difficulty in finding acceptance in Muslim communities. Some describe feeling out of place at the *masjid* because they could not understand the sermon. They have to learn to live in segregated space. While some American-born Muslims are pushing for gender inclusion, more equal space, a few of the converts are less concerned. Some ascribe their negative experience to bad-mannered Muslims: "Although I have been treated badly by some other Muslims, I have come to realize that while Islam is perfect, Muslims are not."[58] Other converts described mixed feelings. "I found that in some aspects I had peace in my life and in others I was in the struggle for my life."[59] A few women mentioned problems with the way in which they were treated as women. One convert complained about praying in a separate area from men, "It's like being back in Alabama in the 1960s with the whites on one side and the blacks on the other."[60] It does seem that the vast majority of converts accept and endorse the traditional gender relationships in Islam, although the younger generation is beginning to ask for inclusion.

While the testimonials sound formulaic, they echo the message of Islam in the West as it is propagated in books, tracts, and magazines, and on Web sites. It is a message that has been honed over years of debate and argument, in many ways the product of Christian Muslim competition for souls. Many converts describe their acceptance of Islam as an individual journey from confusion to peace, from conflict to resolution, from drift to coherence, from emptiness to fulfillment, from loneliness to belonging to a community where one is embraced and celebrated.

It is clear from the testimonials not only that the message of Islam is appealing, but that the methods used in the conversion efforts—the "packaging of Islam"—are effective. However, there appear to be several paths, several adumbrations of Islam, to which women gravitate. While all convert to Islam, there are some distinctions and boundaries between the various interpretations. The majority of the women appear to convert to a modernized traditional interpretation of the faith, one that is conservative theologically and that justifies distinct boundaries based on gender. Most of the testimonials on Web sites and in books published by Islamic missionary organizations appear to fit this category. Believers are identified by adherence to ritual, by dress, and by the environment that they are able to create at home.

A second and much smaller group appears to find the teachings of Muslim women academics, most of whom identify as Muslim feminists in the Unites States, more appealing. A third group appears to gravitate to the practice of Sufi, or mystical Islam. Its members generally do not see themselves as either feminist or traditionalist, but enjoy a sense of equality in a Western context. While they may follow the prescriptions of the law, they are not bound to its minutiae. In their view, Islam liberates humans from any restrictions and binds them to the knowledge and love of God and their experience of him in their lives.

For the traditionalists, Islam liberates them from the struggle to measure up to the dictates of an oppressive American society that is obsessed with women's bodies: how they look, how sexually attractive they are, and how pleasing to men they can be. For the Muslim feminists, Islam liberates them from interpretations of the Qur'anic text in which men have enshrined gender difference. Women are created equal to men, they say, not because they have to struggle with men to achieve equality but because it is guaranteed as God's order for humanity. They are equally accountable before God, as revealed in the Qur'an, and judged by the same criteria based on their contribution to humanity rather than on their obedience to their husbands. For the Sufis, Islam liberates them from bondage to material possessions, to excessive consumerism, and to legal restrictions. They bask in the liberation that God grants individuals as they strive to create a harmonious community dedicated to his glory.

Conclusion

Many elements, then, must be taken into account when considering the conversion of American women to Islam. On the one hand is the fact that a climate for practicing da'wa in America has been created by the activities of missionaries such as the Ahmadis, by the writings and activities of scholars such as Isma'il al-Faruqi and Hammudah Abd al-Ati, and by the affirmation of propagation as a legitimate Islamic activity in the West on the part of Muslim organizations such as the Muslim Student Association, the Islamic Society of North America, the Islamic Circle of North America, and other groups. On the other hand is the set of circumstances that makes conversion an attractive alternative to American women, including the perceived rationality and "rightness" of the faith, the appeal of the Qur'an, the simplicity of Islam as opposed to what has been seen as the complications of Christian theology, the search for an alternative to the general secularism of American society, the desire for community and belonging, and the range of personal reasons women may have for wanting to redefine their identity.

Converts recognize that the model of an ideal Muslim community is yet to be realized, but they express their eagerness to work for its attainment. They understand it to be a goal toward which all humanity should strive, since it is a divine model that guarantees peace of mind to the individual, an ordered and pious society in this world, and a just reward in the hereafter. They realize that the ideal promoted as the Islamic model is just that, an ideal that is yet to be realized, a model that encourages purity, pious living, and service. For some, conversion to Islam involves a rejection of their former faith and a transition to a monotheism that they believe is more theologically clear-cut than Christianity and more inclusive of all humanity than Judaism.

Despite the fact that problems do exist for new female converts—rejection by their families, lack of acceptance by the newly identified Muslim families and communities, racism, discomfort with some of the gender distinctions made in Islam—for the most part converts report that they are very happy with their decision and accept their role as agents of harmonization between Islam and an often skeptical American society. Some understand their responsibility as new Muslims as one of participating in a mission to foster and restore morality to the West. In general, they have found the supportive community that they have been seeking and are happy to trade the individuality of American life for that support.

In general, then, it can be said that female converts to Islam understand their identity not as socially and culturally constructed, but grounded in their original and natural being as a Muslim. They see Islam as providing an alternative to the carefully scripted identity fashioned by American society, which demands that they be attractive, sexually desirable, and competitive with men. As Muslims they can enjoy sexuality within the confines and the protection of marriage, and can play out the special roles assigned to them by Islam as the maintainers of culture and the promoters of the faith.

Whether they are captured by the love of a Muslim man to whom they want to devote their life, or attracted by the Qur'an, which provides them with answers to their quest for self-discovery, or looking for the kind of community that being a Muslim would seem to ensure, converts for the most part appear to have found peace in their surrender to God and through it a safe haven. Surrender and conversion thus serve the multiple ends of spiritual fulfillment, a husband and family, community belonging, and in many cases a newly acquired sense of personal self-assurance.

Notes

1. Interview with a Muslim leader, Washington, D.C., September 9, 2002.

2. Elizabeth Clarke, "Convert Finds Women's Rights in Islam," *Palm Beach Post*, November 6, 2002; Kay Jardine, "Western Women Are Turning to Islam in Rapidly Increasing Numbers," *The Herald*, March 8, 2002; Janet I. Tu, "Muslim Converts Try to Dispel Myths," *Seattle Times*, November 21, 2001.

3. Tamer El-Ghobashy, "Conversions to Islam on Rise in U.S.," *Daily News*, December 26, 2003.

4. Rana Kabbanni, *Imperial Fictions: Europe's Myths of Orient* (London: Pandora, 1986); Muhja Kahf, *From Tergament to Odalisque* (Austin: University of Texas Press, 1999); Reeva S. Simon, *The Middle East in Crime Fiction: Mysteries, Spy Novels, and Thrillers from 1916 to the 1980s* (New York: Lilian Barber Press, 1989); Jack G.

Shaheen, *Reel Bad Arabs: How Hollywood Vilifies a People* (New York: Olive Branch Press, 1984).

5. Ellen L. Fleischmann, "Our Muslim Sisters: Women in Greater Syria in the Eyes of American Protestant Missionary Women," *Islam and Christian-Muslim Relations* 9 (4): 307–324; Annie Von Summer and Samuel M. Zwemer, *Our Moslem Sisters: A Cry in Need from Lands of Darkness Interpreted by Those Who Heard It* (New York: F. H. Revell, 1907); Patricia Hill, *The World: Their Household* (Ann Arbor: University of Michigan Press, 1985).

6. See also his "Legal Debates on Muslim Minorities: Between Rejection and Accommodation," *Journal of Religious Ethics* 22 (1): 127–162.

7. Interview with Zahed Bokhari, Director MAPS Research Program, Georgetown University, Washington, D.C., January 25, 2003.

8. A derogatory term used to designate those who are born into a Muslim family but are deemed "nonpracticing."

9. The package also includes: a translation of the *Qur'an* into English; Fida Hussain Malik, *Wives of the Holy Prophet* (New Delhi: TAJ Company, 1989); 'Abdul Rahman I. Doi, *Women in the Qur'an and the Sunnah* (London: Ta-Ha Publishers, 1993); Abdullah Muhammad Khouj, *Islam* (n.p.: Islamic Foundation of America, n.d.); Abdul Rahman Ben Hammad Al-Omar, *The Religion of Truth* (n.p.: Ministry of Islamic Affairs, Endowments, Da'wa and Guidance of Saudi Arabia, n.d.); Suliman H. Al-But'he, *We Believe in Jesus* (Rabwah, Saudi Arabia: Islamic Propagation Office, 1998); Abu Ameenah Bilal Philips, *The True Religion* (Rabwah, Saudi Arabia: Islamic Propagation Office, 1992); Muhammad Sharif Chaudrhry, *Women's Rights in Islam* (Lahore, Pakistan: Sh. Muhammad Ashraf, 1991; *Islam and Christianity as Seen in the Bible* (Hufuf, Saudi Arabia: al-Ahsa Islamic Center, 1996).

10. Some literature in North America is openly anti-Christian. Ahmad Deedat of South Africa traveled in the United States and challenged Christian preachers to debates. Videotape copies of his lectures ridiculing the Gospels and the Bible for their inconsistencies are widely distributed, as are copies of his pamphlets. Other texts, such as *Why Did They Become Muslims?*, identify useful methods that Muslims could use to turn Christians against Christianity and convince them of the superiority of Islam. The book discusses such issues as the errors and discrepancies of the Bible. At the same time it assures the readers that Muhammad is foretold in the Bible. While affirming that Muhammad's miracle was the Qur'an, it lists a variety of miracles he had performed, including water gushing from between his fingers and his splitting the moon into two.

11. Unlike many Muslim feminists overseas and some Muslim academics in the United States, who have argued that Islam does not sanction polygamy, and that the Qur'an had actually limited the number of partners to one, Abd al-Ati is unapologetic in arguing that polygamy is not only permissible, it is divinely sanctioned in Islam under certain circumstances.

12. *Why Did They Become Muslims?* (Istanbul: Waqf Ikhlas Publisher, 1995), p. 15.

13. I would like to thank my research assistant, Jennifer Lynn Hill, for her work on this section.

14. *Why Did They Become Muslims?*, testimony of Mavish B. Jolly, p. 71.

15. Testimony of Aminah Assilmi, "The True Religion" Web site, http://www.thetruereligion.org.

16. Fatima Heeren, "Testimony of Fatima Heeren," in *Islam: Our Choice*, ed. Ebrahim Ahmed Bawany (Karachi: Begum Aisha Bawany Waqf, 1977), p. 56.

17. Quoted by Giles Whittell, "Allah Came Knocking at My Heart," *The Times*, January 7, 2002, republished at "The True Religion" Web site, http://www.thetruereligion.org.

18. Testimony of Erin/Sumaya Fannoun, "The True Religion" Web site, http://www.thetruereligion.org.

19. Sobia Virk, "Concordia Students Tell of Their Conversion to Islam," *The Link*, February 5, 2002, republished at "The True Religion" Web site, http://www.thetruereligion.org.

20. Alison Kysia, "The Role of Race and Gender Studies in My Conversion to Islam," Typescript (prepared in response to author's questions), May 1, 2003.

21. Quoted by Priya Malhotra, "Islam's Female Converts," February 16, 2002, http://www.newsday.com.

22. Quoted by Virk, "Concordia Students."

23. Testimony of Melanie, "The True Religion" Web site, http://www.thetruereligion.org.

24. Testimony of Amal, "The True Religion" Web site, http://www.thetruereligion.org.

25. Quoted by Tara Dooley, "From Christianity to Islam: A Journey of Faith," *Chicago Tribune*, republished at "The True Religion" Web site, http://www.thetruereligion.org.

26. Quoted by Lucy Berrington, "Why British Women Are Turning to Islam," *The Times*, November 9, 1993, republished at "The True Religion" Web site, http://www.thetruereligion.org.

27. Nick Compton, "The New Face of Islam," *The Evening Standard*, March 15, 2002.

28. Sidra Khan, "A Woman on a Mission," *The Guardian*, May 8, 1997.

29. Marina Jimenez, "New Muslims," *National Post*, January 19, 2002, republished at "The True Religion" Web site, http://www.thetruereligion.org.

30. Quoted in Ibid.

31. Kay Jardine, "Mum, I've Decided I Want to Follow Allah," *The Herald*, March 8, 2002.

32. Testimony of Sister Alyssa, "The True Religion" Web site, http://www.thetruereligion.org.

33. Quoted by Sarah McBride, "Converts in Kuwait," *Kuwait Times*, January 3, 1996, republished at "The True Religion" Web site, http://www.thetruereligion.org.

34. Quoted by Jimenez, "New Muslims."

35. Testimony of Karen, "The True Religion" Web site, http://www.thetruereligion.org.

36. Interview with Anne, March 2, 2002.

37. Kysia, "Role of Race and Gender Studies."

38. Testimony of Penomee, Kari Ann Owen, "The True Religion" Web site, http://www.thetruereligion.org.

39. Quoted by Jimenez, "New Muslims."

40. Testimony of Deanne, "The True Religion" Web site, http://www.thetruereligion.org.

41. http://www.zawaj.com.

42. http://www.singlemuslim.com.

43. Quoted in McBride, "Converts in Kuwait."

44. Jardine, "Mum, I've Decided I Want to Follow Allah."

45. Tu, "Muslim Converts Try to Dispel Myths."

46. Interview with Anne.

47. Ibid.

48. Ibid.

49. Interview with African American Imam, April 5, 2002.

50. Interview with Pakistani American female student at Georgetown University, March 23, 2002.

51. Ibid.

52. Interview with Pakistani American male student at Georgetown University, March 25, 2002.

53. Telephone interview with an African American female convert to Sufism in Los Angeles, May 5, 2003.

54. Testimony of Zainab, "The True Religion" Web site, http://www.thetruereligion.org.

55. Anonymous testimony, "The True Religion" Web site, http://www.thetruereligion.org.

56. Khan, "A Woman on a Mission."

57. Compton, "The New Face of Islam."

58. Testimony of Shakira Graham, "The True Religion" Web site, http://www.thetruereligion.org.

59. Testimony of Nadia, "The True Religion" Web site, http://www.thetruereligion.org.

60. Jimenez, "New Muslims."

References

Abd al-Ati, Hammudah. 1977. *The Family Structure in Islam*. Indianapolis: American Trust Publications.

———. 1978. *Islam in Focus*. Salimiah, Kuwait: International Islamic Federation of Student Organizations; Leicester, UK: Islamic Foundation.

Abou El Fadl, Khaled. 1994. "Legal Debates on Muslim Minorities: Between Rejection and Accommodation." *Journal of Religious Ethics* 22 (1): 127–162.

———. 2000. "Striking a Balance: Islamic Legal Discourse on Muslim Minorities." In *Muslims on the Americanization Path?*, ed. Yvonne Yazbeck Haddad and John L. Esposito, pp. 47–64. New York: Oxford University Press.

Allen, Ernest, Jr. 2000. "Identity and Destiny: The Formative Views of the Moorish Science Temple and the Nation of Islam." In *Muslims on the Americanization Path?*, ed. Yvonne Yazbeck Haddad and John L. Esposito, pp. 163–214. New York: Oxford University Press.

Anway, C. L. 1995. *Daughters of Another Path: Experiences of American Women Choosing Islam*. Lee's Summit, Mo.: Yawna Publications.

Bawany, Ebrahim Ahmed. 1997. *Islam: Our Choice*. Karachi: Begum Aisha Bawany Waqf.

Fleischmann, Ellen L. 1998. "Our Muslim Sisters: Women in Greater Syria in the Eyes of American Protestant Missionary Women." *Islam and Christian-Muslim Relations* 9 (4): 307–324.

Gardell, Mattias. 1994. "The Sun of Islam Will Rise in the West: Minister Farrakhan and the Nation of Islam in the Latter Days." In *Muslim Communities in North America*, ed. Yvonne Yazbeck Haddad and

Jane Idleman Smith, pp. 15–50. Albany: State University of New York Press.

Haddad, Yvonne Yazbeck, and Jane I. Smith. 1993. *Mission to America: Five Islamic Sectarian Communities in North America*. Gainesville: University Press of Florida.

Hill, Patricia. 1935. *The World: Their Household*. Ann Arbor: University of Michigan Press.

Kabbani, Rana. 1986. *Imperial Fiction: Europe's Myths of Orient*. London: Pandora Press.

Kahf, Muhja. 1999. *From Tergament to Odalisque*. Austin: University of Texas Press.

Murad, Khurram. 1983. *Islamic Movement in the West*. Leicester, UK: Islamic Foundation.

———. 1986. *Da'wa among Non-Muslims in the West: Some Conceptual and Methodological Approaches*. Leicester, UK: Islamic Foundation.

Shafiq, Muhammad. 1994. *Growth of Islamic Thought in North America: Focus on Isma'il Raji al Faruqi*. Brentwood, Md.: Amana Publications.

Shaheen, Jack G. 1984. *Reel Bad Arabs: How Hollywood Vilifies a People*. New York: Olive Branch Press.

Simon, Reeva S. 1989. *The Middle East in Crime Fiction: Mysteries, Spy Novels, and Thrillers from 1916 to the 1980s*. New York: Lilian Barber Press.

"The True Religion." Web site with personal testimonies and newspaper article reprints. http://www.thetruereligion.org.

Von Summer, Annie, and Samuel M. Zwemer. 1907. *Our Moslem Sisters: A Cry in Need from Lands of Darkness Interpreted by Those Who Heard It*. New York: F. H. Revell.

Yusuf 'Ali, Abdullah. 1989. *The Meaning of the Holy Qur'an*. Beltsville, Md.: Amana Corporation.

CHAPTER 2

The Shaping of a Scandinavian "Islam"
Converts and Gender Equal Opportunity

Anne Sofie Roald

It is symptomatic that new converts often embrace a specific cultural understanding of Islam, where, for instance, Arabic, Pakistani, or African cultural traits become important in their new Islamic worldview. As most converts go through stages in the postconversion process, their worldview for their understanding of Islam will change. This study will discuss how many of the Scandinavian converts tend to integrate "Scandinavian values" into their understanding of Islam. During my fieldwork among Scandinavian converts in 1999 and 2000, where I handed out questionnaires and conducted interviews with 116 converts from Norway, Sweden, and Denmark, I found that it is mainly those who converted several years ago and in addition are highly educated who are actors in this process of hybridization where "Scandinavian values" become "Islamic values."[1]

In the Scandinavian convert community, I have found a three-stage conversion process relating mainly to the time after conversion. This conversion process deals largely with new Muslims' relations to the born-Muslim community. It also, however, has psychological aspects, its stages being "love," "disappointment," and "maturity." It is important to note that I have observed a similar three-stage process among Muslim converts in other European countries. Although this study mainly deals with converts at the third stage, I will refer to the three stages in order for the reader to get a broader understanding of how the stages related to converts' understanding of Islam.

New Muslims are socialized into a certain cultural context, but, by converting to Islam, there is a total shift of "cultural truths." This cultural shift might put the convert in a contrasting cultural position, where s/he becomes critical of his/her cultural group and tends to look in positive terms at the Muslim group. This is a problematic process, as it might alienate the convert from the previous in-group. At the same time, it might be difficult for the new Muslim to adopt Muslim cultural traits in toto, particularly as this culture, behaviorally and ideologically speaking, is to a great extent founded on patriarchal and traditional ideas alien to many societies in the Western world. In respondents' answers to my questionnaire and in my discussions with new Muslims, I have sensed how many new Muslim converts tend to be enthusiastic about Muslims and Muslim cultures shortly after conversion. However, many of these become more critical of Muslims as a group after a while. The shift of cultural belonging might cause new Muslims to experience a sudden shift of perspective at the beginning of the conversion process. However, as time goes by, the social structure they are primarily socialized into tends to resurface, particularly if there is a wide gap between the cultural traits of the competing paradigms.

This chapter will first give a broad outline of the stages of conversion. Second, it will deal with how "Scandinavian values" tend to be prominent in the Muslim converts' discourse on "Islam."

Stages of Conversion

The initial phase of conversion, where one can be "more royal than the king," is evident in the new Muslims' discussions. Many new Muslims tell of how, in the beginning, they tended to be emotionally obsessed with the new religion. Furthermore, they wanted to practice every little detail of the Islamic precepts. Some of the new converts spoke of how they would sit and read Islamic books every spare moment they had. "I just want to learn every single Islamic rule and start to practice everything I have learnt at once," exclaimed a twenty-one-year-old woman, who had been a Muslim just six months. The phenomenon of absolutism seems to be a universal one among new converts to Islam. A leading British academic convert, T. J. Winters, has termed the phenomenon "convertitis." He explains:

The initial and quite understandable response of many newcomers is to become an absolutist. Everything going on among pious Muslims is angelic; everything outside the circle of faith is demonic; the appeal of this outlook lies in its simplicity. The newly arranged landscape on which the convert looks is seen in satisfying black and white terms of Them versus Us, good against evil. (Winters, http://www.islamfortoday.com)

I was referred to this text on "convertitis" by a new Muslim living in Britain. I recognized the phenomenon, which confirms my own experience with new converts in Scandinavian society in their first stage of conversion, a stage I have called the "falling-in-love stage."

After a while, when the first "intoxication" has worn off a little, many new Muslims realize that they have bitten off more than they can chew. All the new rules and regulations they want to introduce into their life might be felt to be too much. Moreover, at the beginning there is a tendency among new Muslims to look upon the cultural Muslim expressions as "the true Islam." After reading books and having discussions with other Muslims, they realize the difference in Islamic expressions across various Muslim countries.

This second stage of the conversion process is strongly linked to a disappointment with born-Muslim behavior and ideas. Many converts tell how they have suddenly realized that Muslims cannot live according to the lofty Islamic ideals. At this stage, some new Muslims tend to turn away from Islam, as they feel too disappointed.

At this second stage of the conversion process, the convert might also get the feeling of being both "insider" and "outsider" in his/her own society. Just as it is difficult to wholly identify with the immigrant Muslim community, the shift of perspective has made it hard to identify fully with the group of origin. Moreover, a discrepancy develops between the way majority society defines the convert and the way the convert perceives him/herself. The difference between the outer and inner conceptions of the self is illustrated by Amal's reflections. She discusses the difference between her inner self-perception and her visual experience of herself wearing a headscarf; she feels startled when she occasionally catches a glimpse of herself in the reflections of a windowpane and feels that it is another person she sees. "The person I see in the mirror can't be me," she says. She explains this feeling by pointing to the fact that she does not constantly feel herself to be a Muslim. The discrepancy between self-perception and the person's social status, as defined by majority society's view of Muslims and Muslim converts, might lead to a confusion of one's own identity. However, in my experience with Muslim converts, new Muslims choose either to remain within the Muslim cultural paradigm (being cultural converts) or, like second-generation Muslim children, develop "integrated plural identities," where there is a harmonious transcultural oscillation among various patterns of identity (Østberg 2000).

The third stage comes when the new Muslim realizes that Muslims are "human beings and not supernatural creatures," as expressed by one of the converts in this study, and comes to accept intellectually "the discrepancy between ideal and reality," as expressed by several others. At this stage many new Muslims tend to search for new understandings of Islamic ideas and attitudes, and it is at this point that many new Muslims actively start to shape a new understanding of Islam according to the particular cultural context they live in. This stage can be named the stage of "maturity," as many new

Muslims have expressed that they feel they have come "back to themselves." Many have stated how they discovered that "in reality" they are Scandinavian individuals living within an Islamic frame.

This notion of coming back to oneself—being both Scandinavian and Muslim—is illustrated by Østberg's concept of integrated plural identities. Such notions of cultural shifts and plural identities are linked to the question: how does one maintain a religious worldview? Berger and Luckmann (1967) speak in terms of plausibility structures, where a religious person has a plausibility structure that is necessary for the maintenance of "a symbolic universe." Swedish sociologist of religion Eva Hamberg (1999) has discussed how a person's plausibility structure might be disrupted by migration. She discusses various factors in the migration situation and concludes that, because an immigrant loses all contact with her/his own group or with like-minded individuals, it might be difficult to maintain belief in her/his original "symbolic universe," as s/he is not surrounded by a supporting structure that makes this belief plausible.

Hamberg's discussion of immigrants' plausibility structures can be applied to new Muslims' situations. As "religion" involves not only belief but also a complete symbolic universe, the shift to a new belief must incorporate a new plausibility structure. Hamberg regards the plausibility structure in static terms, saying that in the immigrant situation it might be disrupted (Hamberg 1999, 27). In contrast to her view, however, I understand the plausibility structure as in a state of flux. Therefore, it might change according to context.

The influence a new plausibility structure has over the new Muslim depends on his/her life situation. If the new Muslim is living in an environment comprising only born Muslims belonging to one particular culture, that particular plausibility structure has a stronger effect on him/her. However, a Muslim convert who has less contact with born Muslims and more contact with non-Muslims will be less influenced by the born-Muslim plausibility structure. A third alternative is more common: new Muslims of similar cultural backgrounds mix and create a merged plausibility structure built mainly on the Islamic sources, but mixed with the new Muslims' preconversion cultural context. In this case, it is possible for new views and ideas to emerge, built on deconstruction and reconstruction of cultural concepts both from majority society and Muslim cultures.

However, although most converts reach the second or the third stages, some "remain behind" in the first stage for a long time. It is particularly

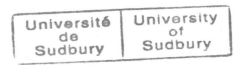

adherents to the "extreme movements," such as the *salafis* and those of the *hizb al-tahrir*, who remained in this first stage. Followers of such movements behave in a fashion similar to many converts in the first stage of "falling in love with Islam," where one adheres to every little Islamic precept. This stage is best illustrated by the example of the *salafi* trend, which promotes the idea that every single Qur'anic verse or hadith should be acted on in a literal way. This direction can be regarded as a particularization of Islam, as it reflects "Arab culture" at a certain period of time, namely the seventh to the tenth centuries.

An important finding of this study is that Scandinavian converts who embraced Islam in the late 1990s do not necessarily go through these postconversion stages. Those who converted in the 1980s and early 1990s were usually socialized straight into an immigrant Muslim context. The growth of the convert community has helped recent converts to be socialized into Islam through other new Muslims. Thus, the "new" converts jump directly into the "old" converts' cultural sphere and internalize convert conceptualizations directly, without having to go through the culturalization process into the Muslim immigrant community. It is thus the convert plausibility structure that creates the "symbolic universe" of the new converts. The development of these postconversion stages, thus, tends to differ according to the time a person embraces Islam, as well as the quality and size of the convert community in the person's area.

Scandinavian converts to Islam experience strong cultural influences both from the Scandinavian and various Muslim cultural spheres. Their understanding of Islam seems to eventually end up as something in between these cultural spheres, particularly in the third stage of conversion, which is the main focus of this chapter. The Norwegian researcher Lena Larsen suggests that new Muslims' shaping of a particular form of Islam in the Western context is an important development. The formation of a strong community of Norwegian Muslims helps them in their intercession between Muslim communities and majority society. Larsen shows that converts are positioned in the middle of society: there is a dichotomy between new Muslims and born Muslims on the one hand and a dichotomy between Norwegian society and new Muslims on the other. Thus, the born Muslims view the new Muslims as "them," and Norwegian society views them the same. Therefore, in Larsen's view, the new Muslims become a separate group: "Norwegian Muslims."

Larsen claims that the separation of new Muslims and born Muslims is caused largely by the Muslim community. However, she conducted her study in the early 1990s, and the situation has changed in the early twenty-first century. Lately, with the growth of the convert community, new Muslims' own "us" and "them" dichotomy has tended to affect the separation between born Muslims and new Muslims. This dichotomy might also affect new Muslims' separation from Scandinavian society: their change in worldview at the time of conversion creates a distance between them and certain Scandinavian attitudes and notions. This distance is expressed in the "us" and "them" dichotomy. In Larsen's model, new Muslims are, to a certain extent, passive and forced into their particular position, whereas the new reality seems to be that Muslims themselves are conscious as well as unconscious actors in the shaping of a particular form of "Scandinavian Islam"/"Scandinavian Muslim" community.

The impression I got from my interviews with new Muslims from Scandinavia is that many regard their particular understanding of Islam as being different from that of the immigrant community. New Muslims often view immigrants' behavior as part of a struggle between "Islam" and "culture"; few grasp the complex relationship that really exists between culture and religion. However, Amal stated that "as the Islamic sources have always been interpreted through cultural filters, we, the Swedish Muslims, might create a Swedish Islam." Larsen has noted a similar development in Norway, saying:

They [the converts] can be regarded as bringing their own Norwegian "cultural baggage," which is of importance when the Qur'anic principles are interpreted in the Norwegian context. The result, in the future, will be a "Norwegian Islam." (Larsen 1995, 175 [translation mine])

"Religion" versus "Culture"

Many researchers on Islam see the Muslim concept of "one true Islam" as being a refusal to accept regional differences in the understandings of the Islamic sources. A Swedish researcher on Islam, Leif Stenberg, sees "Islam" as:

An on-going discourse where different trends are engaged in struggle, and where the successful contender becomes, for the time being, the established tradition, until it is challenged by yet another trend. This is a situation where many "Islams" fight to become the One Islamic tradition. (Stenberg 1996, 15)

Jonas Otterbeck, another Swedish researcher in Islamic studies, has a similar view. In his discussion of the Muslim magazine *Salaam,* he shows how

Muslim writers are looking for a "true Islam" by denigrating other Islamic interpretations as "false Islam" (Otterbeck 2000, 149). He further indicates that Muslims, as well as some non-Muslims, who write about Islam tend to regard Islam as "a reified category that is experienced as an objective reality." In his view it is not understandings of Islam that are presented, but rather "Islam" itself (Otterbeck 2000, 159). I agree to a certain extent with Otterbeck, that in the 1980s and early 1990s this way of presenting "Islamic" ideas was common both among Muslims and non-Muslims. Otterbeck's study does not, however, discuss the huge development of Islamic ideas in the 1990s; rather, it is a historical study presenting ideas in the '80s and the early '90s. Although many Muslims still tend to speak in terms of "right" and "wrong" Islam, the belief in "one true Islam" or "one Islamic tradition" has changed. This change is obvious by looking, for instance, at the Scandinavian Muslim e-group on the Internet, where this concept of "one Islam" is more or less on the way out at the beginning of the twenty-first century.[2] I have also observed amongst new Muslims as well as born Muslims that the acceptance of the diversity of the Muslim community on both a global and local scale is growing. Some accept it reluctantly; others, like Annika, who converted to Islam in the mid-1980s, see the diversity as a "reason why Islam still is a driving force in many Muslims' lives." In my discussion with Annika, she stated that if "Islam" actually were static, it would only be suitable for one place and at one time. "The reason why Islam is still going strong," she says, "is its dynamics that make it suitable for all times and all places."

Otterbeck and Stenberg do not draw attention to the fact that Muslims tend to reject those ideas and actions of other Muslims that they regard to be "harmful" or "bad." This seems apparent in the example to which Otterbeck draws attention in his discussion on "the true Islam," but without discussing it in such terms. Otterbeck quotes a female new Muslim's article in the Swedish Islamic magazine *Salaam*:

A Muslim knows that a child is a gift from Allah, whether it is a boy or a girl, and it has the right to care, cordiality, and guidance. That is why s/he loves his/her daughter just as much as the son: s/he gives the daughter just as good an education as s/he gives the son and s/he shows the daughter just as much appreciation and consideration as s/he shows the son. Anything else would be impossible in the just and global religion of equality, Islam. (Otterbeck 2000, 148 [translation mine]; see also Salaam 8 [87]: 7)

This Muslim convert reacts to what she understands to be injustice and inequality, qualities that, according to her, do not belong within the framework of Islam. She rejects what in her view are "bad" qualities, whereas she would probably accept as "Islamic" what in her view are "good" actions or ideas. The content of what is "good" or "bad" is a cultural as well as personal matter and cannot be discussed objectively. The important thing, however, is that "Islam" for most Muslims represents that which they regard as "good," and they would refuse that which they regard as "bad," seeing it as "un-Islamic."

The English sociologist Bobby S. Sayyid discusses the issue of "Islam" versus "Islams," a debate also tackled by many non-Muslim researchers (see, for instance, Stenberg 1996, 15). He speaks in terms of the signifier (the image) and the signified (the concept). By referring to Jacques Lacan, who believes that the signified is produced by the signifier, he sees Islam as a signifier "whose meaning is expressed by its articulation" (Sayyid 1997, 42). The issue becomes one of identifying how Islam itself is articulated as a nodal point. He gives the example that, in general argumentation, "Islam" connotes many things, such as the Qur'an and the messengership of the Prophet, that "it carries along in any of its articulations within any single Muslim community, and cannot be disarticulated without dissolving the specificity of 'Islam'" (Sayyid 1997, 42). He continues, saying:

This would suggest that, although Islam can be used to suture a large number of discourses, and that in each act of suturing, its identity will be transformed, it still retains traces of its other articulations. (Sayyid 1997, 43)

Sayyid sees the unity of the Muslim community as being the result of "retrospectively constructing its [the community's] identity, through the use of Islam as a nodal point" (Sayyid 1997, 44). Sayyid points to that fact that "Islam" occupies a privileged place within the Muslim discourse and that "the inter-discursivity of Islam is tied up, in large measure, by its significance for the construction of a Muslim identity" (Sayyid 1997, 44). Sayyid argues that even though "Islam" may be used to articulate a multiplicity of positions, this does not mean that there are multiple "Islams." Rather, he says, "Islam has emerged as the means of articulating a multiplicity of positions without losing its specificity" (Sayyid 1997, 44). Sayyid defines this specificity as being "for the majority of Muslims... the definition of good" (Sayyid 1997, 48). In his view, therefore, "Islam" is a "master signifier."

The notion of "Islam" as representing "the good" is reinforced by Otterbeck's example. Otterbeck refers to how writers in *Salaam* understand Islam to be a religion of equality between men and women; a green, ecological religion; as well as a democratic, socially and economically just religion (Otterbeck 2000, 148–149). All the values listed by Otterbeck show how Scandinavian Muslims understand "Islam" as a master signifier of that which is "good" and "lofty."

New Muslims on "Danish," "Swedish," or "Norwegian" Islam

Do new Muslims recognize the emergence of a "Scandinavian Islam,"[3] or do they regard Islam as static and immutable, in keeping with the belief of "one true Islam"? In my discussions with Scandinavian new Muslims I raised the issue and was presented with a different view by nearly every individual. Even within similar currents of thought, I could sense variations in view, and individuals' cultural and social backgrounds, gender and personal dispositions, seem to have as large a part to play in this as the current they represent. Below, I will discuss some of the views.

In my discussions, most new Muslims saw the development of a "Danish," "Swedish," or "Norwegian" Islam as a natural part of the process of Islam's acceptance in Scandinavian countries. However, Mansur, from the *hizb al-tahrir*, categorically opposed the development of a "Danish Islam." He states:

I believe that Muslims cannot and should not form a "Danish Islam." There do not exist many versions of Islam, just as there do not exist many versions of the Qur'an. The attempt to create a so-called "Danish Islam," "European Islam" or "American Islam" is only the over-interpretation of certain Islamic texts. In reality, they are Western thoughts, values and rules that are only dressed up as Islam.

Mansur sees the attempts to develop a "Danish Islam" in terms of conspiracy. "The idea of a 'Danish Islam,' 'European Islam,' or 'American Islam,'" he says, "is aimed at the destruction of Islam and the Muslims." He continues, saying that "such ideas are designed to empty the Islamic worldview and the Islamic legislation of those concepts and laws which are not compatible with Western concepts, norms, values, systems, and legislation." He sees this attempt to destroy Islam as part of Western countries' "global war against Islam," which is manifested in "United States policy in the Muslim world."

Abu Ahmad, who converted six years ago and who has a slightly *salafi* approach, did not accept the concept of "Swedish Islam" either. His view is that "Swedish Islam" would be just a new Islamic Law School. It is interesting to note also, however, his observation that "every country's traditions leave their mark on the way Islam is practiced, but that is something else."

The Danish Imam, Abdul-Wahid Pedersen, regards Islam in a similar way, although he goes further than Abu Ahmad. He says that "Islam is one, but it has many faces." He creates a metaphor of Islam as a string bag full of oranges:

If we change oranges for apples, the bag is still the same, although the fruit changes. I see Islam in this way, if we put Danes or Indonesians or Moroccans in the bag, the bag is still the same, whereas the content, the people inside, change. The people do not change their culture just because they become Muslims. Islam is the gathering factor, but the various Muslim cultures differ from each other.

It is possible to regard Abdul-Wahid's view on Islam as similar to Sayyid's characterization of Islam as a "nodal point." Just as Sayyid believes that "Islam" can be used to articulate a multiplicity of positions without implying multiple "Islams," Abdul-Wahid sees "Islam as one," but with "many faces." Abdul-Wahid's understanding of Islam in these terms rejects the Western notion of "Islams"; he indicates great diversity *within* the Islamic framework.

Abdul-Wahid sees "culture" as being distinct from "religion," indicating a static concept of culture. However, after further discussion, he stated that he sees a close relationship between religion and culture and that "this relationship between the two is the evidence that it is possible to preserve cultural traits within Islam." "Islam is still Islam in Morocco, and Islam is still Islam in Indonesia, although the cultures in the two countries are different," he says.

In my discussions with Abla, who embraced Islam in the mid-1980s, she expressed that "Swedish Islam" for her is "Islam interpreted through Swedish/European experiences." Abla has a degree in humanities and her answers are marked by a reflective attitude both toward "Islam" as a concept and her own role as a Muslim in Scandinavian society. "Swedish Islam," she says, "widens the scope of Islam." She tells how she and other Muslim women—Swedish converts and some first-generation immigrants—have established kindergartens according to the Swedish model of child care, run Muslim women's sports associations, and arranged summer camps for Muslim women and children with outdoor activities, bathing, and canoeing. "These activities are all examples of 'Swedish Islam,'" she claims.

It is, however, in relation to the women's issue that she feels a "Swedish Islam" is most evident in her own Muslim environment. In her view, many Muslim countries have restrictive boundaries for the activities of Muslim women and young girls. "The interpretations of Islam are more limited, traditional, and conventional in Muslim countries," she says. She sees these interpretations as serving the "preservation of culture," in contrast to "Swedish Islam," which, in her view, is an innovative and alternative movement of questioning. "Our way," she says, "is the creation of new culture. Swedish Islam tries to find alternative methods and ways to educate and promote *da'wa*." She further states that in her view "Swedish Islam" incorporates "Swedish" values, such as honesty, punctuality, a work ethic, and the keeping of promises. She says that these virtues are also "Islamic virtues," but they "are not particularly prominent among Muslims."

It is interesting to note that, during the lectures I give to the Swedish public or university students, I usually ask them what they regard as "Swedish ideals," so that we might compare them with "Islamic ideals." The ideals they list are very much in accord with Abla's list of the "Swedish values" she believes penetrate "Swedish Islam." Her view, thus, complies with Sayyid's idea of "Islam" being a master signifier, having connotations of the "good" for Muslims. Abla's Islamic ideals are compatible with Swedish ideals, and "Swedish Islam" becomes a mixture of Islamic and Swedish notions. The innovation in this mixture is its emphasis on the "good": "good" Islamic ideals are mixed with the "good" Swedish ideals, creating a "Swedish Muslim" who is regarded as both the "best Muslim" and the "best Swede." The merging of "Islamic" and "Scandinavian" values indicated by Abla and Pedersen points at the "creolization" of culture. Abla and Pedersen's cultural creolization contrasts with Mansur and Abu Ahmad's idea of one uniform understanding of Islam. The centralized ideology of *hizb al-tahrir* and the *salafi* worldview obviously plays a part in such an understanding. As the ideology of the two movements sticks to the accepted beliefs of Arabic-speaking ideologues, there is no scope for local expressions of Islam. Abla and Pedersen's acceptance of particular Scandinavian expressions of Islam not only highlights the idea of creolization but also shows how converts cause "implosions" within the Muslim community. Abla and Pedersen are both active within the Muslim community and are thus transferring their ideas into a wider Muslim context. The merging of "Islamic" and "Scandinavian" values is a probable outcome of their activities.

Equal Gender Opportunities

As indicated by Abla, "Swedish Islam" allows for Muslim women to participate in activities in which women in Muslim countries are restricted.

In my discussions with Muslim converts, I found that the issue of gender was often raised. The fact that gender issues are prominent among new Muslims has to be regarded in view of how Islam is portrayed as a "religion hostile to women" in the Scandinavian media, as well as in the general Scandinavian discourse. The new Muslims respond to this by presenting counterarguments to such portraits, thus facilitating change in the realm of gender issues. I have observed how new converts tend to defend traditional Muslim gender systems. However, as these new Muslims go through various stages in the conversion process there is a tendency to incorporate Scandinavian ideals on gender relations into the Islamic framework, seeing gender equality as "Islamic" in the pattern of that which is "good" is Islamic. I have discussed elsewhere how there tends to be a rapprochement between the ideas of highly educated Arabic-speaking immigrants and those of the West when it comes to gender relations (Roald 2001). A similar relationship can be observed in the Scandinavian convert community, where views on equal gender opportunities vary according to the level of education and degree of continuous contact with majority society.

Maryam, a young woman who is a sympathizer with the *salafi* movement, states: "In Islam the man is the breadwinner and the woman has to stay at home with her children." Maryam does not wear the face veil that is quite common among *salafis*. She says that she would prefer to wear a face veil, but she is only eighteen and is still at school. Her ideas on the roles of women and men are very much the same as those found in books written by leading *salafis* in Saudi Arabia, Jordan, and Egypt. Books on women's behavior and women's dress from these countries, which have spread to Scandinavia in the late 1990s, promote a strict segregation between men and women and a gender pattern that accords with the Saudi gender pattern in particular. Mansur, of the Danish *hizb al-tahrir* movement, promotes a similar view when he refers to the article on gender written by Taqi al-Din al-Nabhani, the founder of *hizb al-tahrir*. The article states that there is no problem between men and women in "Islam," and Mansur's acceptance of this statement indicates a lack of awareness of gender issues in general.

In contrast to Maryam and Mansur, Håkon does not see any conflict between the ideal of equal opportunities and Islam. He states that there is no problem with equal gender opportunities, so long as one can be relaxed about the issue. "The Arab gender pattern is not necessarily Islamic," he says. "Look at how the Prophet was at home sewing his own sandals and taking part in domestic work in a relaxed way. I do not want to make a big deal out of it and for me I do not see it as a problem." In my discussion with the Danish Imam, Abdul-Wahid Pedersen, I asked him about his view on gender equality. He stated:

There has always been gender equality in Islam. It has been known in Islam for 1,400 years. It is a new thing in the Western part of the world, but there has always been gender equality [ligestilling] in Islam. This gender equality, however, does not mean the two genders have similar tasks [en-stilling], as there is a difference between men and women. Islamic views are based on the real world. Women acquire their rights according to what is stated in the Qur'an, and in the Qur'an men and women are given nearly the same rights and duties.

It is interesting to compare Pedersen's argument with the book written by the Egyptian-Canadian Islamic scholar Jamal Badawi, *Gender Equity in Islam: Basic Principles* (1995). Badawi uses the term "gender equity" instead of "gender equality," seeing the former as more "Islamic" than the latter. He says:

Equity is used here to mean justice and overall equality in the totality of rights and responsibilities of both genders and allows for the possibility of variations in specific items within the overall balance and equality. (Badawi 1995, 47)

Badawi's book was discussed by female convert attendees of a summer camp in Gothenburg in 1997. The discussion centered on Badawi's concept of "equity" and its consequences in "real life." One Swedish convert's impression of "equity" is that, although men and women have the same opportunities, everybody has the right to make personal choices according to his/her own disposition. No position should be regarded as better than another position in her view. She continued by saying that the hierarchical structures in society result from the perceived superiority of men's traditional role over that of women. She believed this standard is still reflected in the modern world's social setup. In the ensuing discussion, another convert commented that the typical necessity for women, due to the economic system in the Scandinavian countries, to work outside the home even though they have small children, is an example of "equality" rather than "equity"; there is no consideration that women have various likes and dislikes. In her view, some women pursue careers, whereas others prefer to stay at home, and the pattern of "equity" takes care of such differences in outlook and disposition. There was a total acceptance of Badawi's concept of "equity," many of the women expressing in interviews that Badawi's book had brought them much relief. One of them exclaimed: "He [Badawi] has named a feeling that many Muslims recognize but have had difficulty expressing." Although I raised the question of how the relationship of power between men and women might influence women's choices, I discovered that there was no real awareness of this among the converts in this discussion. For them "equity" represented a free choice of their own. In the process of defining "gender equity," however, a situation similar to that of the past might arise, where women's tasks, what is Islamic and what is un-Islamic, are established by male representatives of the Islamic faith.

I discovered that with the exception of followers of the *salafi* movement and the *hizb al-tahrir*, by and large Scandinavian new Muslims accept the ideal of equal opportunities, but reject the idea of seeing women and men as "equal." The concept of "equity" seems to cover this distinction. I found that there was no great difference between Shia and Sunni converts on this matter. It is interesting to note that in my discussions with Shi'a Muslims, Gunilla said she feels the Shi'a converts she knows are all "feminists," herself included. In her view, many Sunni converts are more traditional, in that they tend to follow their partners' "Islam," whereas Shi'a female converts are continuously fighting for women's rights within "Islam." I do not know whether she is right or not, but such conclusions seem to reflect more the type of people with whom one mixes. She might feel this way because she mixes with those people she feels comfortable with and who have views similar to hers. There are also more Sunni convert Muslims than Shi'a converts. My discussions with Sunni Muslims, however, have shown that ideas on female empowerment are just as dominant among them as they are among Shi'a Muslims. In further discussions with Shi'a Muslims I discovered that, even in this group, "feminist" ideas are closer to the concept of "equity" than "equality," thus reflecting the pattern in the Sunni Muslim convert community.

In my discussion with Annika, who is a Sunni Muslim, she stated:

In my view "equity" means justice. I believe it is unfair to have to live up to the standard of men. Men are different and have different dispositions, and the creation of a man's world has tended to incorporate the traditional roles of men. If we go back fifty years, this man's world had no place for children. Now look at how much women work. Who should take care of the children? We are working side by side with men in society, but in this "manly" society we have forgotten who is to take care of the family. In the end it all comes down to who is to wash the dishes. The social community represented by the family is dissolving, and I as a Muslim am very concerned about this situation. At the same time, I am very much part of it, as I am a professional woman who does not manage to take care of my family as I would like. If, in Sweden,

we believed in equity instead of equality we might have a better society, where I could
be both a working professional and a good mother and wife.

Annika's dilemma of being a professional at the same time as feeling responsibility for keeping the family together is not specific to new Muslims; it
is a problem for many women in Scandinavian society. It is characteristic of
the new Muslim approach, however, that Annika accepts the woman's role as
being responsible for the running of the family. Annika believes that women
are generally more competent at caring for the family's well-being, and she
would have preferred a society where she could combine her professional-
ism with family maintenance.

The acceptance of men and women's different biological dispositions is
inherent in the concept of "equity." In the official Scandinavian discourse
such argumentation is often termed "biological reductionism," a label that
has negative connotations, and the arguments have been repressed and more
or less defined out of the discourse. In further discussion with Annika I asked
her if she believes that men and women must have different roles due to biological factors. She answered:

In society, I believe that men and women are interchangeable; a woman is as good a
medical doctor as a man, and a man can be as good a nurse as a woman, and so on.
However, on a personal level I believe women feel more responsibility towards their
children than many men. Psychologists and geneticists explain this with the fact that
women, unlike men, can only beget a limited number of children. I believe this has
an influence on the human psyche, at least this is my personal experience. Although
my husband is very concerned with the upbringing of our children, he does not care
to check if they have brushed their teeth properly or if they put on sufficient clothes
when they go out.

In response to my asking Annika how she believes a system of "equity"
would help her in her professional life, she stated that in such a system her
domestic work and her main responsibility for raising the children would be
recognized as qualifications and become part of her official work portfolio.
"If I apply for a job, I should have the right to have this work evaluated as
work experience, which would help me to expand in my job." She continued,
saying that "if women's traditional work were appreciated on an official level
of society, women would have greater possibilities to participate not only in
society as such, but also on a higher level of society."

In the discussion with Pedersen, he stated that women were only re-stricted in leading prayers in a mixed gathering, otherwise men and women have equal opportunities. When I asked a group of female converts about this view, they accepted this limitation on female participation. One convert stated that women might function as imams and lead prayers, but in a female gathering only. Thus, the only limitation for women, she said, is praying in front of men, and she did not see this as a problem. However, she admitted that it might become a problem for some in the future, Muslim girls, for in-stance, who are brought up in a society like that of Scandinavia, where the equal opportunities policy is strong. "But," she said, "we will cross that bridge when we come to it." Another convert stated that she did not regard the issue of women being imams as being as important as that of women becoming Islamic scholars. In her view it is in the intellectual development of Islamic ideas that women are needed in order to correct "the imbalance between the female and the male perspective in Islamic thinking."

Ideas on equal opportunities in the Scandinavian convert community re-semble those of general society. And, just as in society in general, discourses on gender of new Muslims differ according to the educational status of the individuals and the degree of the individual's integration into majority so-ciety. *Salafis*, members of the *hizb al-tahrir*, and less-educated Muslims who are marginalized in majority society tend to accept the traditional Muslim gender pattern. The views of the more highly educated, who are often part of the majority society, tend, on the other hand, to converge with the standard Scandinavian view of equal opportunities. However, the latter group's point of view differs slightly from Scandinavian discourses on gender. The diver-gence can be illustrated in the distinction between the two concepts "equal-ity" and "equity."

Toward a Scandinavian Islam?

Larsen discusses a gradual convergence of "Islamic" and "Norwegian" ac-tivities into a new kind of "Islamic" activity. Norwegian converts have, for instance, started up Islamic kindergartens and have also initiated a specific form of 'id-celebration. In the Muslim world the 'id-celebration is a time when families visit each other during the three or four days that the celebra-tion lasts. New Muslims often do not have Muslim relatives, unless they can include their partner's family. In the Muslim community in Norway there was no real 'id celebration for children until female converts decided to arrange a special party in one of the mosques, al-Rabita (the league), after the 'id-prayer. The new Muslims emphasized the children's need for celebrations and the development of 'id-traditions in the Norwegian context. The giving of gifts to children who had managed to fast and the organization of various competitions became a recurring element in the celebrations (Larsen 1995, 79). Larsen notes that, after a while, even Muslim immigrants took part in this celebration. Even women from other mosques came to attend the celebration, as there were no arrangements for women in their mosques. The new Muslims' 'id-traditions in Scandinavia resemble those of the traditional Christmas observance.

As most converts tend to skip the Christmas celebration (except for those who feel obliged to celebrate with their parents), they have brought the traditions from this celebration into the new Islamic framework. One example of this is the Norwegian converts who have introduced the Norwegian tradition of the "Advent calendar," which contains little pictures and small pieces of candy for each day of Advent, and have adapted them for Ramadan. The calendars are homemade, with an appliqué of mosques, crescents, and other "Islamic" motifs. Larsen writes that these calendars are peculiar in that the children are not to open the gift of the day until after sunset, when the Muslims break their fast.

The publication of a book of Norwegian-Islamic children's songs is another example of how "Islam" has evolved in the Norwegian context. The texts are mainly Islamic songs translated from English, but the new Muslims have composed some songs themselves. It is interesting to observe that the melodies are often taken from well-known children's songs, even Christian songs, from the Norwegian context (Larsen 1995, 167).

During Ramadan 2001, some new Muslims were made responsible for children's activities in one of the mosques in Oslo. In addition to telling Islamic stories, they also worked with play dough. Khadija tells how children queued up to participate in the activities; even those children who often refused to participate in mosque activities were enthusiastic about going to the mosque that year. "They have at last understood that the traditional imams' way of only letting the children sit and read the Qur'an does not work on Norwegian children," she says. "If we want our children to take up the Islamic tradition we have to teach them in an empathetic manner, not in a traditional way."

In Sweden in the town of Gothenburg, a group consisting mainly of Swedish female converts has started up Islamic kindergartens. It is interesting to note that the main methodology used in these kindergartens is the

Montessori system, in which many of the new Muslims have taken classes. The reason they have chosen to follow a Swedish child-care model (the Montessori system is popular in Sweden) is that they regard this model to be in accordance with the "Islamic" pedagogical ideal.

Yet another interesting phenomenon in the development toward a "Scandinavian Islam" is the new Muslim undertaking of "walking with poles," or "exerstriding." Over the last few years this sport, where one walks with ski poles in order to increase the exercising effect, has become popular in Sweden and Norway and particularly in Finland, where it started. Some converts and even some born Muslims walk regularly several miles with poles.

These examples of Norwegian convert activities, the Swedish-Islamic kindergartens and the exerstriding, typify how Scandinavian new Muslims form their own "Islamic" traditions by transferring Scandinavian traditions into an Islamic context. It is also interesting to note how immigrant Muslims participate in the new Muslim activities, as seen in the example of the 'id-celebrations in Norway and in the Muslim immigrants who send their children to the Islamic kindergartens run by new Muslims in Sweden. The new "Islamic" model draws on elements both from the Muslims' own cultural context and from a Scandinavian cultural sphere.

Frank Flinn, a researcher on conversion, discusses a model of conversion in which he proposes that new movements might be formed in response to the converts' perception of a discrepancy between ideal and reality (1999). Moreover, he claims that a convert community might work in a revolutionary way by defying accepted rules and establishing new movements. The process I have described above, where Scandinavian new Muslims are active in shaping a "Scandinavian Islam," reflects Flinn's prediction. The Scandinavian Muslims' defiance of born Muslims' understanding of Islam and their working of new content into traditional theological concepts are factors that might lead to new established theologies within a Scandinavian framework.

Larsen defines the innovation of Norwegian new Muslims using the terms of the sociologist of religion Peter Berger: the "externalisation of a *subjective reality*" (1995, 167). Given Berger and Luckmann's thesis of social reality as a human construction (1967), it is plausible to assume that future generations of Muslims in Scandinavia will internalize the hybrid traditions created by Muslim converts and see them as wholly "Islamic" rather than Scandinavian traditions. These new Muslim activities are the results of a "creolization" process where new Muslims' cultural backgrounds merge with Islamic ideas and practice.

It is, however, important to consider whether the rediscovery of the convert identity built on a merging of Scandinavian and Islamic values, ideas, and practice is a result of a deliberate intellectual endeavor or to what extent it is an instinctive reaction to what can be seen as a downward step in the social ladder. Converts have a great vested interest in remaining "Scandinavian," with all that it implies. By reclaiming the Scandinavian heritage, they can effectively distance themselves from the social, economic, and political problems that are weighing down the Muslim community and keep some of the superior status inherent in belonging to the majority community.

By reclaiming their Scandinavian culture they can claim ethnicity distinct from the "Arabic," "Turkish," or "Kurdish" label, which often connotes inner-city or suburban ghettos, defrauding the benefit system, educational underachievement, poor language skills, and "ignorance," without having to turn their backs on Islam and without appearing racists. On a global level it also means that they can gain relief from the sheer weight of the burden of the Muslim *ummah.* A British convert said that when he became a Muslim it had to do with faith in God, belief, and theology. He said he found it an awful experience to then wake up one day as a Muslim and be expected to take on a dozen political causes. Suddenly he felt responsible for helping to free Kashmir and Palestine, supporting the Bosnian and Kosovan Muslims, feeding the refugees from Afghanistan and Chechnya, and generally arguing the cause of all Muslims around the world. In view of his reflection it seems that being a "European" or a "Scandinavian" Muslim becomes a safer and less stressful option and looks increasingly attractive.[4]

It seems obvious that current Muslim religiosity is influenced by Western attitudes and methodologies in various ways. The new Muslims thus play an important role in the blending of the various traditions. In due course, second-, third-, and fourth-generation Muslims will probably play a similar role as carriers of local Scandinavian traditions into the Muslim communities. On the SFCM e-group in 1998, a Swedish male convert illustrated this blending of traditions thus:

How will contemporary and future young Swedish Muslims look at Islam in this country? "Swedish Islam" will probably, like Swedish Christianity, give rise to a succession of various alternative views, but I believe that the interpretation which is establishing itself as the current Swedish understanding of Islam will, putting it mildly, be very interesting. A calm and balanced Islam rooted in, and with respect for, the Swedish cultural heritage. [An Islam] [w]hich raises up the classical Islamic culture, which is full of nuances, as a beautiful heritage to pass on in the Swedish language. [An Islam] [w]hich represents a deep spirituality rooted in the Islamic orthodoxy as well as in the mystical path of Sufism. (SFCM, April 29, 1998 [translation mine])

Later in his letter he imagined the fruits of this hybrid, combining the Islamic symbol, the mosque, with a strong Swedish architectural symbol, Falun red houses with white corners:

Swedish Islam would hopefully have its own writers, thinkers, and artists, as well as institutions of different kinds, established Swedish imam colleges, people's high schools, and mosques with Swedish architecture. Maybe Falun red mosques with white corners? (SFCM, April 29, 1998 [translation mine])

This new Muslim explicitly expressed his link to both Islamic traditionalism and to Sufism, and his approach to the "Swedish-Islamic" hybrid has to be regarded in view of Gerholm's idea of Sufism as a compromise between the East and the West (1988).

In contrast to this mixture of traditions, which seems to be an obvious general trend among Scandinavian new Muslims, I observe that current interaction between the Muslim communities and Scandinavian society at large flows very much one way. Many of the attitudes and practices of majority society greatly influence Muslims, whereas majority society adopts little except food traditions from the Muslim communities. However, it is impossible to evaluate Scandinavian society without taking the immigrant communities into consideration. Although immigrants in general and Muslims in particular have had little explicit influence on majority society, the Scandinavian countries would probably have looked quite different today without their immigrant populations. Thus there has been an implicit influence that has had and still has an impact on the development of Scandinavian society.

Reflections

Most converts interviewed in this study saw "Islam" in terms of a "Swedish," "Danish," or "Norwegian" Islam. A small minority, mainly recent converts, tended to defy "Scandinavian society" in a pattern of being "more royal than the king." Similarly, sympathizers with the two extreme movements, *salafi* and *hizb al-tahrir*, refused to speak in terms of a "Scandinavian Islam." They claimed that there is only "one Islam" that never changes. These movements are actually marginalized both in the Muslim world and in Muslim communities in Western countries, and such statements reflect the "fundamentalist" nature of these groups in that they interpret the scripture literally and endorse a rigid and at times violent understanding of Islam (see also Roald 2001, 23–28). They have an exclusionist approach to majority society, as witnessed in the *hizb al-tahrir*'s boycott of the Autumn 2001 Danish election. However, many new Muslims in this movement are young people, and here Abdul-Wahid Pedersen's conclusion seems to be pertinent: such movements attract the youth because of the stage of rebellion many young people go through at a certain point in their lives. Furthermore, the harsh climate of that Danish election campaign, which focused on the situation of immigrants, or "foreigners," seems to have triggered the popularity of this movement. In Sweden and in Norway, there is a less fertile soil for such movements to grow, due to a much more careful attitude in the official discourse about the immigrant issue.

As for the great majority of my informants, I observed that, by and large, they accepted the concept of "equal gender opportunities." However, I also discovered that, within the general consensus, there were often slight variations in view compared to the discourse of mainstream non-Muslim Scandinavians.

The idea of an increased individualization in Scandinavian society is reflected in new Muslim reactions against the Arabic gender pattern, as expressed by Håkon. This is another aspect of the spread of an ideology of emancipation, promoting in particular the empowerment of women through a rereading of the Islamic sources. In my study on Arabic-speaking Muslims I found that this rereading is a new trend in Europe (Roald 2001), and European converts seem to have an important part to play in this process. As for the theology of feminism, it is obvious that new Muslims are concerned with the empowerment of women and in opposition to traditional Muslim gender patterns. Similarly, the human rights discourse, with its other subdiscourses, such as democracy, equal opportunities, and rights for individuals of various sexual dispositions, is an important ingredient in the new Muslim discourse. New Muslims' ability to mix ideas is obvious, for instance, in the promotion of "equity" over "equality" in matters of equal gender opportunities.

I observed that Muslims in Scandinavia still feel marginalized in society due to the segregation of society and the fact that many Muslims are unemployed. Few Muslims actively interact with Scandinavian society on a level where the mutual exchange of ideas is possible. In contemporary

Scandinavia, new Muslims constitute the majority of Muslims engaged in a dialogue with wider society. However, the part they play is a defensive one, intended to show that the ideas of Muslims and Islam are not threatening to Scandinavian society. In the near future, second-generation born Muslims will most probably have a similar role to play.

Notes

Author's Note: This research was conducted under the program Religious Minority in the Nation-State, funded by the Swedish Research Council. Parts of the chapter are published in Roald 2004.

1. This study was built on fieldwork conducted among converts in Sweden, Denmark, and Norway in 1999–2000. I distributed a questionnaire and 116 converts responded. I asked most of the respondents whether they were willing to answer before I handed over the questionnaire. Some of the questionnaires I handed over to community leaders, who distributed and then gathered them. I also conducted thirty-two qualitative interviews with twenty-three (72 percent) women and nine (28 percent) men. The quotes in the chapter are from these interviews. As a Norwegian-Swedish convert myself, I have taken part in the converts' discourses and have been a participant-observer in convert gatherings from 1982 onward.

2. See, for instance, http://hem .passagen.se/sfcm/sfcm.htm.

3. It is important to note that the new Muslims themselves do not speak of "Scandinavian Islam." They speak in terms of "Danish," "Swedish," or "Norwegian" Islam. Given the similar cultural traits of these three countries, however, I have chosen to use the generic term "Scandinavian Islam."

4. Thanks to Erica Timoney for making me aware of this perspective.

References

Badawi, J. 1995. *Gender Equity in Islam: Basic Principles.* Indianapolis: American Trust Publications.

Berger, P., and Th. Luckmann. 1967. *The Social Construction of Reality.* New York: Anchor Books.

Flinn, F. K. 1999. "Conversion: The Pentecostal and Charismatic Experience." In *Religious Conversion: Contemporary Practices and Controversies,* ed. Ch. Lamb and M. Darrol Bryant, pp. 51–72. London: Cassell.

Gerholm, T. 1988. "Three European Intellectuals as Converts to Islam: Cultural Mediators or Social Critics?" In *The New Islamic Presence in Western Europe,* ed. T. Gerholm and Y. G. Lithman, pp. 263–278. London: Mansell.

Hamberg, E. 1999. "International Migration and Religious Change." In *Towards a New Understanding of Conversion,* ed. U. Görman, pp. 23–37. Helsinki: University of Helsinki.

Larsen, L. 1995. "Velkommen til en stor Familie: Islam og Konversjon i norsk kontekst." Master's thesis, Department of Religious Studies, University of Oslo.

Østberg, S. 2000. "Islamic Nurture and Identity Management." *British Journal of Religious Education* 1: 91–103.

Otterbeck, J. 2000. *Islam på svenska.* Lund, Sweden: Lund Studies in History of Religions.

Roald, A. S. 2001. *Women in Islam: The Western Experience.* London and New York: Routledge.

———. 2003. "The Mecca of Gender Equality: Muslim Women in Sweden." In *Muslim Women in the United Kingdom and Beyond,* ed. H. Jawad and T. Benn, pp. 65–89. Leiden: Brill.

———. 2004. *New Muslims in the European Context: The Experience of Scandinavian Converts.* Leiden: Brill.

Sayyid, B. 1997. *A Fundamental Fear: Eurocentrism and the Emergence of Islamism.* London and New York: Zed Books Ltd.

Stenberg, L. 1996. *The Islamization of Science: Four Muslim Positions Developing an Islamic Modernity.* Lund, Sweden: Almqvist & Wiksell International.

Winters, T. J. http://www.islamfortoday .com.

CHAPTER 3

Symbolizing Distance
Conversion to Islam in Germany and the United States
Monika Wohlrab-Sahr

It is in vogue in sociology of religion to talk about religion in terms of the market. American sociologists, especially, have advocated theories of a religious market, of religious human capital, and of "rational choice." Some have propagated this approach as a "new paradigm" in sociology of religion. This new paradigm is supposed to replace secularization theory, which has been the predominant theoretical approach for decades (see Warner 1993). In this debate, it is striking how old theoretical assumptions are reinterpreted and given completely different meanings. Whereas for Peter L. Berger (1967) the pluralization of worldviews was a central element *within* a theory of secularization, in the recent American debate it has become the main argument *against* such a theory. For Berger, pluralization implied that religious beliefs and systems of meaning become relative and lose their formerly objectified status. In the recent debate, this view is no longer considered. Instead, a pluralistic supply of religious "commodities" seems to guarantee robust demand (see Stark and Iannaccone 1994; Iannaccone, Finke, and Stark 1997; Finke and Stark 1988). Constant religious needs taken for granted, this approach presupposes a religious actor, who mainly tries to realize the religious human capital that he or she has gathered in the course of religious socialization and practice. Consequently, as Iannaccone (1990) argues, those rational religious actors tend to search for contexts that optimally correspond to their religious competence. If they should undergo any changes— for example, convert to a different religion—they will not stray too far from where they came, and they will do it at a young age in order to amortize their investments. They will look for a spouse with the same religious affiliation, or if their spouse embraces a different religion and has a stronger commitment than they themselves have, they will convert to their spouse's religion to minimize costs and conflicts. Looking at the supply side of the religious market, this approach assumes that a diversified supply and the resulting religious competition will positively stimulate religious demand; that is, "The

more pluralism, the greater the religious mobilization of the population"
(Finke and Stark 1988, 43).

In this chapter, I discuss the reach of this approach using an empirical
study on conversion to Islam in Germany and the United States. Even if personal acts of choice must be considered a necessary constituent of conversion, I argue that conversion can only be understood adequately if the biographical background of such decisions is analyzed as well. The conversion
decision has a specific meaning that is related to the convert's background;
conversion fulfills a certain biographical function. On the other hand, Islam
is not a neutral object of choice. The history of confrontations between the
"Islamic" world and the "Christian" world adds a symbolic connotation to
Islamic conversion that plays into the conversion decision as well. Taking
both into account—the biographical background of conversions and the
symbolic connotations of conversion to Islam in the West—the interpreter
gains a better understanding of the "biographical rationality" of the conversion decision and, by means of that, the profits and losses of that decision.

Conversion, Rational Choice, and Pluralization

At least since the 1960s, and especially for younger generations, it has not
been completely misleading to interpret the religious situation in Western
European countries in terms of a religious market and to consider religious
behavior to be influenced by individual choice rather than by tradition and
social constraint. Broadcast by the growing international mobility and by the
influence of the media, new religious "commodities" are offered on the "market" of worldviews, and there is demand for them, more or less. Formerly
closed confessional milieus—such as in Germany or the Netherlands—have
disintegrated to a great extent, and we see a process of rapid detraditionalization in the field of religion, as well as in morality (see Jagodzinski and Dobbelaere 1993). Even in Catholicism, churchgoing is declining rapidly, and
the consent to essential issues of confessional belief—such as the belief in
Heaven and Hell or the belief in the Hereafter—is weakening enormously,
even among committed church members. On top of these changes, more and
more people choose to abandon religion as a whole. In general, religious affiliation no longer seems to be defined by tradition, social constraints, and
processes of social inheritance. Indeed, religious affiliation has become open
to personal preferences, with the effect that more and more people not only
make their choice *within* the religious market but also decide against religion

in general. Although these developments support some of the theoretical assumptions of rational-choice theory, they do not make religion a commodity like other goods. This distinction is especially important in situations in which not only different varieties of religion, but also the option for religion in general, are at our disposal.

I do not doubt that the phenomenon of conversion is, in itself, part of the process of pluralization of the religious and cultural landscape. If one does not want to subscribe to a simple model of brainwashing, conversion cannot be understood without considering acts of religious choice. The idea of choice is especially true for the phenomenon I will discuss here: the conversions of native Germans and Americans to Islam (see Wohlrab-Sahr 1996, 1998, 1999a, 1999b, 2001).

These conversions would not have occurred without some process of pluralization as a precondition for religious choice. Even though some people in the study may have encountered Islam while traveling to foreign countries, in most of the cases they were introduced to Islam by Muslims in their own country. Some examples from my study: a colleague at work, one's present or former husband, a friend, a woman one wants to marry, the lover of one's mother, or a prominent representative of the local Muslim community. In addition, there must be a societal context that makes religious choice possible; that is, there must be the sense that the society allows thinking about conversion to a religion that seems ultimately foreign to many people in Western societies.[1] For this reason, Muslim converts usually refer positively to a pluralistic situation that allows them to deviate from the religious orientations and behavior of the majority. A German Muslim woman from my study, for example, used to go swimming in a lake in Berlin in full clothing and headscarf. In the interview, she explicitly referred to the example of those who went swimming naked right next to her. "If they dare [to behave in a deviant manner],... so do I," she said (Wohlrab-Sahr 1999b, 160). And a young East German woman commented on her new Muslim orientation by saying, "I can't imagine to be completely without anything anymore.... Because somehow,... maybe we need this to belong to something.... Of course it is not irrelevant what you belong to, but you can choose what you like" (Wohlrab-Sahr 1999b, 324).

But even if "you can choose what you like," the commodities offered in the religious market are not completely arbitrary; they have specific social and historical connotations. These connotations are available in the stock of knowledge of a given society in the form of typifications and become part of the would-be convert's definition of the situation. Conversion to Buddhism has a different connotation from conversion to Islam. Those who convert to Islam enter the context of a history of polarization that has lasted for centuries. Even in the historical imagination of European nations, especially in the mythological narratives about their origins, Islam is primarily addressed as "Europe's absolute antithesis and negation, against which the only option was battle" (François and Schulze 1998, 25 [translated by author]). Whether they want to or not, converts participate in this history of polarization. Usually they do not only participate in this history as "victims," but also consciously make use of it, more or less. Conversion, then—scientific observers take note—is used as a means of distinction.

Nevertheless, the behavior of converts to Islam contradicts the assumptions of the religious human capital approach in many respects. Converts turn to a religion that is disconnected from the religious competence they have gained in their life. Their choice produces enormous conflicts and costs. The life that they have been living, the social relationships that have been relevant, the places that they have been going, cannot be referred to easily after conversion. Does this kind of religious choice make sense? From the perspective of the rational-choice approach, we would have to assume that in the background of bicultural marriages (the adjustment to a spouse with a stronger religious commitment, in most of the cases a Muslim man) is the attempt to avoid conflicts in marriage and to harmonize the public presentation of the family. In my research I found conversion decisions based on such backgrounds. If a religiously committed Muslim man and a less committed or religiously indifferent woman with a Christian background get together, conversion to Islam may be used to gain common ground in the relationship. In other cases, conversion may play a role in the power balance between the marriage partners. The wife may use her status as a convert as a kind of symbolic and cultural capital, based on which she can legitimately argue with her husband about the right interpretation of Islam and its consequences for daily life. In these cases, however, most people change their religious membership without undergoing the more fundamental transformation process that we term "conversion."[2]

The rational-choice approach explicitly ignores differences among various commodities on the market. The "essence" of religion, as Iannaccone (1990) states polemically, is of no more interest to this approach than the essence of an apple. In his critique of the rational-choice approach, Steve Bruce has stressed that religion, as well as love, is closely connected with personal identity. Even if we find ourselves on marriage markets and on markets of worldviews, the commitments that take effect, the motives that drive us, and the idealizations that operate are inconsistent in many respects with the behavior of a "rational" actor trying to maximize benefits. Thus we can approach religious orientations sociologically only if we can also conceive of what Alfred Schütz in his phenomenological sociology has called the "Because-motive" (1960, 123). In short, the Because-motive is the background that the actor comes from when he or she confronts a specific situation of choice with a variety of possible options. The options that a person has in a certain situation may be more or less attractive because of that person's specific biographical background. The same choice taken by different people may have different meanings because of this background. The various "situations" in which a choice is made have different histories, and because of that, different implications. Using the language of rational-choice theory, one could say that only if we reconstruct the "biographical rationality" of the conversion decision, can we understand the profit and loss of conversion.

The Approach: Biographical Analysis in a Functional Perspective

My study combines biographical analysis with a functional perspective. The function that conversion fulfills for a person's biography is at the core of my research. My approach uses Schütz's Because-motive as the experiential background based on which specific life plans are developed. Corresponding to this term in functional theory—as represented by Merton (1968) or Luhmann (1970a, b, c)—is "reference problem," in reference to which a certain act or arrangement becomes a "problem solution." Because-motives, like functions, can only partially be conceived of by the actor himself or herself. There are blind spots for every person involved in a specific setting. For this reason, functional theory talks of "latent functions."[3] Of course, sociological observation has its blind spots as well; the sociologist will see things differently from a religious actor or a theological interpreter.

Obviously, a functional approach relates disparate things to each other when it looks for the connection between religion and biography. This approach might seem suspicious to observers from within the religious field because they usually claim a *religious* foundation for their conversion decision, for example, discontent with Christianity, problems with the idea of the Trinity, etc. Consequently, they choose religious terms such as "illumination" or "revelation" to explain the conversion process. A religious phenomenon, then, is explained by reference to religion.

Trying to explain religious conversion sociologically, and from a functional perspective, is considered by others especially suspiciously when the religion is Islam. Because it is a religion, some critics feel obliged to defend it against the dissecting view of a sociologist. Because it is a foreign religion, it even seems to need special protection. However, my interview material shows no evidence that conversion to Islam results from inner religious conflicts. Even if converts sometimes referred to such conflicts in the interview, for example, problems with the idea of the Trinity or the idea of the Immaculate Conception, it became clear that this problematic view only developed *after* these people came into a milieu of other converts. Consequently, these conflicts have to be interpreted as resulting from a discourse among converts that confirms their new social identity and draws a distinction between it and the old one. In other words, these conflicts are the result of *identity politics*. Thus it would be a fallacy to conclude a conversion motive.

Certainly I cannot exclude the possibility that there might be people somewhere who converted to Islam as the result of "theological" problems with Christianity. But my research shows such theological virtuosos are rare. The converts I interviewed did not have problems with their religion at the time they converted. Rather, they had withdrawn from the religious field in the course of their adolescence. Through Islam, religion gains new relevance for them.

Biographical analyses indicate a close connection between processes of biographical crisis and the conversion decision. Even if this perspective were not in line with the religious self-description of Muslim converts, it would be a problematic restriction of the sociological analysis to shrink from formulating such a connection. In the context of functional theory, the relationship between biographical crisis and religious conversion can be described as the relationship between reference problem and problem solution.

People usually do not become converts in a procedure of conscious self-therapy. They do not convert *in order to* solve problems. Doing so would destroy the religious nature of their choice. Furthermore, it would reduce them to strategists in the religious field, like the figure of Casanova in the field of intimacy. Certainly this type of conversion may happen, but it is probably rare and not likely to last. Nevertheless, biographical narratives deliver the necessary material for a sociological interpretation and for the reconstruction of reference problems and problem solutions. To look upon biographical material in functional terms means to look upon it as an observer. The observer depends on the convert's narrative, but he or she does not hear only the intended message of the convert's self-theory. It is latent functions or latent meanings that the analysis aims to uncover.[4]

Collecting interview material based on which connections between the biography and the conversion decision can be detected raises some methodological problems. As Luckmann and others have shown in their work about the conversion narrative (Luckmann 1986, 1987; Ulmer 1988; Snow and Machalek 1983, 1984), converts make use of a certain narrative *form* when they are asked how they became converts. This insight revolutionized the sociology of conversion during the last thirty years and has been labeled the "linguistic turn" in conversion research (Krech 1995). Consequently, sociologists developed an approach focusing on the forms of religious communication and on the strategies of self representation through which converts convincingly present themselves *as converts*. The convert was looked upon as a social type, who could be recognized first of all by a specific rhetoric (see Snow and Machalek 1983, 1984). Some researchers even claimed that it is *only* this specific presentation and communication that make a person a convert. It was the "conversion narrative" as a specific "genre of communication" (Taylor 1976; Sprondel 1985; Luckmann 1986, 1987; Ulmer 1988) that was especially interesting for sociologists, although these narratives became more and more suspicious as sources of exploring the *causes* of conversion. Compared to former approaches, this perspective was fruitful for sociology of conversion because researchers became aware of the specific social forms within converts' self-presentations. Consequently, they moved beyond the naïveté of just collecting converts' narratives in order to find out about the causes and paths of conversion. Unfortunately, these insights do not seem well known among present analysts of religious conversion.

In spite of such progress, this approach, which claimed to be specifically sociological, also implied a narrowing of the perspective to the refinement of forms and strategies of presentation in a specific social context. What fell completely out of sight was this question: Why does it make sense to an individual to participate in a procedure that the majority of people find strange? In other words, researchers did not discuss the structural relationship between a specific sort of typified social presentation (conversion narrative) and a specific biographical identity.

Nevertheless, the methodological problem remains significant. If there are stereotyped ways of talking about one's conversion decision, the empirical investigator who is interested in the relationship between biography and conversion must find a way to avoid the reproduction of such stereotypes.

For this reason, I decided not to ask people how they became converts. Instead, I asked them to tell me about their whole lives and about conversion as a part of their lives. There was only one person among my interviewees for whom this distinction did not work: a man with a leading role in the Muslim community who had often talked (and written) publicly about his conversion decision before. In this case, the attempt to generate an ad hoc narrative failed, whereas in all the other cases it worked well. In spite of the process of reorientation that converts have gone through, usually they are well able, as other people are, to talk about their lives in different ways. The "conversion narrative" is only one mode of telling about their lives, and it is used in specific situations as a kind of "claims-making," and oftentimes has at least some missionary implications. But an ad hoc narrative about their whole lives is another possibility. This approach enables observers to see the setting of a person's life of which conversion is a part.[5]

Empirical Investigation: Conversion to Islam in Germany and the United States

Between 1992 and 1996 I conducted forty-two biographical interviews with Muslim converts in different cities of Germany and the United States. It is difficult to estimate the total number of Muslim converts because conversion to Islam is not very formalized, and Muslim communities have a low level of bureaucratic organization in general. There are no statistics about "members," as in the Christian churches. For these reasons there are no reliable records about converts and few reliable numbers about Muslims in general, especially in the United States.

There are some recent estimates that the Muslim population in the United States is about 5 to 6 million (Siddiqi 1992, viii), whereas in Germany, during the time of my research, there was a Muslim population of about 2.2 million. Since then, the Muslim population in Germany has grown to between 3 and 4 million. Compared to the United States, Germany's population has a much higher percentage of Muslims, most of them Turkish immigrants. But the number of converts is hard to determine and must not be confused with the number of German Muslims in general. There are probably a few thousand Muslim converts in Germany.[6] Several Muslim organizations estimate that about two-thirds are women. Looking at a total of 121 conversion documents of the Community of German-speaking Muslims in Berlin in 1992, I found a ratio of 68 women (56 percent) to 53 men (44 percent). However, these numbers do not necessarily reflect the general ratio of men to women, because most conversions are not documented in that way.

Compared to Germany, the United States has a much smaller percentage of Muslims in its population; however, it has a much higher percentage of converts. In 1986 Yvonne Haddad estimated that about one-third of American Muslims were African American converts (1986, 1; Weeks 1988, 53), whereas she estimated only ten thousand were white converts, most with a strong preference for Sufism.[7]

In my research, the German sample was composed of seven men and twelve women, among them two women who had grown up in the former German Democratic Republic (GDR). The American sample was composed of eleven African American men and twelve women of different ethnic origins, most of whom had been living with African American men for at least a while. Again, the composition of the sample hints at the different milieu-context in each country. Even if conversion to Islam does not have a primarily political background today, as it did during the time of black nationalist movements, conversion to Islam in America is still mainly an African American phenomenon, which is predominantly passed on within this ethnic group. In Germany, conversions are often related to intercultural contacts, especially marriage to a Muslim spouse.[8] Nevertheless, most of the interreligious marriages do not involve conversions. And if they do, conversion cannot be explained by marriage alone. In some of the cases, conversion comes first, and only afterward does a partner from the new religious context enter the picture. In other cases, marriage and conversion are two moments in a process of reorientation that lead in the same direction and stabilize each other (see Haddad 1986, 7).

There are certainly cases in which Muslim men (or their families) pressure their wives to convert to Islam. More striking, I found the opposite in my research. In many cases, the male Muslim partners were looking for a "Western" woman rather than for a convert and neither wanted nor enforced their wives' reorientation. On the contrary, it was often the female converts that pushed their partners to adhere more faithfully to their Muslim origins and to practice their religion. In spite of these varieties of mutual influence, Muslim partners have an important role in conversion because in many cases they are the significant others who bring the new religion onto the would-be convert's horizon. In addition, they are part of the biographical dynamic in the course of which conversion occurs. To say it pointedly: They "deliver" the material that can be used biographically.

I am especially interested in the relationship between conversion as a change of worldview and life orientation, and the biographical background and biographical reflections of those who undergo such a change. To formulate this relationship in terms of functional analysis: My aim is to reconstruct the problem that conversion refers to and to work out the specific problem solution that goes along with conversion.

Results: Three Types of Conversion

Ultimately, the biographical analysis does not aim at understanding the single case as such. It aims at understanding general elements or typical features of the case. In my research, which is based on biographical case studies, I reconstructed three functions or types of conversion to Islam. In spite of specific differences, I found all three types in both countries. The distinctions among these three functions are ideal-typical distinctions, whereas in concrete biographies these functions might overlap. The three types of conversion refer to three different realms of experience and characteristic problems associated with each (i.e., typical reference problems). Through the process of conversion, people could articulate these problems and find specific solutions.

The first sphere of problems refers to issues of sexuality and gender relations. Characteristic experiences are personal devaluation resulting from the violation of norms regarding sexuality and gender relations or from the dissolution of a gender-related social order. Conversion to Islam enables the symbolization and articulation of these experiences, and through this process problem-solving can begin. With the establishment of new boundaries, rules, and interpretations, a new order implying a revaluation of the person is created. I label this solution, and the function of conversion associated with it, "implementation of honor" (see Wohlrab-Sahr 1996).

The second sphere of problems refers to issues of social mobility. Characteristic experiences are failed attempts to move up socially and economically and the loss of personal acknowledgment associated with such failure. Conversion to Islam enables these failed attempts to be stabilized or referred to as an alternative career, thus new acknowledgment can be gained. Stabilization is closely connected with the religious reorientation and takes the form of a "methodization of life conduct" (see Weber 2002), the second function of conversion to Islam.

The third sphere of problems refers to issues of nationality and ethnicity. Characteristic experiences are those of precarious belonging that become relevant not only in the public, but also in the private, sphere. Of specific importance is the ascription of collective or social identities that, for certain reasons, cannot be taken as one's own or which define social exclusion. It might also be that old forms of distinction and affiliation do not work under new circumstances and for this reason new commitments become relevant. Conversion to Islam in these cases fulfills the function of "symbolic emigration and symbolic battle." Through Islam a new kind of global association in the sense of an "imagined community" comes into play (see Anderson 1991).

These spheres of problems, and the types of experiences associated with them, show that without referencing the specific biography of a person, conversion can be understood only on the surface level. According to my findings, the specific dynamic of conversion results from biographical crisis experiences that cannot be solved with other, nonreligious means, but through conversion can be articulated symbolically and ritually within a religious frame of reference. The problem solution is connected to this articulation. Therefore I speak of conversion as the *symbolic transformation of crisis experience.*

Part of this problem-solving process is different forms of moralizing that refer to the realms in which devaluation, failure, and disintegration were experienced: the moralizing of sexuality and gender relations, of personal discipline, and of political and social order.

I reconstructed all three types of conversion in the samples from both countries. Cases that seemed to be quite different in the beginning—the conversion of a black American man and the conversion of a white German woman, for example—turned out to be quite similar in the end. Obviously Islam as a point of reference influences which spheres of problems Western converts associate with it. Nevertheless, there are characteristic differences pointing to the different religious "landscapes" in the two countries.

Implementation of Honor

Regarding the first type of conversion, "implementation of honor," the German interviews mainly referred to individual experiences of devaluation and stigmatization. The interviewees narrated experiences where they as individuals, or significant others in their family, violated a normative order or fell out of such an order. Clearly there was no collectively shared frame of reference that they could refer to in order to articulate these experiences, or there were severe reasons that hindered them from referring to such a frame of reference.

One of my male interviewees—coming from a middle-class background—converted to Islam during the 1960s at the age of sixteen. Prior to his conversion, his mother had started an affair with a Tunisian man, and later she divorced her husband. Soon her lover, who had a wife and children in Tunisia, moved into the son and mother's house. The interviewee responded to this situation—in their environment certainly stigmatizing—by refusing confirmation, which was "a shame" in his mother's eyes, and certainly a significant nonconformity at that time in Germany. At the age of sixteen the interviewee converted to Islam, which in his family was interpreted as the mother "losing" her son. The narrative indicates that there was some aggression at play in the sense that he was responding to his mother's sexual nonconformity with his own religious nonconformity. But at the same time, through conversion, he challenged the new man in the house by overpowering him in his "own field": Islam. He sought information about Islam through the man's pious brother and started to lead a strict Islamic life, focusing mainly on the moral implications of Islam. He even thought about marrying a Muslim girl in Tunisia whom he had never seen privately.

A female convert had several problematic sexual relationships in her past, she had undergone four abortions, and she had a history of alcohol abuse and violence in her family. Her attempts to finish high school and get a professional education had failed. Her son had severe problems in school. One day she started learning Arabic and eventually married her teacher, a Palestinian man of her father's age. Soon she converted to Islam and started wearing the headscarf. She motivated her husband to stop drinking alcohol and to practice his prayers. She argued that her long hair was the cause of her unsatisfactory past sexual relationships, and that she was able to control the effects of her hair with the headscarf. This personal theory is interesting in two respects: she externalizes the cause of her problems and, at the same time, externalizes the problem solution. She uses the headscarf to establish external boundaries that, for specific reasons, she cannot set on her own. Beyond the specifics of this case, the woman's biography shows that establishing external boundaries is usually a solution arising from an "emergency" and has the features of this emergency attached to it. For this woman, the attempt to impose external boundaries on her fifteen-year-old son completely failed. Her son became a male prostitute, and she ended all contact with him.

Unlike these personal crises, in the American cases, conversion refers to issues of sexual and gender order in a more general sense. The narratives, especially of African American men, are more about the general distinction between manliness and womanliness (e.g., being a "real man" or a "sissy"), or the distinction between homosexuality and heterosexuality. In the interviews with African Americans, the order of the sexual is often implicitly paralleled with the order of the black milieu, and the dissolution of the sexual and gender order represents the dissolution of the black milieu. In one interview, the idea of an original order of the black milieu was even reproduced in the linguistic form of presentation. In an extremely detailed narration, the interviewee recalled street names and street numbers and described specific scents and sounds of childhood, drawing a highly interconnected black cosmos. Even segregation, corporal punishment, and violence were integral constituents of this cosmos, in which everything had its clear place. But according to the logic of the narration, this order was undermined and destroyed by homosexuality and by gender relations that were thrown out of balance.

In the German context, the problem-solving associated with Islam refers to individual experiences of devaluation, whereas in the American context the general "problem of order," which nevertheless is experienced personally, is of greater importance. In the German cases, covering and sometimes circumcision for men become symbols for the re-creation and revaluation of the person. This process is emphasized by specific familial or social settings with clear-cut spheres of responsibility. In the American cases, Islam and the concepts of gender identity derived from it become a substitute for what is considered the "original order" of the black milieu. For blacks, a situation that is experienced as being out of control, can, at least symbolically, be put in order again. Under these circumstances covering is not only related to the individual person, but also to the surrounding milieu. The headscarf symbolizes membership in a new order and distinguishes the wearer from the neighborhood and the dangers of the "street" (see Wohlrab-Sahr 1998). It also implies the moral distinction between oneself and one's black neighbors.

Because the black lower-class milieus in American cities are known for their problem of single mothers and absent fathers, it is not surprising that family issues are of importance in groups of black converts to Islam. But what at first sight is supposed to signal the responsibility of the black Muslim man for his wife and family, is worth taking a second look at. The following example illustrates this second look. During my stay in California I regularly participated in a Muslim women's group. The group was chaired by the two wives of the community's imam. One day, the group discussed an excursion that they wanted to make with their children. A young woman had planned this trip carefully, suggesting a hike in a nearby national park. After she finished her presentation, the imam's wives informed the group that they had spoken to "the brothers" about these plans, and that "the brothers" were concerned because there might be wild animals in the national park. Therefore, they considered the trip too dangerous for women and children and suggested going to the park of a city college, which had a fence around it, instead. The two wives emphasized that the brothers' concerns were only for the women's safety. Although the young woman who planned the trip commented that women could not be kept within fences, the group agreed to go to the city college park.

This scene can be interpreted as an attempt to reestablish a patriarchal arrangement in the word's original meaning: the husband is the head of the family, and he is responsible for protecting wives and children and providing for them materially. What makes the scene paradoxical is that this model is applied to a social setting in which black women have become much more successful in terms of education and jobs than black men. Whereas a big part of the actual responsibility for family welfare rested on the women's shoulders, the community tried to symbolically reestablish the myth of the man as the family's patriarch. The outside world ("in the woods") was constructed as dangerous, whereas the men—despite having severe problems providing the necessities of everyday life—were "invented" as frontier heroes who needed to protect their families against lurking dangers.

Methodization of Life Conduct

Another difference between the cases in Germany and the United States can be found in the second type of conversion, "methodization of life conduct."[9] Common in the samples for both countries is the reference problem of failed attempts at upward mobility. Here again for the American cases, there is a reference to the social milieu. Black milieus are referred to as negative horizons, which threaten one's attempts at stabilization with drugs, teenage pregnancy, and violence. So the street and its dangers become a negative symbol, which one must be alert to and, at the same time, be distinct from (see Wohlrab-Sahr 1998). For African American converts of the lower classes especially, conversion to Islam is used as a means of resocialization. Male converts from this group also tend to practice a disciplined kind of sport, like boxing, and refer positively to their military experience.

The motif of methodization also plays a role for those converts whose parents managed to be upwardly mobile, but who themselves could not reproduce this status. Whereas their parents, usually supported by the community of a church, gained social distinction through economic success or through education, the children could not keep up with them. These converts use Islam as a means of moral distinction because it implies leading a "difficult," disciplined way of life. One of my interviewees, whose parents were successful entrepreneurs in a social welfare organization, was not very good in school, but he finally managed to get a job as a teacher. When he talked about his conversion, he described the home of a "Muslim brother" who introduced him to Islam as thoroughly clean and well ordered but located in a neighborhood full of dirt, drugs, alcohol, and violence. In his view, the Muslim's home was like "a castle in the ghetto" (Wohlrab-Sahr 1999b, 198). Certainly the ghetto was not a likely place for this young man to end up, even if he did not succeed in reproducing his parents' success. Whereas Islam on the one hand became a means of disciplining himself, on the other hand it served as a means of moral distinction that substituted for distinctions based on economic and educational success.

In these cases, Islam as a religion is contextualized in a specific social milieu, and there are role models associated with this social background as well, for example, black boxers and black musicians. Besides that, there is little reference to specific milieus for converts to Islam. Usually, conversion provokes conflicts with one's family of origin, and oftentimes it supports the disengagement from this social context and from its demands for status reproduction and upward mobility. The attempts to become part of a milieu of Muslim migrants, which is more common for German Muslims than for American Muslims, often remain precarious.

Symbolic Emigration and Symbolic Battle

In both countries, the last type of conversion, "symbolic emigration/symbolic battle" (see Wohlrab-Sahr 1999b, 2001), is characterized by problems of belonging and of distinction. The most typical examples in the German sample are two women from East Germany, but the function of symbolic emigration is also of some importance in other cases.

In one case, for the interviewee's family, and for the communist state of the GDR, a programmatic antifascism was an important part of the collective worldview. But the biographical past of this family, especially the father's role during fascism, was more ambivalent. He was imprisoned in the concentration camp of Auschwitz during the Nazi regime because he was a communist. But then he was released and forced to live in a village side by side with Nazis, to work for them, and to establish a family there. At the same time, thousands of Jews were killed in the camp every day. After the breakdown of the Nazi regime, the family was engaged in building up the new communist state of the GDR, and they were considered "Heroes of Resistance" by the state. The father was engaged in the "Auschwitz committee," but he never talked about his own experience. It was never clear to the family's daughter what her father's role during the Nazi time actually was. For the daughter, this contradiction created massive conflicts that could not be solved within the system of the GDR. Conversion to Islam, which in this case was coupled with fleeing to the West and marrying a Turkish man, enabled the daughter to leave the conflicting frame of reference and to adopt a new social identity in a far-reaching sense. Whereas she could only convert to Islam, she tried to force her children into adopting a "Turkish" identity, even though their father, whom she divorced after a few years, had lost his Turkish nationality and never intended to go back to Turkey.

In the second East German case, the ways of making oneself distinct from "the ordinary way of life" and the ways of associating with like-minded others, which in the GDR were enabled mostly through communities in the Protestant church, did not work anymore after the German reunification. For this woman, converting to Islam and marrying a Muslim immigrant from Albania became instruments for expressing her sense of alienation in the unified Germany ("We both lost our homelands") and symbols of an imagined withdrawal from "being German" and the wish to become part of an idealized community of Muslims. But her integration into such an Islamic community, which she imagined to be like a huge family, had not yet become reality at the time of the interview and probably never would. After being married for four years, the young woman still had not been introduced to her parents-in-law, even though her husband visited them for several weeks each year.

In the American context, such problems of belonging usually have an ethnic dimension. A young African American man, for example, opened the interview by suggesting to me that I should also conduct interviews with people who were born Muslims in order to compare them to converts. From his point of view, just to be born a Muslim did not count, if the person did not choose a Muslim existence. This plea for a form of social and religious affiliation that is not a matter of cultural heritage but a matter of individual *choice* has a specific meaning in the background of this biographical narrative. The young man was born the illegitimate child of his black father and his white mother. In the interview, he referred to his mother's European descent by excessively listing European countries, almost "all of Europe." He used his mother's ancestors as illustrations of the "melting pot," which, as he explained to me, "does not exist outside of European Americans." When he told me that he was the offspring of an extramarital affair between his African American father and his white mother, he said, "I guess you would say I'm a bastard."

The plea for a religious affiliation not based on social inheritance but on individual achievement and choice, in this case, obviously corresponds to the background of precarious belonging within one's own social and cultural context. A definition of the "melting pot" that only includes European Americans excludes the speaker himself. The self-stigmatizing label "bastard" supports the finding that a problem of precarious belonging is one of the main issues in this case. In the interview, this problem is transformed into the interviewee's idea to go to Iran someday, study the Qur'an there, and finally fight in an armed war against the United States. To this man, the United States was an evil regime that deserved nothing but destruction.

In these examples, Islam functions as a contrasting principle and ideology enabling the person to leave the conflictive symbolic frame. For the East German women, conversion primarily has the function of symbolic emigration, whereas for the American man, conversion has the function of symbolic battle. In both contexts, the problem of precarious belonging is turned against the system that makes belonging problematic. The moral devaluation of the old system corresponds to the envisioning of a moral Muslim community.

Religion and Morality

A functional analysis must consider functional equivalents. If conversion to Islam for Germans and Americans fulfills the latent function of symbolically transforming experiences of devaluation, degradation, and disintegration, the question still remains: Why do people refer *to Islam* as their way of dealing with these problems? One part of the answer is the presence of significant persons in their surroundings who brought Islam to their attention, and who participated in the dynamic resulting in the conversion.

But my research also shows that—compared to other kinds of conversion—conversion to Islam implies a specific form of problem-solving. In his critique of rational-choice theory Steve Bruce has argued for a culturalist explanation. Religion, in his view, is strong when it connects to issues of ethnicity, and when it fulfills the function of "cultural defense" (1999a, 25).

In this perspective, religion is strong when it has to do with a more general establishment of "we-groups."

My thesis is that conversion to Islam represents the opposite side of this function. It is only against the background of the close relationship between religion and cultural defense that conversion to Islam gains its provocative meaning. But obviously provocation is not an end in itself. It is those people who choose Islam who also experienced situations in which they fell out of the dominant order.[10] They experienced stigmatization, failure, or disintegration within their own context, and they articulate these experiences with reference to a "foreign" religion. However, conversion creates a paradox: Converts symbolize maximal distance from their own society or social surroundings, but they do it from within this society and amid these surroundings. As opposed to other forms of symbolizing distance—such as the use of fascist symbols by right-wing juveniles—Muslim converts refer positively to a pluralistic common sense, which gives space to their kind of articulation.

But there is a further argument for the specific reference to Islam. The process of detraditionalization and church decline since the 1960s has been accompanied by a decline of moral rigorousness, especially in the field of sexual morality. Today, even members of the Catholic Church consider issues of sexuality a subject of personal decision. Some may see a secondary effect of this liberalization in the reluctance of liberal Christian churches to provide a platform for certain problems, which in former times could easily be dealt with in the realm of the churches and be interpreted in terms of sin and forgiveness or of shame and grace. What remains a possibility—aside from psychotherapy—are Christian sects (see Liebsch 2001) or those religious communities that insist on a close and sometimes rigid relationship between religion and morality in general.[11] To formulate this idea in terms of a revised market theory: Different religions or religious communities obviously supply different segments of the religious market and enable people with specific problems to relate to them. The converts' biographies also show that in modern universalistic societies, personal and collective devaluation and moral degradation may result in serious problems, which need to be solved by individuals or groups. The process of symbolic transformation attending conversion to Islam implies a process of remoralizing in a double sense: first, through the moral rehabilitation of the person, and second, through the creation of an imaginary moral cosmos that establishes a clear order and allows one to distinguish oneself from the dominant context. Remoralization works through moral distinction from a context in which the person was morally discredited. In this respect, the social "costs" of converting to Islam may be outweighed by the "profits" of biographical problem solution. Even though converts did not "rationally" choose Islam *in order to* solve biographical problems, biographical analyses nevertheless reveal a specific "rationality" of conversion decisions, whether they are in line with commonsense notions of "rational behavior" or not.

Notes

1. The most recent conflicts about conversion in different countries—e.g., in India—clearly indicate that the right to change one's religion cannot be taken for granted at all.

2. For the distinction between conversion and change of membership see Snow and Machalek (1984, 171).

3. I refer to the functional analysis that has been developed by Luhmann (1970a, b, c) with critical reference to Merton (1968). In Luhmann's theory the former idea of the "maintenance of continuance" has been replaced by the idea of problem-solving with respect to certain "reference problems."

4. Methodologically this refers to procedures of data analysis that aim at the reconstruction of latent meaning, in this case the method of "objective hermeneutics" (see Oevermann 2000).

5. But—from within the religious field—talking about one's biography outside the framework of a conversion narrative may nevertheless seem dangerous. In an interview an African American convert told me a story from his life that was very revealing with respect to his gender identity. He told me that his son, when he was graduating from high school, was, like all the others, supposed to take part in a dance ritual during the school-leaving ceremony, in which the girls were to wear football uniforms, while the boys were dressed as cheerleaders: a symbolic reversal of gender-identities before the students entered "adult life," with its clear-cut identities. The interviewee nevertheless saw this very differently. He told me that he was so upset that his son was supposed to wear a woman's dress that he put immense pressure on him not to participate in the ritual. As a result, his son was the only boy in school to be wearing jeans and T-shirt during the ritual. While the interviewee was telling this story, his wife came in and asked with a cutting voice: "What has that to do with Islam?" Obviously she was very much aware that biographical narrations hardly stay within the limits of a conversion narrative.

6. Muslim organizations today talk of eleven thousand converts in Germany; in earlier times much higher numbers—which were probably wrong—were given. Since nobody knows or can verify the sources these numbers come from, they can't be considered reliable.

7. When I was doing my research in the United States in 1996, a big Sufi conference was taking place in San Francisco. The audience was predominantly white. At the same time there was a conference of Warith Deen Muhammad's followers in Berkeley, with almost no white person attending.

8. The high proportion of female converts obviously does not relate specifically

to Islam, since Islam allows Muslim men to marry Christian or Jewish women, but not vice versa. But it relates to the general feminization of religion in Europe, as well as in the United States. If religion is mainly an activity of women, also converts will be mainly women.

9. This term has been taken from Max Weber's *Protestant Ethic*. See Weber 2002.

10. This shows, on the other hand, that even in an "individualized" society there are dominant forms of order that you can "fall out" of. But it is getting increasingly difficult to interpret such "falling out" as a collective experience.

11. Another option would be the reference to kinds of moralizing communication in the media, e.g., on talk shows. But because of the very short periods of attention that those shows offer, they can hardly serve as means of problem-solving in the long run.

References

Anderson, Benedict. 1991. *Imagined Communities: Reflections on the Origin and Spread of Nationalism*. London and New York: Verso.

Berger, P. L. 1967. *The Sacred Canopy: Elements of a Sociological Theory of Religion*. Garden City, N.Y.: Doubleday.

Bruce, St. 1999a. *Choice and Religion: A Critique of Rational Choice Theory*. Oxford: Oxford University Press.

———. 1999b. *Religion and Modernization: Sociologists and Historians Debate the Secularization Thesis*. Oxford: Oxford University Press.

Finke, R., and R. Stark. 1988. "Religious Economies and Sacred Canopies: Religious Mobilization in American Cities." *American Sociological Review* 53 (1): 41–49.

François, E., and H. Schulze. 1998. "Das emotionale Fundament der Nationen." In *Mythen der Nationen. Ein europäisches Panorama*, ed. M. Flacke, pp. 17–32. Berlin: Koehler & Amelang Verlagsgesellschaft.

Haddad, Y. Y. 1986. *A Century of Islam in America: The Muslim World Today*. Occasional Paper No. 4. Washington, D.C.: American Institute for Islamic Affairs.

Iannaccone, L. R. 1990. "Religious Practice: A Human Capital Approach." *Journal for the Scientific Study of Religion* 29 (3): 297–314.

Iannaccone, L. R., R. Finke, and R. Stark. 1997. "Deregulating Religion: The Economics of Church and State." In *Differenz und Integration, 28. Kongress der Deutschen Gesellschaft für Soziologie—Dresden, Kongressband II*, ed. K.-S. Rehberg, pp. 462–466. Opladen, Germany: Leske und Budrich.

Jagodzinski, W., and K. Dobbelaere. 1993. "Der Wandel kirchlicher Religiosität in Westeuropa." In *Religion und Kultur. Special Volume 33 of Kölner Zeitschrift für Soziologie und Sozialpsychologie*, ed. J. Bergmann et al., pp. 68–91. Opladen, Germany: Westdeutscher Verlag.

Krech, V. 1995. "Was ist religiöse Bekehrung? Ein Streifzug durch 10 Jahre soziologischer Konversionsforschung." *Handlung, Kultur, Interpretation* 4 (6): 131–159.

Liebsch, K. 2001. *Panik und Puritanismus. Über die Herstellung traditionalen und religiösen Sinns*. Opladen, Germany: Leske und Budrich.

Luckmann, Th. 1986. "Grundformen der gesellschaftlichen Vermittlung des Wissens: Kommunikative Gattungen." In

Kultur und Gesellschaft. Special Volume 27 of Kölner Zeitschrift für Soziologie und Sozialpsychologie, ed. F. Neidhardt et al., pp. 191–211. Opladen, Germany: Westdeutscher Verlag.

———. 1987. "Kanon und Konversion." In *Kanon und Zensur. Beiträge zur Archäologie der literarischen Kommunikation*, ed. A. Assmann and J. Assmann, pp. 38–46. München: Fink.

Luhmann, N. 1970a. "Funktion und Kausalität." In *Soziologische Aufklärung, Vol. 1*, pp. 9–30. Opladen, Germany: Westdeutscher Verlag.

———. 1970b. "Funktionale Methode und Systemtheorie." In *Soziologische Aufklärung, Vol. 1*, pp. 31–53. Opladen, Germany: Westdeutscher Verlag.

———. 1970c. "Soziologische Aufklärung." In *Soziologische Aufklärung, Vol. 1*, pp. 66–91. Opladen, Germany: Westdeutscher Verlag.

Merton, R. K. 1968. *Social Theory and Social Structure*. New York: Free Press.

Oevermann, U. 2000. "Die Methode der Fallrekonstruktion in der Grundlagenforschung sowie in der klinischen und pädagogischen Praxis." In *Die Fallrekonstruktion. Sinnverstehen in der sozialwissenschaftlichen Forschung*, ed. K. Kraimer, pp. 58–156. Frankfurt am Main: Suhrkamp.

Schütz, A. 1960. *Der sinnhafte Aufbau der sozialen Welt. Eine Einleitung in die verstehende Soziologie*. 2nd ed. Vienna: Springer.

Siddiqi, M. 1992. "Preface." In *Islam in North America: A Sourcebook*, ed. M. Köszegi and G. Melton, pp. vii–viii. London: Garland Publishers.

Snow, D. A., and R. Machalek. 1983. "The Convert as a Social Type." In *Sociological Theory, Vol. 1*, ed. R. Collins, pp. 259–289. San Francisco: Jossey-Bass.

———. 1984. "The Sociology of Conversion." In *Annual Review of Sociology* 10: 167–190.

Sprondel, W. M. 1985. "Subjektives Erlebnis und das Institut der Konversion." In *Soziologie und gesellschaftliche Entwicklung. Verhandlungen des 22. Deutschen Soziologentages in Dortmund 1984*, ed. B. Lutz, pp. 549–558. Frankfurt am Main and New York: Campus.

Stark, R., and L. R. Iannaccone. 1994. "A Supply-Side Reinterpretation of the 'Secularization' of Europe." *Journal for the Scientific Study of Religion* 33 (3): 230–252.

Taylor, B. 1976. "Conversion and Cognition: An Area for Empirical Study in the Microsociology of Religious Knowledge." *Social Compass* 23 (1): 5–22.

Ulmer, B. 1988. "Konversionserzählungen als rekonstruktive Gattung. Erzählerische Mittel und Strategien bei der Rekonstruktion eines Bekehrungserlebnisses." *Zeitschrift für Soziologie* 17 (1): 19–33.

Warner, St. 1993. "Work in Progress toward a New Paradigm for the Sociological Study of Religion in the United States." *American Journal of Sociology* 98 (5): 1044–1093.

Weber, M. 2002. *The Protestant Ethic and the Spirit of Capitalism*. London and New York: Routledge.

Weeks, J. R. 1988. "The Demography of Islamic Nations." *Population Bulletin* 43 (4): 5–54.

Wohlrab-Sahr, M. 1996. "Konversion zum Islam als Implementation von Geschlechtsehre." *Zeitschrift für Soziologie* 25 (1): 19–36.

———. 1998. "Konversion als Resozialisation." In *Zeitschrift für*

Sozialisationstheorie und Erziehungssoziologie 18 (4): 373–388.

———. 1999a. "Conversion to Islam: Between Syncretism and Symbolic Battle." *Social Compass* 46 (3): 351–362.

———. 1999b. *Konversion zum Islam in Deutschland und den USA*. Frankfurt am Main: Campus.

———. 2001. "'Ich hab das eine gegen das andere ausgetauscht sozusagen.' Konversion als Rahmenwechsel." *Psychotherapie und Sozialwissenschaften* 3 (3): 224–248.

PART TWO. DISCOURSES AND NARRATIVES

CHAPTER 4

Gender, Conversion, and Islam

A Comparison of Online and Offline Conversion Narratives

Karin van Nieuwkerk

In this chapter, conversion narratives of female converts to Islam collected during anthropological fieldwork in the Netherlands will be compared with self-presentations of new Muslimas on the Internet.

During my research among Dutch female converts to Islam in 1997 and 1998, I was often impressed and puzzled by the diversity of the women's stories. I conducted in-depth interviews with twenty-four women, and of half of them I also interviewed relatives or friends.[1] In addition, I joined twenty-five meetings of two organizations for converts and analyzed their monthly magazines.[2] During these meetings I had many informal talks with converts. After most interviews I came home with the feeling that I could understand this particular woman's choice for Islam, but that her motivation was rather specific and quite dissimilar from the motivations and the life stories of the women I had spoken to before.

I thus often found it difficult to understand these women's choice for Islam in a sociologically satisfactory way. It was hard to relate their conversion to (a lack of) religious affiliation, educational background, family milieu, and psychological crises, or even to their marriage with Muslim partners, because this was not the case for five new Muslimas. Although most were married to Muslim partners, were of a middle-class background, and were well educated, these factors did not give much insight into the reasons for and meaning of their conversion. It appeared that each conversion story made sense only within the framework of the complete life story. For one of them a psychological crisis and medicine addiction convinced her of the natural and healthy character of Islam; for another woman sexual harassment made her realize the importance of a certain distance between the sexes. Some women tried to rebel against dominant mothers; others tried to find a "place to belong." Several converts were attracted to the spiritual and all-encompassing nature of Islam; many were attracted to the rational character of Islam. Some converted to establish a harmonious marriage relationship or to realize a unified upbringing of the children; others converted without a Muslim partner.

Within the diversity of the converts' stories, however, there are also commonalities. Despite their divers trajectories, the converts are all women who are living in the West and decided to become Muslim. They thus share important aspects of their identities related to ethnicity, religion, and gender. These important aspects of the converts' identities are crystallized in a structured narrative or discourse. Most conversion stories contain a biographical narrative (why they as individuals took the path to Islam), a religious discourse (why Islam), a gender discourse (why they as women chose Islam), and finally an ethnic or national discourse (why they as Dutch/Western women chose Islam). Together these four discourses give insight into Islam's appeal to women in the West. Whereas the biographical narratives are heterogeneous, the other discourses show recurrent patterns. The religious discourse in particular shows a high level of congruency.

In the meantime, I was fascinated by the growing amount of conversion stories on the Internet. I was excited to find this extra source of information because it is well established in anthropology that the stories and narratives gathered in interviews are strongly influenced by the interactive context of the interview. The fieldwork setting and the converts' perception of the researcher as a non-Muslim Dutch feminist professional could influence the content and style of these narratives (Rabinow 1977; Clifford and Marcus 1980). The Internet offers the convert the possibility of presenting her story in her own words without any interference and questions. Self-presentation on the Internet is potentially a free and unconstrained way of creating and expressing new identities (Schmitz 1997; Watson 1997; de Groot 1997). Narratives online, as bodiless expressions for an anonymous public, offer possibilities for autonomous identity constructions absent in an ordinary anthropological setting of fieldwork and interview.

I eventually collected more than a hundred stories of female converts from the Internet. They came from personal homepages, special sites for converts, and e-mail discussion groups. Most of them are in the meantime put together on the site "The True Religion."[3] Of this sample, I selected fifty stories of female converts from the United States, Canada, and Europe from a Christian or secular background. I also joined two e-mail discussion groups, each for about half a year, that were mostly aimed at and run by new Muslimas.[4]

At first sight, these Internet stories amazed me as much as those derived from interviews, but for a quite opposite reason. All the stories did look so much alike! After reading the fifteenth story I was bored; they merely seemed a repetition of each other. I expected a wide range of voices on the Internet, yet the opposite seemed to be the case. No diversity, but standardization. In order to analyze the Internet stories I did not need intricate biographical analyses, because most stories did not dwell at length on personal backgrounds and motivations. The four discourses I observed in the conversion stories of Dutch Muslimas are also visible in the Internet accounts, but seemed to have a smaller range of variety as well. I was intrigued by this observation and decided to conduct a closer comparison of the discourses written by converts on the Internet and those gathered through interviews.

In this chapter, I will try to make sense of these differences. What are the similarities and differences in the biographical narratives and in the gender, religious, and ethnic discourses? How can we explain them? How far can we understand the differences by looking into fieldwork and Internet as different sites of production? This chapter is thus not only aimed at analyzing the content of the narratives but also at contrasting the modes of presentation in a face-to-face interview situation with self-presentation on the Internet. First, I go into conversion narratives as a genre. Second, I compare the biographical, gender, ethnic, and religious discourse of the conversion stories collected during fieldwork and from the Internet. Lastly, I try to account for the similarities and differences between the online and offline narratives by examining Internet and fieldwork as sites of production and (self-)presentation.

Conversion Narratives

Conversion narrative as a genre has received some interest from anthropologists and sociologists (Stromberg 1993; Beckford 1978; Whitehead 1987; Harding 1987). It is acknowledged that these narratives have to be taken cautiously because of their constructed character. Several issues merit attention. First, conversion narratives are created backwards; that is, they are told after the conversion. Past events are reinterpreted in light of current convictions. The stories should therefore not be understood as containing factual information on the conversion process. Second, this reconstructing process does not only take place at the individual level but also at the group level. Lehman draws attention to the collectively constructed character of conversion narratives in an "Erzählgemeinshaft" (in Hofmann 1997, 17–18). Converts come together to discuss their experiences and incorporate common narrative elements into their stories. In the process of telling and retelling their conversion experiences, they create a common model. Beckford (1978) has taken these ideas a step further. He points out that conversion narratives should be understood in light of the ideology and organization of the religion or denomination involved. The narratives are remodeled and refashioned in line with the structures and purpose of the converts' new convictions. According to Beckford, converts do not simply reproduce a rehearsed script but include elements of the religion's ideological rationale in their narratives. Third, Stromberg (1993), in his interesting study on conversion narratives, calls attention to the phenomenon that telling the conversion story itself can be part of the conversion process. In his case study on evangelical Christianity, he indicates that his interviews with converts were a ritual rather than an ordinary interview setting (see also Harding 1987). It is thus important to analyze the purpose of telling the conversion story. Finally, not only the purpose, but also the context in which the narratives are produced, should be examined. I first apply these precautions to my fieldwork material and then to the Internet narratives.

During the interviews, it was often clear that new Muslimas interpreted past events, behavior, and ideas in light of their current convictions. For instance, they made remarks like "I have always been conservative in the way I dressed," "I never used makeup and fancy clothing," and "I never drank alcohol or ate pork." Or they said: "As a child, I already questioned the Trinity and could not make sense of it." During their meetings, I could also observe how they created a common script. This script was particularly related to such gender issues as polygamy, wife beating, work outside the home, the headscarf, and women's rights in Islam. Most converts shared experiences of parents and friends who abhorred the fact that a Dutch "emancipated" girl could turn toward such an "oppressive religion." They discussed ways of dealing with these assumptions. The construction of a common script became very clear to me during an interview with a new Muslima who converted eight years prior to the interview. I asked her how she responds to questions about women's issues in Islam like polygamy, obedience to the husband, and women's share in inheritance, suggesting that she might often be confronted with these types of questions. She replied: "Yes, you are right, especially in the beginning I talked a lot with other Muslimas about this and read books about women's rights in Islam. But in the meantime I forgot the right answers."

During the interviews there was a clear awareness of and reaction to aspects of my identity. I suspect that particularly my gender identity and being Dutch influenced their conversion narratives. They often told me: "I know Dutch people think that women are oppressed in Islam, but..." Or, "You probably think I am a very conservative woman but..." Because I also asked permission to interview one of their significant others—from among parents, relatives, and friends—they probably felt obliged to reveal details of their biographies. Some of them said: "Well, if you talk to my mother she will probably tell you about . . . I better tell you my side of the story." Others refused to let me interview a parent because of a strained or severed relationship. Also, the fact that I interviewed them at length at home, sometimes twice, probably explains the extent of information I gained about their personal trajectories.

The fifty selected stories from the Internet also have the character of "telling backwards." As one of them writes: "If you would have told me 5 years prior that I would embrace Islam, I never would have believed you. In retrospect, Allah's guidance was so subtle yet consistent, that now I see my whole life as leading up to that moment."[5] In only one story does a convert quote her own diary to give insight into her feelings and doubts before conversion.[6] Most accounts are reconstructions in which present convictions or behavioral styles are reinscribed into their life stories. Besides the intellectual doubts most of them appear to have had about the Trinity and salvation from a tender age, they describe moral issues that they can now relate to their "Islamic" inclinations. One of them, for instance, writes about meeting a man "in whose culture it is not normal to touch until marriage. . . . This held me in awe, though I enjoyed the story I never thought that the same incident could occur again."[7] Also other lifestyle aspects, which only become meaningful after conversion, are represented as already there.

It is not easy to establish how far converts on the Internet can be considered a community that acts as an "Erzählgemeinshaft." Several clues, however, point in that direction. For some converts, the Internet was the main means through which they came into contact with Muslims. They visited sites for converts and chat rooms on Islam or became members of e-mail discussion group such as the New Muslim Woman. E-mail discussion groups, especially, are comparable to a community in which lively discussions, knowledge, advice, and conversion stories circulate. In particular, the Niqab Support e-group gave the impression of a close community. Its members not only supported each other in dealing with problems concerning the *niqab*, the face veil, but also with regard to marital problems, health problems, and childbearing and -rearing. They also helped each other to keep steady in their religious devotion and to increase their knowledge of Islam. A common sentiment was that the sisters of these virtual groups were more like real family than their own non-Muslim relatives. This virtual community also figures as "Erzählgemeinshaft" for conversion stories. For instance, the conversion story of Hudda Droll was circulated, followed by an appeal to write one's own stories as a source of inspiration for others.[8] Several participants in the discussion groups had their own homepages, on which they put their conversion stories, as well as links to the stories of other members. Several stories from the selected sample thus start with "I have been reading everybody's stories and hope mine will be an inspiration as well." These linkages and circulation of stories create models and scripts online.

Whereas in a fieldwork and interview setting narratives about identity and religious change are constructed in an interactive context, the selected stories from the Internet are self-presentations. How does identity enactment take place on the Internet? The actors on the Internet are potentially free to emphasize or deemphasize elements of their identities. They can also choose to remain anonymous, as some converts did. The Internet is a medium, or a new space, in which identities can be detached from embodiment and other essentialist anchors. One could thus even fake being a Muslim. This apparently happened in one case in which a woman participated in an e-mail discussion group on Islamic matters. She pretended to be a Muslim but got so many questions that she decided to study Islam seriously and read the Qur'an. This eventually led to her conversion.[9] Miller and Slater (2000) theorize two major relationships between identity enactment and the Internet. First, the Internet can be a means through which one can enact a version of oneself that is perceived and presented as the "real self." The Internet provides the instrument through which the "real self" can be fully realized. One can establish oneself as a member of a culture or community that is regarded as old or originary. That is, through the new means of the Internet one can become what one thinks one really is or belongs to. Miller and Slater label this process "expansive realization" (2000, 10–12). Second, the Internet may allow an actor to envisage a quite novel idea of what one could be. The Internet, then, offers the potential to create new identities. This aspect is called "expansive potential" (Miller and Slater 2000, 13–15).

How does identity enactment take place on the Internet in the case of the conversion narratives? Is the Internet a place where (would-be) converts can glimpse new identities or a place where they can fully realize themselves as Muslims? In the final section of this chapter, I will compare fieldwork and the Internet as different contexts for identity enactment. First, I discuss and compare the identities and discourses that are most central in the convert stories collected during fieldwork and from the Internet.

Discourses and Identities

Most interviews with converts contained four narratives connected to major aspects of their identities. Besides their biographies, the stories include a
religious, a gender, and a national or ethnic discourse. These discourses also
figure into the Internet accounts, but—as we will see—with a somewhat different content and accent.

Biographical Narratives
During fieldwork I was particularly intrigued by the linkages between the
discourses, for instance, by the ways in which the personal life stories provide relief for understanding their religious or gender discourses.[10] Such an
analysis is difficult to pursue with the Internet accounts. Most of the Internet stories give hardly any clue to personal trajectories and motives other
than the most basic facts such as the place of birth and former denominations. Only a few stories give insight into the way Islam fits into converts' life
histories. For instance, an American convert of Southern Baptist origin was
divorced and felt guilty about that. Her pastor affirmed that she was right in
feeling guilty. After meeting Muslims at the university and participating in
activities of the Muslim Student Association, she started reading Islamic literature and felt it to be "so uplifting. It made me feel good about myself." She
found out that divorce is allowed and that her ex-husband was to blame because he committed a grave sin (adultery). She converted within a month.[11]
Also a few long stories give insight into the way Islam made sense within
converts' lives. Most stories give insight into why Islam is "the best religion,"
but not into the way Islam is connected to the life stories of their narrators,
that is, why it is the best for them personally.

The personal backgrounds of the converts in both cases appear to be comparable. The Dutch new Muslimas converted to Sunni Islam, except for one
convert who was inspired by Sufism. With regard to the Internet stories, I
also tried to select conversions to Sunni Islam, although it was not always explicitly mentioned. Most converts appear to be of a middle-class background.
They meet Muslims and become curious about Islam. The Internet converts
often mention a university as the place where they first come into contact
with Muslims. Dutch converts meet Muslims while in secondary school or
at the workplace and not that much at a university. In both cases, marrying
Muslims was an important reason to study Islam; a notable number, however, converted without marriage to a Muslim. Most Dutch converts had a

religious background but were no longer actively involved, whereas the Internet converts were still practicing at the time they become curious about Islam.[12] Most Dutch Muslimas thus converted from a secular position to Islam, whereas most American converts were practicing Christians.

Whether the background is religious or secular also influences the ensuing conversion process. Dutch women were simply curious to know more of their husbands' culture or religion and started to read about Islam. None of them was trying to convert her Muslim friend or husband to Christianity. On the contrary, a Dutch Muslima said that she was not religious, and when she met her prospective husband, who was studying mathematics in Paris, she thought: "How can such an intelligent person be a believer? I will talk this out of his head." In the Internet narratives, however, the conversion process contains religious conflicts. A common route to conversion in the Internet narratives is a religious person who meets a Muslim while in her twenties. She tries to convert her new Muslim acquaintance to her own religion, but in order to do so, she has to be knowledgeable about Islam and thus she starts reading the Qur'an. In this process she discovers that all kinds of religious questions she used to have as a child are answered in a convincing and rational way. Several variations on this theme exist. For instance, a young woman who belonged to the Church of Christ dated and eventually married an "Arab." She witnessed her roommate's conversion to Islam and felt guilty for not having "saved" her. She secretly studied Islam to reconvert her friend and to convert her husband as well. Yet, by reading Muslim literature she became convinced of its ultimate "truth."[13] Several Internet stories are written by proselytizing Christians who realized that they could no longer defend Christian beliefs and doctrines and therefore converted. The personal narratives are thus statements of their religious motivations rather than elaborate life stories. Whereas the life stories gathered through interviews are heterogeneous, the online narratives show a high level of standardization in the personal trajectories.

Discourse on Gender

During my fieldwork, gender issues and "the position of woman in Islam" were often discussed. The new Muslimas felt obliged to defend themselves against the Dutch perception of Islam as a religion oppressive toward women. They articulated their own discourses, which entailed criticism of Dutch constructions of gender.[14] These critical views were inscribed in the whole life story but most clearly articulated at two phases of the story: at the initial part of the conversion story and when explaining the narrator's opinion on veiling.[15] I will go into the three main aspects of the stories' gender discourse, those connected to sexuality, the construction of gender, and motherhood.

First, these Muslimas feel that the freedom in the West or in Dutch society is exaggerated, particularly the sexual freedom. In Dutch society everything is "so open and related to sex." They consider the restrained behavior between men and women in Islam a way to prevent disorder. Islamic rules, if applied properly, contribute to clarity and stability in familial and marital life. Furthermore, several new Muslimas feel that in Islam they are less perceived as sex objects than in the West. By covering, they also believe they can escape "the terror of fashion" and the ideal of slenderness. They feel that their body is a very "intimate thing" that should not be publicly exposed. They hold that "In Islam you are not considered a sex object. You don't wear flashy clothes and makeup; you are seen as your own self. You are respected for what you are, not for what you look like." They thus express views that resemble feminist thinking.

Second, with regard to the construction of gender, the new Muslimas are convinced of the equality of men and women in Islam. They do not regard themselves as "oppressed." On the contrary, they perceive themselves as emancipated and equal to their partners. Even the converts themselves admit that they had this idea of women's subordination in Islam before becoming a Muslim. They had long discussions with their husbands about their rights as women and scrutinized Islamic sources on the status of women before they dared to convert. Several new Muslimas link tensions in the beginning of their marriages to their "overassertiveness" regarding sex role patterns. They are convinced that Islam gives women equal rights, although they immediately explain that many Arab or Islamic countries do not grant women the rights they should have according to Islam. They usually distinguish "religion" from "culture," a distinction they regard as particularly valid with regard to women's issues. The Dutch new Muslimas think they are quite capable of distinguishing between "religion" and "culture" because they have not grown up with a variety of Islam embedded in a native cultural context.

Whereas Dutch new Muslimas hold that the sexes are of equal value, most converts do not consider them of equal nature. Most of them do not aspire to equality between men and women in all respects. Many new Muslimas adhere to the notion of "equal but different" (see also Roald, this volume). The Islamic idea that the sexes are complementary is attractive to them. Some of them formulate views that are similar to a brand of feminism, the "differential feminism," that stresses the differences between the sexes and the inherently positive values of womanhood.[16] Several new Muslimas criticize Dutch society for its equality policy. They hold that in the Netherlands you "must be a man" or "you must be a man and a woman," that is, "you should make a career and take care of the children as well." According to them, this is not necessary in Islam. "You can be yourself." "If you want to, you can make a career, but you don't have to." "You can live according to your *fitrah,* your nature."

Lastly, this feminine *fitrah* is strongly related to care and motherhood. Islam is "friendly" to women because it permits women to stay at home and take care of the children. Motherhood is highly valued and mothers are greatly respected in Islam. Since women give birth, several Dutch new Muslimas deem it natural that women with small children are protected and have a right to maintenance. They criticize Dutch society, in which even women with small children are obliged to earn their own income.

Dutch new Muslimas who stress the different nature of women do not see any contradiction between their ideas and the ideas of women's emancipation. Some women stress their "emancipated" Dutch background in addition to women's rights in Islam. They describe situations in their daily lives to show they live an emancipated life and earn their own income. The difficult position of their immigrant husbands on the labor market causes many new Muslimas to be the main breadwinner of the family. Several converts who told me that women are naturally predisposed to take care of children were in practice breadwinners, whereas their husbands were "housemen."

The new Muslimas' understandings of the meanings of emancipation are varied. They might understand it as independence, earning their own income, or equality in value to men; often, though, they use it in the sense of "developing yourself." "Developing yourself" is a personal emancipation strategy and can mean "living according to your own nature" and "living according to your own choices," including the religious choice. I have the impression that emancipation in the sense of independence and equality is more strongly expressed by women who recently converted, whereas those who converted several years ago stressed their freedom to develop themselves in the way they choose. Most Muslimas thus locate themselves within an emancipation discourse. Whereas most new Muslimas see no contradiction between Islam and emancipation, only a few identify themselves as feminists. Feminism is associated with a rigid notion of equality in all fields.

In comparison, the Internet stories are rather silent on the "women's question." In cases where it figures into the conversion accounts, it is in the same two phases as in the interviews, that is, right at the beginning or in connection with covering, either *hijab* or *niqab*. In a few stories, converts mention that they were prejudiced against Islam and tried to find fault by looking into women's issues such as polygamy and veiling, but then discovered that their judgment was totally wrong. Like the Dutch converts, they stress the negative aspects of sexuality in the West, which they characterize as a "slave market of sexual competition and violence."[17] Another American convert states that "In popular culture women are portrayed as very sexy, ladylike, independent enough so that men have no real responsibility towards women and children." She holds that in Islam she found a system that gave her ultimate respect for being a mother.[18] Yet generally there is little discussion about their conversion as women and the appeal of "Islamic" constructions of femininity.

The second stage at which convert discourse on gender and sexuality appears relates to covering. There is a separate genre of stories on the Internet, "the *hijab* stories," "proper *hijab* stories," or "*niqab* stories," and there is an e-mail discussion group of *niqabi* converts in which veiling is the dominant topic. I collected about fifteen *hijab* stories and fifteen *niqab* stories. These stories describe underlying religious motivations and the different steps in veiling, as well as difficulties converts meet with regard to non-Muslims and Muslims alike. Gender and sexuality, although not absent, are clearly subordinate themes.[19] A few *hijab* stories mention that the *hijab* is liberating because it forces people to judge a woman according to her intellect instead of physical appearance.[20] A Canadian convert states that she wears a *hijab* because: "I am a Muslim woman who believes her body is her own private concern." The *hijab* gives back to women "ultimate control of their own bodies."[21]

The discourse on gender and sexuality on the Internet, though, is a rather insignificant theme in the *hijab* stories, and in the conversion stories it is rarely expressed. The ideas occasionally expressed are rather similar to the Dutch converts' gender constructions. The gender discourse is a more central and organic part of the Dutch conversion stories. Dutch new Muslimas convert to Islam as individuals and as women, and feel obliged to explain both aspects of their identities. They voice critical opinions on Dutch constructions of sex and gender and redefine notions of emancipation.

Ethnicity

The relative importance of gender issues for Dutch converts becomes clear also when we examine their discourse on being Dutch or Western. In Dutch society new Muslimas are sometimes regarded as weird and strange, and veiled converts are sometimes treated as foreigners. The combination of veiling and being Dutch is questioned. The image of women who wear a veil and wooden clogs is sometimes used in the media to ridicule Dutch converts, as well as to convey a message of the incompatibility of veiling and being Dutch.[22] The most important construction of Dutch national and cultural identity vis-à-vis converts is related to sex and gender. During the interviews with relatives of Dutch converts, they often explained that to them the most amazing thing is how an emancipated Dutch girl can become a Muslima. The self-image of the Dutch is that the Dutch, in contrast to Muslims, are very liberal and emancipated. The Dutch narratives on nationality or ethnicity are thus very much linked to the gender discourse.

Most converts identify as Dutch and Muslima, or—put together in a single label—as Dutch Muslimas. They stress that they have become Muslim but did not adopt the Turkish, Moroccan, or Egyptian nationality of their partners. Although they changed their views on Dutch society and have become critical of several aspects of Dutch culture, they are not totally estranged. They sometimes feel like "symbolic migrants." They moved away from central Dutch values, but do not feel they are outsiders. Islam offers them an alternative system from which they criticize Dutch views on morality and such Western values as individualism and materialism. Islam provides them a way of distancing themselves from their Western background. A few converts claim that neither nationality nor ethnicity is an issue, that their new identity as Muslima is central. They are not Dutch Muslimas, but simply Muslimas.

The Internet material shows more heterogeneity in national background.[23] Most converts are from the United States. In the Internet stories, the reaction of relatives and ruptures with American culture are occasionally touched upon, particularly with regard to veiling or Christian celebrations. It is interesting to note, however, that ethnicity is generally played down. The majority of American converts are reported to be African Americans, and according to the research of Wohlrab-Sahr (1999), there are differences in motivations and discourses between white and African American converts. Historically, there is a strong connection between Islam and black nationalism (Wohlrab-Sahr 1999, 34–47; McCloud 1995; see also Simmons, this volume). The issue of race and ethnicity could be expected to be a feature in the Internet stories. This part of these new Muslimas' identity, however, is hardly mentioned. Exceptions are infrequent statements such as those of a convert who had a painting in her room of Jesus as a black man and wrote, "He was black like me," [24] and another who stated, "I couldn't be a Muslim. I was American and white." [25] In most stories, however, no clues are given to the racial or ethnic identity. In the Al-Niqab Support Group (ANSG) the differences between "new Muslims" and "Arab Muslims," or "born Muslims," are occasionally touched upon. An African American Muslima complained that "most Arabs do not *salaam*" her or do not wish to stand shoulder to shoulder in prayer. Several new Muslimas share similar experiences. So the issue of ethnicity and nationality is important, yet it is condemned as "*fitnah*" and sinful. The discourse that is dominant on the Internet appears to deliberately underplay the ethnic or racial component. Islam is presented as the universal non-national religion, and occasionally this is mentioned as one of the attractive things about Islam. "In Islam there is no prejudice at all. . . . Muslims do not judge a person on their skin color, place, status of birth, male or female. The only way a person can be better than another is if they are better Muslims." [26] "Islam gave true equality not only to men and women, but to all races and social classes, judging only by one's level of piety." [27] The ethnicity discourse thus shades into the religious discourse, to which I will turn now.

The Religious Discourse

A comparison between the religious discourse of the online and offline conversion stories shows similarities and differences. In the fieldwork, I could not only discern linkages between the personal story and the religious discourse, but also between the gender discourse and the religious discourse. Rather specific examples were sexual abuse and Islam's regulation of sexuality, parental divorce and Islam's promotion of a stable family life, and alcohol addiction of one's father and Islam's prohibition of drinking. Islamic prescriptions concerning lifestyle made sense within these biographies. Besides the direct relationship with individual biographies, the Dutch converts' religious narratives showed certain consistencies and centered mostly on three themes. First, Islam is perceived as the ideal social and moral religion, providing a stable family life and regulating the relationships between the sexes. Second, Islam is perceived as a pervasive, practical religion that is grounded in nature. It gives a clear guidance to spirituality through the direct accessibility of God and regular moments of prayer. Religion thus becomes embedded in daily life. Islam is a natural, social, and complete way of life. Third, Islam is a rational, scientific, and logical religion, and this makes it the most convincing religion as compared to the other monotheistic options.

Particularly this last discourse on rationality was prominent. Islam's rational and logical character was illustrated with reference to rules regarding eating, drinking, and the sexes, as well as to theological arguments on the Trinity and salvation. The Dutch converts found it important to challenge common ideas about Islam as irrational and religion in general as scientifically unsound. A university graduate heavily emphasized the convergence of the Qur'an with science in order to legitimize her choice.

In comparison to the fieldwork material, the Internet sample's religious discourse is more standardized and is strongly focused on the last-mentioned discourse, the logical, rational, and scientific character of Islam. This discourse contrasts Islam and Christianity, using such examples as the concept of the Trinity versus the unity of God; Jesus as the son of God versus Jesus as a prophet; the Bible as written and changed by human hand versus the unchanged perfection of the Qur'an; and the presence versus absence of the idea of original sin. Last but not least, the Bible is in contradiction with modern science, whereas the Qur'an is held to be compatible.

Not only is Islam appealing because of its rationality, but it also offers an intellectual route to conversion. The act of reading the Qur'an is in many stories described as a decisive factor in the conversion process: "It gave me a good feeling, I could understand it and I couldn't put it down."[28] The initial reason for studying the Qur'an is usually the acquaintance with Muslims and sometimes observing practicing Muslims. One of the converts on the Internet writes, for instance: "I was in awe at how someone could have so much certainty in what he believed and followed."[29] The fact that Islam is not just "faith," but also provides "proof," makes this religion beyond doubt. As one of the converts on the Internet argues about Islam: "Here is a religion of truth, which can stand up to any test of logic and reason! Just as I always thought religion should be. It should make sense, it should be logical."[30]

This theme of Islam's logical, scientific, and rational character leads to another interesting trope, that of recognition, of realizing that in fact one is already a Muslim. Some of them describe how they find their own solutions to theological problems and then realize that these self-discoveries happen to be aligned with Islam. They have always rejected the ideas of the Trinity or Jesus as the son of God, but were not aware of the existence of an Islamic alternative. "The more knowledge I acquired about Islam, the more . . . I found that many of the beliefs that I already had were actually Islamic not merely 'common sense.'"[31] Others feel they have always been Muslims but did not know. "If anyone were to ask me when I became Muslim, I guess the only feasible answer would be that I was born Muslim, but just wasn't aware of it." [32] They are dormant Muslims, who can only recognize this fact after being led to Islam through meeting Muslims and then study.

The idea of being already Muslim is most strongly expressed in the Internet accounts and taken a step further. "I was Muslim but just wasn't aware of it" slides into the ideology of "all people are born Muslim," that is, in a "state of Islam." "We are all born in a state of Islam but what is unfortunate is that many people never recognize this fact." [33] Everyone is born a Muslim, since all human beings are born into a state of "submission to the will of God." Therefore, conversion is not a correct notion and should be replaced by "reversion." Several converts also prefer to speak about "embracing Islam" rather than "turning to Islam." This expresses the same idea that Islam is not something new and strange but an originary and familiar religion.

To conclude this section on the online and offline conversion narratives, several similarities and differences are discernible. First, concerning the content of the accounts, there are no striking differences. The gender discourse is more or less similar, and the religious discourses overlap. The focus, or accents, in the two case studies, however, are different. Whereas in the fieldwork case the personal and gender discourses are prominent and linked to the religious discourse, in the Internet case the religious discourse is dominant. Other discourses, such as the personal, gender, and national discourses, are subsumed under the religious discourse. Second, in both cases, a certain amount of standardization of the discourse is visible. Yet the extent of standardization in the Internet material is greater. This is particularly the case with the religious discourse of the Internet narratives. The idea of the logical, scientific, and rational character of Islam is dominant in most accounts. Whereas the fieldwork narratives consist of varied discourses and different voices, the Internet accounts are rather depersonalized, standardized religious narratives.

Fieldwork, Internet, and the Production of Conversion Narratives

Why is there more stress on the religious discourse in the Internet accounts and more on gender in the Dutch case? Is this related to the different national contexts, as most Internet accounts are from the United States? Why is there more standardization on the Internet? Why is there a depersonalized discourse instead of a variety of expressed identities and voices on the Internet? Contrary to the expectations created by the Internet's status as a medium for a free and unconstrained expression of identities, we observe a depersonalized and standardized discourse in the case of the conversion stories. How are identities expressed through the Internet, and how is identity enactment different during an interview?

A clue to this rather unexpected turn can be found in an interesting experience I had during fieldwork. I visited a lecture at the El Tawheed mosque in Amsterdam organized by a small group of Dutch converted Muslimas and their Muslim husbands. They are educated in Arabic and Islamic studies, and give lectures in Dutch and Arabic. They wear *niqab* and are known for their dedication to the cause of Islam. I tried to do interviews with them, but they refused. I eventually managed to take one of them aside for half an hour. She explained why they refused to do interviews. They felt that my anthropological approach and interest in personal trajectories were not relevant. The only thing important to them was God, and their lives were dedicated to serving him. They, as persons, were not important except for their religious work and devotion. During the interview, she thus refused to go into biographical details, but was quite willing to explain why Islam was the best religion, meant for all times and all human beings.

The explanation she gave for her refusal is interesting because she chooses to stress one aspects of her many identities, that is, her religious identity. All other sides of her personal identity—being a white, middle-class Dutch woman married to an Egyptian and the mother of several children—are discarded for her religious identity as a Muslima. Her account is close to the Internet accounts. Having a mission appears to be the key word to explain the difference between her account—and the Internet accounts—and the other converts' narratives collected during fieldwork. This means that we have to investigate the purpose of telling or writing the conversion story. Is it to witness, to confess, to defend, or, as Stromberg observed, is testifying part of the conversion itself? Three elements thus merit attention in understanding the difference between the fieldwork narratives and the Internet discourses. First, the difference in national contexts needs to be considered. Second, the different purposes of telling or writing conversion stories should be compared. Finally, it is important to examine the different contexts of the production of narratives, that is, fieldwork versus Internet.

First, with regard to the national context, the most obvious difference appears to be related to secularization and emancipation. In the Netherlands, people have a strong self-perception of belonging to an emancipated society. This self-definition is particularly articulated vis-à-vis Islam. In the Dutch

secularized context, Islam's Otherness is not defined in terms of different religious ideologies, but mainly in terms of gender and sexuality (Prins 2000).
Accordingly, gender issues and sexuality are prominent in the discourse on
Islam both among Muslims and non-Muslims.[34] Islam is perceived as the ultimate Other in contrast to Dutch national identity. Whether this gender discourse with regard to Islam is less outspoken in the Unites States is difficult
to assess based on my research. Yet it partly explains the stress on the gender
discourse in the Dutch case study. In the Unites States, on the other hand,
there appears to be more religious vitality in the various denominations or
new religious movements than in the Netherlands (Bruce 1999). And as explained above, the religious commitment of the converts from the Internet
sample was considerably higher. Many Dutch converts were either secular
or at least no longer practicing at the time of conversion, whereas the Internet converts reported higher religious attachment. This could be part of the
explanation for the greater stress on the religious dimension in the Internet
accounts.[35]

Second, if we look at the purpose and public of the narratives, we can see
the divergence. The missionary aspect was largely absent in the fieldwork
narratives. The Dutch Muslimas sporadically said that they hoped I would
convert one day, as they had the experience "that it made them so happy to become Muslim." Occasionally they described their efforts to correct false views
of Islam as a form of *da'wa*, calling to the faith. They sometimes mentioned
that testifying to the glory of Islam would bring them closer to paradise. Yet
they were explaining their conversion rather than engaging in an explicit
form of *da'wa*. The missionary aspect was less important than defending
their rather "unusual" or "weird" choice to become a Muslim. Parts of their
accounts were simply explanatory, others dealing with issues like gender and
emancipation were defensive and critical, and Dutch morality was criticized
and condemned. Yet the explanatory and defensive voices were dominant.
Their purpose was to explain their situation for the public of Dutch acquain-
tances, condensed in the person of the researcher, that is, me. As a result of
their perception of me as an exponent of Dutch society and probably as an
"emancipated woman or feminist," the gender discourse was prime.

The purpose of the Internet stories appears to be different. Some of the
converts chose to put their stories on the Internet as a source of inspiration
for others. Others were asked to write their stories so that they could be
linked to special sites for converts or potential converts. The Web site "The
True Religion" has an explicit missionary aim. Its goal is "to introduce the

reader to Islam, the natural religion of man, as well as to give an overview of core beliefs, compelling evidence and rational arguments for the truth of Islam."[36] The stories form just one link connecting general information about Islam, comparative religion, revelation, God, and the prophets. The subsection on converts provides, besides the stories, such guides as how to become a Muslim, "so you just embraced Islam, here is what you must know," "looking for a Muslim name," "learning how to pray," and advice from other new Muslims. In particular, the testimonies of former priests and missionaries are recommended as inspirational and thought to be powerful instruments for proselytizing. Whereas not every individual story needs to be written as a missionary effort, most are aimed at this goal or function as such in the way they are presented at such sites as "The True Religion."

The observation of Beckford (1978) that converts include elements of the religion's ideological rationale in their narratives seems to hold for the Internet case study as well. The content of the religious discourse in the Internet narratives is related to a specific missionary ideology. Poston's study on Islamic *da'wa* in the West (1992) gives insight into the various debates on missionary activities and strategies. Of particular interest is the attempt at applying Islamic missiology to Western countries. One of the prominent writers in this field is Khurram Murad, who lives in Great Britain but also has extensive influence in North America and Western Europe. In his booklet, he explains the conceptual and methodological aspects of *da'wa* among non-Muslims in the West (1986). His basic idea is that the message of Islam, though essentially the same in all ages, must be conveyed through a medium that is understood by the addressees. So the stress should first be on commonalities between Islam and Western religions. The most important way to reach the missionary goal is stressing that Islam is not a new religion but the foundational and natural religion for humankind. He argues: "We do not invite people to a 'new' religion, we invite them to the oldest religion, indeed to their 'own' religion, the religion of living in total surrender to their Creator, in accordance with the guidance brought by *all* His Messengers" (1986, 18). He continues: "Indeed, if I am not misunderstood, we may be bold enough to say that we do not invite anyone to change his 'religion,' to transfer his allegiance to a rival religion. For, by our own admission, Islam is not a new or rival religion among the many competing for human allegiance; it is the natural and primordial religion" (1986, 18). As Poston argues, this missiology sets the stage for a common Muslim appeal that choosing to follow Islam is not "conversion," but rather "reversion." According to Murad, this message should be spread by Western converts to Islam. They are regarded as more effective in proselytizing than born Muslims. Converts should be messengers to their own people because they can be truly effective in showing others the way to their "own" religion. Converts as fellow citizens should thus bring Islam home. So writing or telling the conversion story is not directly part of the conversion itself, as Stromberg argued; it can, however, be an instrument for converting others. Testifying to your conversion is an important form of *da'wa*. The idea of Islam as the original and natural message for all people, to which non-Muslims should return, is thus part of a missionary ideology (see also Haddad, this volume).

Lastly, the difference between the online and offline narratives is related to the different contexts of production. As Miller and Slater stated, the Internet can provide a space for enacting core values, practices, and identities. People can "realize" themselves. People can even bring about a state that had been realized but then lost. They can enact a version of themselves in which they make happen what they think they really are or should be. Yet people can also envisage a quite novel vision of what they could be through the Internet. That is, the Internet can provide an expansive potential.[37]

For the converts, the Internet has provided both options but at different stages in the conversion process. Many American converts relate that the Internet was a very important medium in their search for information about Islam. Several women describe how the Internet is their only medium for communication and knowledge about Islam. Without the Internet they might not have become acquainted with Islam. A convert from Iceland related that she entirely converted through the Internet. She first learned about Islam through the Internet, stumbled upon a chat room about Islam, chatted extensively with Muslims, and asked many questions. After some time she wanted to take *shahada*, the declaration of the faith, while she was chatting with sisters. She decided to see if it was possible to do so on the spot and found several sisters online prepared to witness. She declared her faith online and became Muslim by way of the Internet. She thus found a new space and identity through the Internet.[38] The same sister now has her own Web site with her own story and stories of other Muslimas.

This constitutes the second stage at which the Internet functions as a means to realize the new identity. New Muslimas can bring about a form of online community that most of them lack offline. They can feel themselves part of a virtual Islamic *ummah* and actively expand this community by creating their own Web sites and writing their stories. They can inspire other potential converts by sharing their stories and experiences. Conversion stories, then, feature structured narratives or scripts and show a high degree of "expansive realization." Converts can realize themselves not only by testifying to their conversion, but also by finding a place to belong.[39] The Internet thus provides a good opportunity to realize one's "true or original self" and to expand this message globally.

Whereas the difference in the national contexts sets the stage for the stress on gender in the Dutch case and the emphasis on religion in the Internet case, this tendency is further strengthened by the different purposes for the testimonies and the contexts in which they are produced. The Internet provides a medium to select one's identity, so that it can be as varied or limited, as expansive or narrow, as one wishes. In the case of the Dutch Muslima who refused to be interviewed on personal details, I still gained information about aspects of her life other than her religious identity by simply sitting face-to-face with her. Representations on the Internet can be "bodiless" for an anonymous public. On the Internet one can leave out sides of one's identity that are inescapable in a fieldwork setting. On the Internet one can select which aspects of identity are presented as primary. This freedom, however, does not necessarily lead to a multiplicity of voices and expressions, as is often assumed. Depending on one's purpose, one can select or feign an identity. One can thus choose to focus solely on the religious identity and the religious discourse thought to be most effective in promoting the new conviction. Identity enactment on the Internet can be a powerful tool for *da'wah*.

Conclusion

The aim of this chapter is to analyze the different discourses that can help illuminate why Islam can be attractive for women in the West. Beyond personal trajectories and specific biographical themes, Islam's appeal is related to gender (why converts as women are attracted to Islam), nationality and ethnicity (why they as Dutch/Western/American individuals are attracted to Islam), and religion (why Islam). The gender discourse mainly centers on gender roles, sexuality, and motherhood. Islam provides converts with constructions of gender that allow them to live according to their *fitrah*, their feminine nature, without being treated as sex objects. They feel respected as women. Islam thus gives them a counterdiscourse on gender that is in their view compatible with notions of emancipation, while simultaneously providing a framework to criticize the West. Islam also offers a possibility of distancing oneself from an ethnic background, either through a discourse on the universality of Islam and the irrelevance of the ethnic dimension, or by critical reflection on such Western values as materialism, individualism, or views on sex and gender. Islam as a religious system is attractive because it is grounded in nature and it is a social and moral religion. Last, but not least, Islam is rational, scientific, and logical and therefore the most convincing religion. The Internet stories add a more specific religious discourse to this. Islam is felt to be a rational and natural religion into which everyone is born. Many converts describe their feeling of being a dormant Muslim. They are already Muslim without realizing their true nature.

Despite similarities between the online and offline conversion narratives, it appears that the conversion stories collected by means of fieldwork are somewhat different from the Internet accounts. The gender discourse is prominent in the interviews, and the religious discourse is paramount on the Internet. The missionary tendencies and standardization of narratives are also stronger in the Internet discourse. It is not absent in the fieldwork narratives, but these voices are more diverse and multifaceted. Whereas the difference in the national contexts sets the stage for the stress on gender in the Dutch case and the emphasis on religion in the Internet case, this tendency is further strengthened by the different purposes for the testimonies and the contexts in which they are produced. Not only are the Internet narratives written and the fieldwork accounts spoken, the first are also self-presentations for an anonymous public, whereas the latter are presentations of self in an interactive context. In the interactive context of face-to-face interviews, the narratives include responses to the interactive context. The speaking subject is multiply situated and embodied. In the Dutch case this particularly implies converts defending themselves on the ground of Islam's assumed oppression of women, an issue they as "emancipated Dutch women" cannot avoid.

Whereas Dutch new Muslimas feel obliged to defend themselves through a gender discourse, converts who publish their stories on the Internet try to convince through a religious discourse. We have seen not only that the Internet is a good medium for performing *da'wa*, but also that converts themselves are considered perfect instruments for proselytizing. Their stories, as part of an "Erzählgemeinshaft," contain elements of Islam's ideological message that can be convincing to new members. The Internet is potentially a space where new identities can be constructed, or "real" and "originary" identities can be reconstructed. New Muslimas, in their "bodiless" presentation of self on the Internet, can choose which issues to address, identities to present, and narratives to write. This does not, however, necessarily lead to a multiplicity of voices, but can result in standardized narratives of the ideal (religious) self used as a device to convert others.

Notes

1. In the Netherlands, there were about six thousand converts in 1990. Approximately two-thirds of them were women. There are no recent estimates (Wagtendonk 1994, 6; Speelman 1993, 145; Crijnen 1999, 8).

2. There are two organizations for converts. Al Nisa is a liberal organization that helps new Muslimas find their place in Islam. Al Nisa provides a place to meet and to pray. It also sponsors lectures and publishes a monthly magazine. El Tawheed is linked to a mosque and has a reputation for its strict, or Islamist, interpretation of Islam. The converts of this organization provide lectures in Dutch and Arabic.

3. http://www.thetruereligion.org/converts.htm. Other sites are: http://www.isgkc.org/stories; http://www.islamia.com/reverting; http://www.usc.edu/dept/MSA/newmuslims; http://www.al-islam.org/begin/newmuslims; http://www.muslim.net/islam. Some of the stories were only half a page in length and contained hardly any information on the .conversion motives, so I skipped them.

4. I followed the e-group ANSG, the Al-Niqab Support Group, from October 2000 until the end of May 2001. Since the information about this group is confidential and only for members, I will not cite from this e-group. I will use the information only in a general sense or when it is also available at other sites on the Internet, since cross-posting is a common practice.

In addition, I followed the New Muslim Woman from January 2001 until the end of July 2001. This group is for Muslim and non-Muslim women.

5. http://www.usc.edu/dept/MSA/newmuslims/karima.html.

6. http://www.thetruereligion.org/khadija.htm.

7. http://www.usc.edu/dept/MSA/newmuslims/kaci.html.

8. Hudda Droll's story is also available at http://www.thetruereligion.org.

9. http://www.thetruereligion.org/hanifa.htm.

10. See van Nieuwkerk 2006.

11. http://www.thetruereligion.org/nadia.htm.

12. The religious background of Dutch converts is as follows: ten Catholics, five Protestants, three atheists, two secularists, one Dutch Reformed Christian, one Jehovah's Witness, and one Jew. This refers mainly to the religious affiliation of the parents and the church they visited as children. They were no longer involved at the time they meet Muslims and considered conversion to Islam, except for two women. The religious background in the Internet stories is as follows: twenty-two "Christians" (not self-identified by denomination), eleven Catholic, five Southern Baptists, three Protestant, two secularists, two unknown, one Church of Christ, one Church of England, one Quaker, one Jew, and one Evangelical Lutheran. Besides the two secularists, seven other women

mention that they were no longer religious at the time of conversion.

13. http://www.usc.edu/dept/MSA/ newmuslims/afrah.html.

14. See van Nieuwkerk 2003.

15. Half of the Dutch converts I interviewed are veiled in Dutch public space and two wear the *niqab;* the others are not veiled or only when they go to meetings for Muslimas. Others were considering veiling, but were not ready to face possible hostile reactions.

16. In the feminist movement in the West two traditions developed. The "equal rights" tradition contests ideas of an essentialist womanhood, whereas the radical feminist idea, or differential feminism, struggles for the acknowledgment of the inherently positive values of women. The tradition of "equality feminism," however, has gained dominance, and differential feminism is often depicted as conservative. See Aerts 1984 and Scott 1989.

17. http://www.usc.edu/dept/MSA/ newmuslims/penomee.html.

18. http://www.islamfortoday.com/ phreddie.htm.

19. An exception is, for instance, Sharifa Carlo's conversion story and *hijab* story, which are linked to and circulated on several converts' sites and in e-mail groups. In her conversion story, she is silent on gender issues; in her *hijab* story, however, she voices strong opinions on this matter. She states: "I was a modern woman, educated and liberated. Little did I know the awful truth. I was more oppressed than any Muslim woman in the most culturally oppressive village in the Muslim world. I was oppressed not by an inability to choose my clothing or to choose my life-style, I was oppressed by an inability to see my society for what it really was. I was oppressed by the idea that a woman's beauty was public,

and that lustful admiration was equal to respect. It was when Allah guided me to Islam, and I put on the *hijab,* that I was finally able to step out of the society in which I lived and see it for what it really is. I could see how the highest paid women were those who exposed themselves to public display, like actresses, models and even striptease dancers. I was able to see that the relationship between men and women was unfairly stacked in the man's direction. I knew I used to dress to attract men. I tried to fool myself by saying I did it to please myself, but the painful reality was that what pleased me was when I was admired by a man I considered attractive" (http://www.muslim.net/islam/ story.html).

20. Opinion on veiling expressed in the e-group the New Muslim Woman, August 6, 2001.

21. Muslim Internet Directory, http:// www.2muslims.com.

22. See van Nieuwkerk 2004. Interestingly enough, a picture of a Moroccan Muslima who was veiled and wearing wooden clogs also provoked reactions of laughter, but conveyed the meaning of integration and inclusion instead of exclusion.

23. The national background of the selected narratives are as follows: USA, thirty-two; not known, eight; Canada, two; Australia, two; UK, two; Iceland, one; Sweden, one; Ireland, one; and Germany, one.

24. http://www.islamfortoday.com/ phreddie.htm.

25. http://www.thetruereligion.org/ aminah.htm.

26. http://www.usc.edu/dept/MSA/ newmuslims/aamina.html.

27. http://www.usc.edu/dept/MSA/ newmuslims/karima.html.

28. http://www.thetruereligion.org/zakiyyah.htm.

29. http://www.usc.edu/dept/MSA/newmuslims/kelly.html.

30. http://www.usc.edu/dept/MSA/newmuslims/diana.html.

31. http://www.usc.edu/dept/MSA/newmuslims/lara.html.

32. http://www.usc.edu/dept/MSA/newmuslims/themise.html.

33. Ibid.

34. Roald (2003) mentions a similar tendency for Sweden.

35. Wohlrab-Sahr (1999), who did research comparing Germany and the USA, observes that there were other characteristic differences between the two contexts that also informed the conversion process and narratives. She particularly mentions the collective nature of the African American conversion versus the individual character of this choice in Germany. This could also influence the difference in the extent of standardization of the narratives. Yet as the ethnic identity of individuals in my sample is often unknown, it is difficult to verify her observation.

36. The site "The True Religion" claimed to be run by a "Muslim family living in New York" and to be a "completely voluntary, self-funded and independent-operated effort, unrelated to any organization or government."

37. In their case study on Trinidad, Miller and Slater concluded that contrary to the expectations that the Internet would lead to a reduction in national identity and nationalism, its clearly global scope assures that it is constantly used to represent Trinidad. In the diasporic situation of Trinidad, the global Internet is constantly used as a medium to perform Trini-ness and to reestablish a "local community." The Internet primarily serves originary ideals and structures.

38. http://www.geocities.com/Athens/Rhodes/7797.

39. It is interesting to notice that even the content of their stories testifies to the theme of "realizing a state that had been lost," that is, "reversion."

References

Aerts, M. 1984. "Gewoon hetzelfde of gewoon anders? Een feministisch dilemma." *Wending*, February 1984, pp. 82–89.

Beckford, J. A. 1978. "Accounting for Conversion." *British Journal of Sociology* 29 (2): 249–263.

Bruce, St. 1999. *Choice and Religion: A Critique of Rational Choice Theory*. Oxford: Oxford University Press.

Clifford, J., and G. E. Marcus. 1980. *Writing Culture: The Poetics and Politics of Ethnography*. Berkeley: University of California Press.

Crijnen, T. 1999. *Veertien portretten van Nieuwe Nederlandse en Vlaamse Moslims*. Amsterdam: Bulaaq.

de Groot, I. 1997. "Het verhulde geslacht. Over de (on)mogelijkheid om geslachtsloos te communiceren op internet." In *Virtueel verbonden. Filosoferen over cyberspace*, ed. Y. de Boer and J. Vorstenbosch, pp. 60–76. Amsterdam: Parrèsia.

Harding, S. F. 1987. "Convicted by the Holy Spirit: The Rhetoric of Fundamental Baptist Conversion." *American Ethnologist* 14 (1): 167–181.

Hofmann, G. 1997. *Muslimin werden. Frauen in Deutschland konvertieren zum Islam.* Frankfurt: Universität Frankfurt.

McCloud, A. B. 1995. *African American Islam.* New York and London: Routledge.

Miller, D., and D. Slater. 2000. *The Internet: An Ethnographic Approach.* Oxford: Berg.

Murad, Kh. 1986. *Da'wah among Non-Muslims in the West: Some Conceptual and Methodological Aspects.* London: Islamic Foundation.

Poston, L. 1992. *Islamic Da'wah in the West: Muslim Missionary Activity and the Dynamics of Conversion to Islam.* Oxford: Oxford University Press.

Prins, B. 2000. *Voorbij de onschuld. Het debat over de multiculturele samenleving.* Amsterdam: Van Gennep.

Rabinow, P. 1977. *Reflections on Fieldwork in Morocco.* Berkeley: University of California Press.

Roald, A. S. 2003. "The Mecca of Gender Equality: Muslim Women in Sweden." In *Muslim Women in the United Kingdom and Beyond: Experiences and Images,* ed. H. Jawad and T. Benn, pp. 65–91. Leiden: Brill.

Schmitz, J. 1997. "Structural Relations, Electronic Media, and Social Change: The Public Electronic Network and the Homeless." In *Virtual Culture: Identity and Communication in Cybersociety,* ed. S. G. Jones, pp. 80–102. London: Sage Publications.

Scott, J. W. 1989. "Deconstructie van gelijkheid-versus-verschil. De bruikbaarheid van de post-structuralistische theorie voor het feminisme." In *Het raadsel vrouwenge-schiedenis. Jaarboek voor vrouwengeschiedenis* 10. Nijmegen: SUN.

Speelman, G. M. 1993. "Mixed Marriages." In *Muslims and Christians in Europe: Essays in Honour of Jan Slomp,* ed. G. Speelman, J. van Lin, and D. Mulder, pp. 138–150. Kampen: Kok.

Stromberg, P. 1993. *Language and Self-Transformation: A Study of the Christian Conversion Narrative.* Cambridge: Cambridge University Press.

Van Nieuwkerk, K. 2003. "Multicultural-iteit, islam en gender. Visies van Nederlandse nieuwe moslima's." *Tijdschrift voor Genderstudies* 2003 (3): 6–21.

———. 2004. "Veils and Wooden Clogs Do Not Go Together." *Ethnos* 2004 (2): 229–246.

———. 2006 (forthcoming). "Biography and Choice: Female Converts to Islam in the Netherlands." In a volume edited by C. Notermans

Wagtendonk, K. 1994. *Islam, godsdienst-wetenschap en de ideeën van al Nisa.* Amsterdam: Universiteit van Amsterdam.

Watson, N. 1997. "Why We Argue about Virtual Community: A Case Study of the Phish.Net Fan Community." In *Virtual Culture: Identity and Communication in Cybersociety,* ed. S. G. Jones, pp. 102–133. London: Sage Publications.

Whitehead, H. 1987. *Renunciation and Reformulation.* Ithaca, N.Y.: Cornell University Press.

Wohlrab-Sahr, M. 1999. *Konversion zum Islam in Deutschland und den USA.* Frankfurt: Campus Verlag.

CHAPTER 5

The Shifting Significance of the *Halal/Haram* Frontier
Narratives on the *Hijab* and Other Issues

Stefano Allievi

The question of the *hijab*, the most common Arab name for what is often imprecisely called the "veil," as well as other gender issues, has always been a very sensitive issue in European countries' perception of Islam. It seems that, more than the issue itself, it is its symbolic perception that is crucial. The subject of women in Islam is in fact a burning issue and a source of polemics and mutual incomprehension.

At the risk of excessive simplification, two dominant positions can be distinguished in the public discourse. For the West, the Muslim woman is by definition downtrodden, and the symbol of her oppression is the *hijab*, the veil, which she is forced to wear. For some Muslim women—and for Muslim men—it is Western women who are slaves to their obligation to be beautiful and available, on pain of being rejected, and so it is they who are not free. Furthermore, Muslims say, except for in certain situations the veil is a choice, not, as the West sees it, an obligation. The *hijab* is therefore a symbolic banner, waved on both sides by those who are either for it or against it.

In addition, there is a kind of "semantic war" being waged about the *hijab* that seems to be of some significance. The Arab word *hijab* is sometimes translated with no great semantic accuracy, as is the case with the French *foulard*. But often the choice falls on stronger words: the French *voile*, the English *veil*, and the Italian *velo*. The word *veil* itself dramatizes the debate, referring at least implicitly and certainly psychologically to something that separates, conceals, masks, or blocks the view (not to mention the word *chador*, often used in Italian, erroneously but perhaps not innocently, as an equivalent for the preceding terms). Even if, on a symbolic and etymological level, the word is polysemic and ambiguous, in this debate the veil is always "that which covers," not "that which re-veals" (the Latin root of these words shows more directly the link between veil and revelation). The semantic aspect is thus not neutral, aseptic. It turns out to be strongly ideological. The choice of words used reflects the exact way we want to put the question, and also points to the responses we wish to receive.

A significant example comes from the main European comparative research project on moral and religious values, the RAMP Project (Religious and Moral Pluralism). One question asked in the RAMP questionnaire was introduced as follows: "All religions require the faithful to do certain things (like for example cover their face or head) [the two actions in themselves not identical] or they forbid them to do others," and interviewees were asked if they agreed "that girls should go to school with their head covered, if that forms part of their religious customs." In the Italian sample the "definitely don't agrees" came to 66 percent, to which must be added those that are in a middle position on a scale that goes from 1 to 7. (Allievi 2003b, 294–295). Let us imagine how different the result would have been if the question had been about Muslim girls' *right* to wear a *hijab* (that is, a headscarf), not the *obligation* to do it.[1]

In Italian there is a proverb that says: "The tunic does not make the monk." *Mutatis mutandis*, a garment does not make a Muslim. But Muslims—and even more so Muslim women—are continually being faced by the problem of what they wear. If not through their individual will, through the social pressure of the surrounding Islamic community. If not through this, through the no less indiscreet pressure of non-Muslim society. Muslim women are questioned if they follow a presumed Islamic code of conduct and even if they do not. This is in certain ways paradoxical and so all the more significant to understanding our way of perceiving Muslim women. Quite often it is surrounding society that creates the problem of the veil, and in a way "insists" on it as part of the cliché of the Islamic woman. In a certain sense there exists a "social demand" that associates the veil with Islamic women, and so expects it, almost insists on it.

This can be seen in many debates on Islam typical of the French situation—from the first, in 1989, in the wake of the case of the three schoolchildren of Creil suspended from a state school, to the latest, in 2003, more or less with the same dynamics. I give another example, in many ways paradigmatic, but in no way unusual. This is the case of Fouzia Ez-Zerqti, thirty-nine years old, a Moroccan living in Padua. She has worked in Italy for many years, is emancipated, perfectly integrated and at the same time religious. A RAI-TV (the Italian public television) team asked her for an interview on her experiences and the story of her life. The proposal was first accepted but then refused because RAI *insisted* on filming her wearing a *hijab*, which she had never actually worn. So in her place they interviewed and filmed another woman who conformed more to the stereotype. On the contrary, a famous convert,

Barbara Aisha Farina, a woman with radical ideas, always gets invited for interviews on television, which she does dressed in the Afghan *burqa* (Allievi 2003a). But then, from the point of view of the journalist, how can you tell if she is a Muslim (especially if converted) if she is not wearing a veil? This is just one example among many of the social reproduction of stereotypes.[2]

We may observe from these examples how issues related to the situation of women in Islam, and particularly those concerning the *hijab*, are raised and debated, from two different and often opposing points of view: first, that of society at large; and second, that of individuals and Muslim social actors, including male and female converts. In the following section I shall analyze the point of view of society. The point of view of individual and social Muslim actors will be integrated into the point of view of converts. Converts refer to debates that are anything but new in Islam, and frequently conducted in many Muslim countries, yet they are obliged to compare them with their own European background. Before discussing these opposing points of view I shall outline diverse trajectories of conversion.

Trajectories of Conversion

The greatest number of conversions to Islam is the result of something that has little to do with the search for spirituality, that is, marriage. As is well known, following the Islamic *sunna*, a non-Muslim man cannot marry a Muslim woman without converting first. This reason for conversion may contradict the principle of freedom of religion and freedom of conscience as it has developed in the West, but it is not normally perceived as being particularly problematic by many of these candidates for conversion, who are often hardly religious at all, and consequently not particularly disturbed by their choice.

These conversions generally have no great impact on the lives of individuals and couples, and often not even on those of their offspring. Conversion under these circumstances is a means of attaining another goal (marriage), not a goal in itself. And it concerns men mainly, at least as a legal obligation. It may also concern women as a *social* obligation, for them to be accepted by the family of the Muslim partner, or by the ethnic and/or religious community to which he belongs, and whose judgment he might fear in case of exogamy.

In a previous book (Allievi 2002) I devoted a chapter to so-called "mixed" couples, in which I distinguished not only between exogamy and endogamy, as it is usual to do, but also introduced the category of "selective exogamy," which from another point of view might be called "enlarged endogamy." It concerns, among other cases, couples in which ethnic and cultural exogamy is in some way "compensated for" by a religious endogamy. In those cases in which one of the two partners is a convert, he (or more frequently she) is "pushed" toward conversion through social and psychological pressure.

However, other trajectories to conversion, which, like the previous ones, may be called "relational," even if far less numerous, are those that have the greatest impact: on the lives of individuals, and also on the life of Islamic communities in Europe. In this list can be included the "discovery" of Islam by meeting Muslim believers, while as a tourist or on a business trip to Muslim countries, or by meeting an immigrant in Europe and possibly falling in love with him or her.

A different model of conversion is that of "rational" conversions.[3] We can refer to intellectual conversions—"cold," so to speak—which are due to reading the Qur'an, even by chance, for all sorts of reasons and in the most diverse situations: either because it is received as a gift, as happened to one of the most well-known European converts, former pop singer Cat Stevens, who became Yusuf Islam, or because it was found in the prison library. Others have become acquainted with Islam through books on Islamic mysticism, especially Sufism, which have attracted a wide Western readership.[4] Books that have influenced conversions are those of traditionalist authors such as René Guénon, Fritjof Schuon, and Titus Burckhardt, who have all become Muslims. Both the intellectual way and the mystic—more frequently, probably, the second, at least in my own experience—are followed by large numbers of women.

Sufism is, however, a specific way of entering Islam, or rather a special facet of it, and leads to embracing Islam through the role of *tariqa*, not necessarily and not often connected to the "Islam of the mosques," where immigrants of Muslim origin can be found.

For many converts the background of conversion is political, and can be either (even extreme) right or left. Islam, the religion of praxis that does not on principle distinguish between the "city of men" and the "city of God," just prefers to overlay them, and seems to be an ideal way of "spiritualizing" a militant commitment that previously was only social or political. It is no accident that we find these converts in the leadership and at the intermediate levels of many Islamic associations of different European countries, in mosques, and in promoting political initiatives such as requests that Muslims be recognized by the state as a minority. In short, these converts are normally closely in touch with the Islam of immigrants.

In my research,[5] however, this way is much more—if not exclusively—a male trajectory. This is probably due to general problems of acceptance of women as part of the leadership of mosques and associations—particularly, but not only, where first generations of migrants are concerned.

Conversion, as entry into another culture and another religion, presupposes strong moments that symbolically sanction the conversion itself and reinforce its significance as a radical change and clean break with the past. It is a process that in the definition of conversion proposed by William James (1902)—containing a few literary archaisms and yet widespread in the self-perception of converts, for whom it is always a "novelty"—is characterized as passing "from the darkest night to the most brilliant light of things." This "stepping over the threshold" symbolizes and means "joining a new world" (van Gennep 1909).

The first and principal rite is obviously the *shahada*, the public declaration of faith. But others take on a significance, from the point of view of social recognition, that is almost equally important. One of these we could summarize with the Latin motto *Nomen omen*—the name "determines" the man (and the woman). Let us see what this means for converted men and women.

The choice of name, in the case of Islam contextual to the *shahada*, is perhaps the most important and symbolically characteristic, because it also changes the identity of the person in some way—is a typical "bridge-burning event" (Hine 1970). Not by chance, it is often connected not only to entry into a religion, but also to the taking up of a commitment and a greater responsibility inside that religion, as is the case, for instance, with Christian monks, and on up the chain to the pope. And again, *nomina sunt numina*, naming things means bringing them into existence, giving them meaning.[6] Within relationships with Muslims, this process takes place especially where it is decided to highlight this choice by making it public. It could also have a public sanction in some official way even at the bureaucratic level, as with requests by individual converts and Islamic organizations of various European countries to be able to change names even on ID documents. That would make the Islamic religious affiliation visible also on the level of personal details in registry offices, and incidentally the change would also be a guarantee of nonreturn, almost an insurance policy for the community that neo-Muslims will not change their minds, or will anyway have more difficulty in doing so. In the end, it is a sign of weakness, more than a sign of power.

Changing names is not actually *sunna,* an obligation. In Islamic tradition the story of the delegation sent by Muhammad to the Coptic governor of Egypt to convert him to Islam is well known. The governor declined the offer, but sent numerous gifts to Muhammad, among which were two Coptic slaves, Mariya and Sirin. They both converted to Islam, the first becoming the Prophet's concubine, but kept their original names. Besides, in Islamized countries what prevails is the traditional custom: if Arab Muslims obviously have Arab names, that is, also Qur'anic, as the revealed Qur'an is in that language, elsewhere there is normally a coexistence of Islamic (Arabicized) traditions and pre-Islamic ones in the local language. Whereas in the West, and especially with converts, the stakes of the choice of name seem to have become symbolically higher: an element of distinction assumed and to a certain extent displayed, a distinction at times seemingly more "against" something (surrounding society, Christian tradition, etc.) than simply "for" something.

Men and women converts are careful, more than, for instance, Arabs or other born Muslims, to take Islamic names, not only traditional Arab names. In this case it really is a case of *nomina sunt numina.* This is why the most common names start with the prefix 'Abd (servant) followed by one of the ninety-nine names for Allah; or the name of one of the prophets named in the Qur'an, or of historical figures particularly famous from the Islamic point of view, such as the first four caliphs called the *rashidun,* the well guided; or naturally the seal of prophecy itself, Muhammad. For female converts, Aisha, the favorite wife of the Prophet, or Khadija, his first wife, or Fatima, his favorite daughter, are popular names.

The "naturalness" of the choice of an Islamic name is so obvious that aspiring converts are not even informed that it is optional, not an obligation, some only becoming aware of this for the first time after our interview questions. Some have repented their choice and tend to make less use of the Islamic name or to abandon it. Others have put up with it, as almost a kind of compulsory toll, being sacrificed on the altar of good socialization with original Muslims. Finally others, and they are in a certain way the newest cases, belonging to more recent conversions, have had the social courage to reject this path and keep their original names. With regard to the naming of children, some converts have chosen the practice of a double name, which allows a double appropriation. Besides changing names, changing appearance is a central and controversial identity issue.

The Point of View of the Host Society: *Hijab* as a Public Manifestation of Individual Rights?

The *hijab* is an important symbolic issue for a non-Muslim society. Differences in how the *hijab* is perceived by society at large, the media, the religious milieu, etc., mark differences in its symbolic acceptance by these groups, related also to the acceptance of Islam itself. Many studies have already analyzed this aspect of the question, so I will here just recall some "highlights" from debates in various European countries (see Maréchal et al. 2003).

It is a common statement—often made by Muslim women and women converts—that just the appearance of the *hijab* in the public space can "produce" reactions like insults, protests, or simply insistent curiosity. But it can also produce forms of *intra*-Muslim tension, which are not usually noted in the arena of social representation by the media and other professional observers. Actually, many issues related to women's condition must be included among these intra-Muslim tensions: between ethnic groups, between different nationalities, and more commonly, between urban- and rural-background populations, between persons of contrasting levels of education, with different opinions and attitudes of mind (more liberal or traditional, more or less militant), but also between men and women, and between immigrants and converts.

We might say that the debate over the *hijab*, as a state affair, is essentially a French problem. Yet it has taken on more universal connotations through specific controversies, which have been solved in different ways, depending on the country and the particular moment. Everyone who has had the opportunity to hold courses, seminars, or lectures on Islam knows just how sensitive the question of the *hijab* is: it is almost a touchstone for reflection on the presence of Islam in the public space. But everyone who has had experience of fieldwork among Muslims—in particular, converts, and, especially, women—knows well how significant this issue is to them as well.

As regards the host societies, this is surprising if examined as a principle, because the question of freedom of dress should not even be raised in the West, except possibly within the limits of respect for decency and its legal consequences.

In a certain sense, the question of the *hijab* is a nonissue, or an issue without real content. Most probably, what is real in this debate is not its object at all. The most well-known debate in Europe—which has been the paradigm of many others—sprang from the decision not to let three pupils wear the *hijab* in a lycée in Creil, following the introduction of a new school rule, in the autumn of 1989, at the beginning of the new school year. This was also the year when France was celebrating the bicentenary of the French Revolution and its principles, which probably had something to do with the sensitivity around the issue. This led to a major debate all over France and elsewhere. It went through three main phases. The first was in 1989 and 1990, with the events of Creil; then again in 1994–1995, when, following this long discussion, Minister Bayrou's statement of September 1994 condemned "ostentatious signs" of religious affiliation, while, however, accepting "discreet" ones. In between we can record a long process of official and unofficial positions, ranging up to the highest authorities of the state, administrative decisions at all levels up to the Council of State, consultations, debates in the media, political controversy, and electoral contests. But the case was also revived more recently, in 2003, when Minister Sarkozy confirmed, in a statement at a congress of the Islamic organization Union des Organisations Islamiques de France (UOIF) (an official presence that was in itself unprecedented), that wearing the *hijab* would continue to be officially banned. The case continued through October, this time at a lycée at Aubervilliers, where the same story was repeated. Ironically enough, in this case of expulsion of two sisters— neo-Muslimas recently converted, daughters of a Jewish nonbelieving father and a Catholic-raised nonbelieving Kabilian mother—immigration was not involved. The case ended up, as is well known, with the proposal, made by a Commission des Sages led by Bernard Stasi, for a legal ban on the *hijab* and other "ostentatious" religious symbols. The proposal for a ban law was supported by President Jacques Chirac, and its final chapter was the approval, by a large majority of the French Parliament, of a controversial law on this matter in March 2004, applicable by the beginning of the school period *(rentrée scolaire)* of the same year.

The discussion also had the militant aspects of an ideological battle, making some observers speak of secular fundamentalism *(républicain,* in French terms). Most of the magistrates involved in past decisions, before the ban law was approved, ruled that the girls and their motivations were in the right. In some places, contorted and at times surprising compromises were sought, requested by some headmasters as gestures of goodwill, such as the suggestion to tie the *hijab* at the back instead of the front, seriously made by a headmaster in Colmar, while elsewhere the *hijab* was forbidden during lessons but allowed on the school premises (Straßburger 2000). At still another school, the solution found was to authorize the veil only in the presence of male

teachers. Quite a paradoxical and sometimes surrealistic discussion! Furthermore, it is interesting to note that whilst French *laicité* declared war on the
hijab, French Catholics accepted some of the girls who had been excluded
from state education into their schools, so that, in an interesting reversal
of positions, religious figures of different faiths accused *laicité*, in its French
form, of sectarianism.

There have been similar cases, but not with the same "nervous" exacerba-
tion, in many other European countries: the Netherlands, Belgium, Germany,
etc. (even though, following the French example, things seem to be undergoing change). And in some countries, such as Great Britain, this is not a real
issue. The fact that different countries react differently to the *hijab* is not at all
insignificant, and in many ways revealing. What creates the problem is not
necessarily the *hijab* in itself, but the way it is perceived. The role of context—
a basic statement for every sociological assumption—is decisive. To give one
example: the same argument French Minister of the Interior Sarkozy chose
to justify the banning of the *hijab* for ID photographs (Catholic nuns are also
forbidden to wear their veils) works the other way round in other contexts.
In Italy the fact that Catholic nuns are allowed to cover their hair in ID photographs has been used to allow Muslim women to do likewise. In both cases,
the basic reference was the same: the principle of equality before the law, and
of equal treatment of citizens. The difference was in the content of the law.

It should be noted that the *hijab* can in some cases become an element of integration of the presence of Islam into the public space. It happened in the case
of Nabila Benaïssa, the sister of Loubna, a little girl murdered by a pedophile in
Belgium. The popular mobilization around the case and the protests against the
shortcomings and covering-up in conducting the investigations were enormous,
leading to the immense "Marche Blanche" in Brussels in 1997. The figure of the
young Nabila, displaying her Muslim identity with simplicity and discretion
(she always appeared wearing the *hijab*), and showing her perfect social integration (speaking French perfectly and reasoning calmly), made a strong contribution toward creating a less offensive and threatening, "polite" so to speak, perception of Islam. The drama helped to trigger a process that on that occasion I was
tempted to call "assimilation through grief" (in Dassetto 1996).

On the other hand, the debate over the *hijab*, and the *hijab* itself, often cata-
lyze what could be called "reactive identities" on both sides. On the side of
the host society, the reaction to the *hijab* allows hidden or "sleeping" identities to emerge, as is the case when, faced by "them" (the *hijabi* women and the
appearance of the *hijab* in the public space), an "us" starts to be evoked by the

different entities (we women, we Westerners, we Christian civilization, we the secular state, etc.). On the Muslim side, the reactive identity can be seen when the *hijab* becomes a symbolic banner raised in order to counter society and its symbols, especially in certain militant milieus. It can be especially observed among women unaccustomed to wearing the *hijab* in their country of origin deciding to wear it in the host country—but also among converted women.

The Point of View of Converts: Narratives and Rationalizations of the *Hijab*

A second approach to the question seems to have been less studied and analyzed. Fewer studies have, in fact, been conducted on the weight of social practices concerning the *hijab* and their meaning *inside* Muslim communities. For instance: how are converted women seen, and how differently, if they do or do not wear the *hijab*, especially in mosques and in associated milieus? What is the meaning of this practice, for the women involved, in terms of acceptance of the mainstream local Islamic culture? Is the *hijab* necessary for women to be *accepted* by the (mainly male) Muslim social actors? And what is its role in terms of self-positioning toward non-Muslim society?

If we specifically examine the variations in narratives and rationalizations of the *hijab*, and more generally the *halal/haram* frontier, with special reference to women, offered by male and female converts, we are tempted to look for certain specific features. Both male and female converts have in common the fact of *not* being related to any "traditional" or "ethnic" interpretation of Islam, a situation that is specific to immigrants. But their arguments often *are* related to "traditional" or "ethnic" interpretations of Islam. They necessarily have to be rooted, in order to become accepted arguments, in Islamic traditions, and more specifically, those of the community to which they refer (often a local and in some way ethnically characterized Muslim community, such as a mosque or the *zawiya* of a Sufi *tariqa*).

Nevertheless, the fact of being men or women often puts converts in a different position, and it is interesting to understand how and why, and what the gender consequences are. I will attempt to do this by comparing rationalizations about the *hijab* and other gender issues proposed by some converted men and women.

The question of the *hijab* is part of a more general issue: the *haram/halal* frontier. *Haram* and *halal,* the pure and impure, the licit and illicit: these are the categories on which the thinking, juridical more than theological, of Islam rests. That is, the criteria marking this frontier are the separation of good and evil, and the recognition and separation of Muslims with respect to the rest of the world. As noted by Weber, the personality of Muhammad

is free from any kind of "tragic" sentiment of sin—a character that has remained fixed in orthodox Islam. "Sin" appears there as a ritual impurity, or as religious sacrilege (such as polytheism), or disobedience to the positive commandments of the Prophet, or class unworthiness for violation of customs and proprieties. (1922)

This is an attitude considered typical of Islam, and similar to Orthodox Judaism (taken up in the distinction between sacred and profane proposed by Durkheim). But, as Durkheim (1912) himself implies, it is present inside almost all religious traditions, to a greater or lesser degree, in that there are immediately comprehensible and hence well-known criteria of recognition of the goodness of one's conduct and the laws one can and must follow. Laws that, however unfounded or irrational, offer an easy and immediate guide: orthopraxy knows immediately where to seek inspiration and who if anyone to seek advice from. In case of doubt there is always the ultimate instance of conscience; but first, and it is a particularly important fact for Islam, there are the *ulama*, the *imam*, those who know a little more, books, and, second-to-last, the jurists, some of whom (if we think of Yusuf al-Qardhawi or, for the younger generations, Tariq Ramadan) are real pop stars.

A Muslim, even an immigrant, can immediately comprehend and absolutely identify with the logic and practice just mentioned. But a convert? Is the practice accepted or rejected, or possibly mediated and accepted with reservation? And if it is accepted, is it a cultural acceptance or, at most, a response to a psychological need, a lightening of the anxiety of individual responsibility? And how much does the acceptance of a convert "cost"? Because there *is* a price to pay, as Primo Levi (1986) noted: "Changing a moral code is always costly: all heretics, apostates and dissidents know that." The behavior declared (but also that which is observable) definitely goes in the direction of acceptance of revealed law as religious obligation, but in a certain sense with reserve, with mediations and nuances that, at least in part, lead back to the internal forum again, to the conscience. The law is not to be discussed, it must be accepted; better still, we must become one with it. In its application, however, its severity can be modulated, usually more severe in the initial phase of conversion, and more tempered in the more mature stages.

For men the problem is less explicit and above all has much less to do with religion in the strict sense. As underlined by one of our interlocutors, responsible for an important Islamic center, whose beard is admittedly quite short, "It is not written anywhere that I have to dress like the Prophet and wear my beard long like him. If I do, it will be to my merit, but if I don't, it will not be a demerit." There are no real religious obligations, except possibly the recommendation on the part of some *hadith* not to wear gold, silk, and precious garments, as part of that sobriety and measure that is typical of Islam. Apart from that, there is only the possible literalism, at times even fanatical, of some contemporary "exegete."

However, the question of the Islamic veil is more problematic.[7] The *hijab* is, in fact, a symbolic banner of a certain importance: both for Muslims, *among* Muslims so to speak, in establishing the boundaries between Muslims and non-Muslims, and the host society as such. Muslim men and women face this problem in various ways. In synthesis, the difference is between a literalist attitude, an acceptance of Arab tradition (in other Islamic lands the veil is rare or unknown, or only a militant symbol), and a "modernist," interpretative attitude, with a symbolizing tendency.

It is particularly difficult in the case of the *hijab* to speak of a prevailing attitude. For some, wearing it is a symbolic act, which is followed more or less willingly, but anyway without problems, in the case of prayer in the mosque and other possible encounters of an Islamic character. For others, refusal, asserted discreetly and never too strongly, prevails. In any case the veil is considered *maktub*, that is, "it is written," meaning sanctioned by the Qur'an, even if the scriptural references are questionable, and so it is better not to talk about it. Refusal also marks the difference between acceptance of the original customs and a more spiritualizing and "Western" interpretation, if not pure and simple apathy. For others, again, it is a banner of an identity. And, in the case of men, perhaps a *conditio sine qua non* for matrimony, for the search for a wife: in the marriage columns that can be found in European Islamic magazines and on the Internet, there is an extremely high percentage of men, immigrants but also often converts, who specify that they want a *hijabi* wife, veiled.

As it is not a question of personal experience (a man can have his opinions, but it is not he that wears the *hijab*), the male arguments probably reflect a greater degree of abstraction and intellectualization, both in the case of acceptance (or obligation) and that of refusal (or of a silent freedom of choice). This is how one of our interlocutors, Abdul Hadi, justifies his position, quite common also among women:

We find ourselves faced by the conflict that exists between the spirit and the letter of something. If the veil as a precept is to have a function, it is not to attract the gaze of men; but, in an environment like the West, a woman, especially if she is a Western woman who has decided to wear a veil, ends up by becoming the center of attention, especially if she lives in an environment in which there is not a minority presence of a Muslim religious community for which, let us say, this behavior has become habitual. This woman walks along the road and becomes the center of attention. So in this case a desire to stick to the letter produces an effect that is exactly the opposite of the spirit of the norm. For some converts who have decided to wear a veil a certain dose of exhibitionism plays a very important role. The aim of converting to Islam is not to make women pass from nonveil to veil: it is to teach women and men a certain morality and a certain kind of behavior in relations with other human beings. The fact that originally, in the environment in which Islam was born, this precept ended up in the veil does not change the fact that it is necessary to proceed and maintain this attitude even in the face of changed conditions. This is the risk that there is in all readings of the sacred text that stop at the letter.

Female arguments appear more interior and more centered on experience, both if they go in the direction of acceptance and if they are oriented toward refusal of the veil. It is interesting to listen to some of the voices of the converted, because their arguments on wearing the *hijab* or not do not belong to their ethnocultural legacy and are perhaps more authentically religious. Aisha, a militant convert, summarizes all the reasons for wearing the veil: displaying identity, protection, self-control, formalization of belonging, condemning deviant behavior, even practicality in an Islamic key:

Then one day I decided that I had to wear the veil. It's not so much the veil in itself, but I think they notice you more if you have a veil. However, apart from the fact that it is written in the Qur'an, I think the veil protects you, because that way everyone knows that you are a Muslim—apart from those that think that I am a gypsy. So everyone knows my religion, which means they treat me accordingly, or at least they should. However, at least inside the community, they treat me like that and then, it sort of helps me to feel inside me. For example, now that I go around in a veil I know that I have to behave accordingly, because I am like a walking symbol.

And then it's true that there are people who are rude to us in the street. I find that distressing, I don't like it, really. At times I'm upset; sometimes in the course of the day so many things happen that I feel like crying even in the street and say, "I can't take any more, why can't they leave us alone?" ... But it's as if there is protection all the same. I was reading the history of the Jews and the kippah: *the reason they wear it is to keep Heaven separated from Earth ... that is, to remember that they are subjected; and as in Islam* aslama *means "to subject," it's the same thing. It's like a sacralization of the whole person.*

The "identity banner" dimension is here taken in its strongest terms, to the point that Aisha has become a public figure after an interview in *Corriere della sera,* the most important Italian newspaper, and following on this has been invited for interviews by various women's magazines and for some television appearances for having insisted on having her photo in a *hijab* on her identity card and passport. She is the reason for the ministerial circular that allows it to be worn, as with the nuns' garb. Today Aisha, even more militant and radical after entering a polygamous marriage (not officially, of course) with a combative Senegalese *imam,* and after creating a newspaper with the programmatic title of *al-Mujahidah (The Woman Combatant),* gives interviews dressed only in an Afghan *burqa,* and from under it expresses support for the Taliban and Saudi Arabia (the only real Islamic regimes in the world, in her opinion), Bin Laden, and the Palestinian *shahid.*

The need to show and identify with one's community of reference is often present. Exemplary in this sense is the attitude of Nura, another convert, who was confronted with the misunderstandings that the veil can create. To start with, there was the time that the veil was the reason for her being dragged into the Questura, the Italian police station:

Yes, and . . . I really enjoyed myself, al-hamdulillah, *because they were carrying out a swoop and they got me, and they were nasty. They asked: "Have you got a permit of sojourn?" I looked at the policeman and said: "No," but actually they didn't even give me time to speak; they grabbed me and took me to the police car. I had never been in a police car before—they drive like crazy, I was a bit scared, these rough people . . . and so I found myself at the police station. They took me up, dragging me by the jumper, and took me upstairs. At a certain point a policeman sent me to another person, who does the registering of names. So I gave my name, date of birth, and everything. And so we went to the Commissar, he was given this sheet of paper: so there we were standing in front of him and the Commissar said: "Who is this lady M.F., born in . . . ?" I looked at him and said "Me." "Who? You? But . . . you're . . . Italian!" And the Commissar said: "But why didn't you say so before?" I said: "Look, you asked me for my permit of sojourn. It's obvious that I haven't got one. But if you had asked me for ID, I would have said OK, here it is! You can't treat people like this!"*

This was not an isolated episode for Nura:

At times on the bus it really came to violence because of my refusal to admit to being Italian. Because they took me for a Moroccan. One person said to me, "Move over, Moroccan!" and gave me a punch, literally. I said to him: "Who do you think you are, you bully, who do you think you are? Do you really think you can shove people around like that even if there's plenty of room?" So one of them gave me another punch and said: "But you're not ... Moroccan." And I said: "Yes, yes, I am." In that moment I insisted that I was Moroccan; never would I have admitted for any reason in the world that I was Italian.

For Shahida, on the other hand, the veil is inscribed in a sort of family continuity:

I always used to wear one, ever since I was small. We went to church and wore a veil. I lived in the country, down in Potenza [in southern Italy], and in the summer period it was boiling hot, and then there was the cutting of the corn, the harvest, we were always out, around, there was the threshing with us all around. Incredibly hot, and so we wore a scarf over our heads, and so we had it on all the time ...
Q: It was like going back to your childhood?
A: Yes, it was a return, practically, yes. A headscarf has never been a problem for me; and anyway I don't like luxury, nor showing off, so I don't want to wear things to make people look at me.

If for Shahida it is a return to the past, for other women it is something new and problematic. Fatima, whose parents separated, lives with an elderly granny, who followed her granddaughter's gradual approach to Islam closely and with a certain apprehension. Fatima, much better than anyone else, stressed how much the problem is not so much the conversion of the heart (the "circumcision of hearts" of which Saint Paul speaks) as the complex, intrusive, and above all overvisible "contour" that accompanies it (the "circumcision of the body," to remain inside the Pauline metaphor):

When I put on the veil I was practically thrown out of the house. Just as well, it was August, so I took it as an opportunity to go on holiday. Jokes apart, I stayed with friends for a while. You know, I live with my grandmother, and my grandmother naturally with her mentality—mind you, I'm not blaming her—was upset by what had happened. The family, it's not that they have anything against Islam, it's the veil, that is, the outward show, the fact that everyone knows that I am a Muslim.

Other converts, however, take a position of doubt, of individual refusal. This position hardly ever extends into a general refusal, even less a condemnation.

Zeynab has interiorized its meaning:

I've changed in these things, in this way of thinking: that's why I'm not interested in them anymore. Even if I admire those sisters who are trying to affirm their identities, wanting a photo in a hijab *on their identity cards, I understand: you have to be able to choose . . .*

Q: Do you understand it and admire it or do you understand it and that's all?

A: No, I say that you have to be able to choose, you have to be able to have the right to pray in the workplace, if you want your photo in the hijab *you must have the right to have it.*

Q: But you don't feel the need for it . . .

A: No, I don't feel the need. I can't wear the hijab *in my office, I have never asked but I know I could never do it. Anyway I'm not interested in these outward signs; I have realized that the* hijab *is the symbol of a kind of behavior. . . . In my opinion that's all it is: like lots of other things, like the rules for starting to walk with your right foot, using your right hand, according to me they are just symbols.*

Maryam thinks the same, with some timidity in front of those who wear the veil, and so looks for more social reasons:

Each one of us must be ourselves, even in Islam, and live our lives a bit . . . in our own way. Even if there are rules, and I know perfectly well that there are. Me, for example, I don't wear a veil outside the mosque, and Muslim brothers often make observations on this. But seeing that in Islam the finest thing we can discover is exactly this direct relation with God, without intermediaries, so there is no priest who absolves you and . . . So, I know perfectly well that there are just me and Allah before me. Allah knows the reasons why I don't wear the veil because . . . I also think that some things were introduced during the period in which the Qur'an came down to us.

Q: So it is really your choice, this; I mean, it's not a transition stage.

A: No, I don't know if I'll ever wear it. I've got no preconceptions against the veil, because I know anyhow that it's a beautiful thing, because when you put it on for prayer that's when you have the real value of the veil, in that moment. But for the rest of my life, no, because I live in Italy, I'm not living in a Muslim country, where everything would help me to live my Muslim being.

More widespread among Muslim women by birth is a defensive position corresponding to that of Cardinal Bellarmino in Bertolt Brecht's *Galileo*, who, faced by the hypothesis that it is the sun, and not the earth, that is at the center of the solar system, is worried by the fact that if we start by putting one little thing in doubt the whole edifice will then collapse. In sociological language it is the position stated by Berger on more than one occasion, when he theorizes the fundamental role of "plausibility structures" in helping to uphold one's religious faith. Plausibility structures are even more important as religious pluralism increases and, hence, as society does not "confirm" for us the evidence of our faith and our belonging, especially if we belong to a minority. They are even more important if we have been converted to another religion, which explains the tendency of many new converts to marry people belonging to the new religion that they have embraced.

Berger maintains that for a religious faith to be upheld in a person's conscience, it must form part of the plausibility structure that is peculiar to that very faith, which means, above all, that in the social environment of that person there must be a community continuously professing this faith. "It will be rewarding if those who have the greatest emotional importance for the person we are speaking about (that is, those called by George Herbert Mead the "significant others") belong to the community that professes this faith. It will not count very much if the person's dentist is not Catholic [in the present case, Muslim], but everything will certainly be better if his wife and most intimate friends are" (Berger 1969).

Yet the position taken by many women converts, as well as women of Muslim origin, not to wear the *hijab* is also important. Of these, however, less is said for the precise reason that they are not noticed. Some reached this decision after having thought about it, even if perhaps fleetingly; others did not even consider it a problem.

The question of the *hijab*, in any case, can be considered only as a case study of a more general problem, which should be related to other issues concerning the *halal/haram* frontier, particularly relating to the behavior allowed between men and women. We will see how converts deal with this.

Women and the *Halal/Haram* Frontier: A Further Comparison

The pure/impure dichotomy touches upon many aspects of relations between the sexes. A frequent problem, and one that is widespread throughout society, as it is a question of a sign actually preceding or at least accompanying knowledge of someone, is shaking hands. The problem is that whereas a Muslim man knows perfectly well that it is not done, a non-Muslim usually knows nothing of these practices, and so his ignorance can be a source of misunderstandings. Latifa, a Shi'ite convert, says:

If I am talking with a person and this person wants to shake my hand, I can't say that I can't give him my hand because Muslims cannot touch. Because it will seem that that is all Islam is interested in. Whereas it's nice if a fellow Muslim doesn't offer his hand, because he knows what the situation is. It's a different respect that exists between us, because we are brothers in Islam. If a Christian gives me his hand, I know

that his intentions are honorable; if I leave him there with his hand outstretched he
will be left with a bad impression of me, too hard.

In this case, too, a more pragmatic attitude can resolve the cultural problems
of incomprehension that may arise. Latifa develops her theory further:

The fact of not being able to shake hands and other little prohibitions have never been
a problem. But I'm quite old and maybe a young girl would find them bigger prob-
lems. In my work [as an interior designer], when I sometimes meet a person for the
first time and he wants to shake hands I shake hands the first time because otherwise
I might give a bad impression. Then I explain that there is this rule that it's better
for men and women not to have direct contact unless they are close relatives, and I
apologize if the following time we don't shake hands. Everyone has understood this
and they have never created any problems. Probably if on first meeting I refused to
shake hands I might be considered stuck up, or anyway I wouldn't be understood, but
this way no. What's more, in my job it often happens that a customer sends me to an
acquaintance and I've noticed that they've already been informed, they get in touch
with one another. So often I have no need to shake hands because they have already
been told about these rules. Anyway, 90 percent are women customers, not men. He
[she is referring to her husband, who is present at the interview and converted to Shi'a
Islam many years before her] is more drastic than me and often appears with some-
thing in his hand so as not to have to shake hands with a woman, or he immediately
tries to broach the subject.

On the other hand, there are many male converts who prefer not to shake
hands with a person of the female sex, sometimes with awkward affectations
of naturalness, and sometimes with a deliberately provocative attitude. In
this way they may damage their relations with non-Muslim women, who
may consider this a lack of respect toward them. This exaggerated form of a
kind of behavior, which immigrant Muslims practice relatively infrequently,
is a demonstration of refusal on the part of the person in question to accept
any physical contact with a person of the opposite sex outside the marriage
bond.

A case similar to shaking hands—and *a fortiori* kissing the cheek during
greetings—is connected with respect for other eminent cultural norms typical of the Arab world, such as those that regulate relations between the sexes
within the private sphere, the home. It is especially related to norms that forbid a man and woman not of the same blood to be alone in the same room.
When, for example, I went to interview Samira, divorced from her former

Egyptian husband, at her house, even though she knew there would be no Islamic witnesses, out of respect for those rules she was waiting for me with a Christian female friend, who had come especially for the purpose, and who at the beginning of the interview retired to the neighboring room:

Q: You have chosen a rigorous attitude in practicing Islam. Even this fact that I was coming here and as I was a man you invited a female friend of yours to be present is something that no Western women would have felt the need to do . . .
A: There are rules and I like to follow them. When I decide to do something I like to do it properly. I have thought carefully about it, because it wasn't just a question of deciding overnight. I thought hard, and when I was sure of myself, I was at peace with myself, I was serene, I took this step. And having taken this step I now want to respect what there is to have respect for.

The *Hijab* and Identity: The Price to Pay (Full Identity for Half the Cost?)

Wearing the *hijab* has a price. To what extent are women willing to pay this price? And what are the consequences in their lives? Let us give a clear example of a price that is not just psychological or symbolic: how to deal with the question of looking for a job.

We'll start with a positive example. The decision to wear the *hijab* does not always have a high socioeconomic price. The above-mentioned case of Latifa, interior designer before and after her conversion, is in this sense interesting:

I have never had any sort of problem at work. I am an interior designer and my work takes me to the homes of people of various social levels, from low to high class, but they have never said anything to me. . . . If anything, I can say that I noticed an increase in confidence in me after I became a Muslim. It has been a great experience. The girls I go around with who are younger than me and so give more importance to clothes, I say to them that if they wear it proudly, but without being ostentatious, normally, calmly, they will see that people will respect them. I've had no problem in getting on with others. The only problem I had to deal with was in the beginning, inside myself. I was nervous about being rebuffed, in fact I stopped wanting to go to my customers, because I didn't know how they would react. This fear lasted for two months, and I didn't put my headscarf on when I was at work, but only on other occasions. At a certain point I asked myself what sort of Muslim was I anyway, and so I decided to wear it, and no one said anything.

Not all experiences are so positive, however. On the contrary. It is not so much the risk of losing one's job, even if some women decide out of fear not to even try wearing a *hijab*. The risk is greater for those who do not yet have a job and know that their range of possibilities will be reduced drastically. Aisha (the radical militant mentioned above), at the beginning of her conversion, when she still wore the *hijab* and not the *burqa* (a choice that coincided with her leaving her job for a militant and womanly commitment full-time), was in telemarketing. The problems she had were not that much with the customers—they did not see her and she did not see them—but with her workmates. This is what she said in an interview at that time:

They ask me the most absurd questions, whereas I just wanted to be left alone to work. As it is, I do a job there that drives you crazy. If between one call and another you have to explain what the tawheed is, it's impossible. But you have to answer somehow. You're torn between two things. On the one hand you would like to be left in peace—but perhaps that's not my role, to be left in peace. . . . And so I am forced to accept the confrontation with the others, it's only natural. Because if I stay in my corner and say that I am living my own life and am not going to speak to anyone, well, what am I doing here? I've got to transmit this [the Islamic faith] and so it's normal for you to talk to people.

Finally, for others, the fact of wearing the *hijab* will lead them to inventing and setting up *religious* (or *cultural*) *businesses* connected to Islam (teaching Arabic, or teaching in Islamic schools, or Islamic publishing) or the veil itself, as in the case of those who have opened Islamic fashion boutiques or even begun designing *Islamically correct* clothes. The veil is an infinite source of discussion and polemics, even among Muslim women. Various sensibilities emerge: "ethnic" (Arab women often appear to converts as more in conformity with tradition than sub-Saharan African women) or "cultural" (converted women appear to be more extreme than nonconverted). Khalida gives a good description of this conception:

I have this idea that, as the only Muslim women that I see are Somali women, and they don't wear a veil or they wear it in their own way, perhaps they have a way of seeing things that is closer to my way than Arab women and other converted Italian women.

The discussion between the converted women who accept or even uphold the *hijab* and those who on the contrary do not accept it or leave it in the background is not one of the easiest: the former pay a price that the latter do not consider worth paying. And given that the cost of this practice is not low, it is difficult to agree to share a "full" identity with, or recognize the identity of, those who insist on paying a price that is undoubtedly much lower. A university teacher of the Arabic language, a convert, gives an example:

I had the opportunity of meeting a woman student who was strongly drawn to Islam, who had studied a lot, and who asked me to introduce her to some women of the community. She came away from the encounter absolutely terrified and she changed her mind, just because of the rigidity and intolerance shown by these women.

This seems understandable, however, and explains the harshness of the dialogue between these two kinds of converts: the "rigorists" and the "flexibles." The first are paying an extremely high price for their choices of identity, and they therefore do not wish to concede a similar "identity license" to those women who have chosen to pay, so to speak, only half price. Half the price in their eyes is not worth an entire identity. *Hijabi* women will often think that the others are after all not *real* Muslims or not enough so, or at least less so than *hijabi* women. This is why these two kinds of converted women do not only resemble two tracks running parallel and never meeting up. Often, rather than tracks, they are scissors whose blades start from a common point (the choice and moment of conversion) and gradually diverge and separate irremediably. The former will, in fact, often mix with other "rigorists" to confirm to each other the fullness of their identity and their exclusive legitimacy. And the latter will no longer find a common terrain of confrontation and will drift off, often more due to a feeling of exclusion than to any precise decision. After all, the latter do not deny the former any legitimacy—nor could they—and might even want to continue having relations with them. But it is the former that are less interested in these relations, which for them are destabilizing. And they use their greater "centrality" to progressively marginalize, even exclude, the others. An interesting aspect is that often the support of male cultural power and cultural legitimacy is used in this process, as well as male attitudes toward the *hijab* itself (whether those expressed by classic theology or by the district *imam*).

The arguments of those women who wear the *hijab* often show a gradual drift toward a "feminist" position, defending the practice of wearing the veil (see also Badran, Roald, and other articles in this volume). Layla, an ex-feminist, bears witness:

And what have they [feminists] become? If we have an army of women all using the same lipstick, perhaps that vivid mauve lipstick is in fashion that I used once, and everyone wears it, all the same miniskirts, and anyway they all follow the same pattern, and then they have the nerve to ask me, "Why do you wear that?" I can't stand

it. . . . Because they are different, but from what? They are more conventional than me in the end, that's what it is; and then what I can't stand anymore is all this competition, this frenetic emphasis on how you look.
Q: In fact in the past you have been involved in fights for abortion, for divorce, for freedom of choice, for . . .
A: The first two years after my conversion I spent asking God for forgiveness. Every evening I asked God for forgiveness for these things, because I didn't understand . . .

She goes on:

At the bottom of all this there is something very profound, which has something to do with the equality of women, real equality . . . which is not in the fact that . . . I show myself like this or like that, but it really consists in the fact that all of us, at least on a physical level, are all equal before God.

The harshness, from the Western point of view, of Islamic rules concerning women makes their conversion decidedly a more "heroic" and in any case a more costly affair (at least in its social consequences) than that of men. "For a woman it is not easy to change her garments, she needs courage. For a man it is easier because if nobody points it out to you, you don't even realize, whereas we are immediately picked out," one of my interviewees told me. This high visibility does not stop women from converting in proportionally significant numbers, and not only for marriage.[8]

Some active Shi'ite groups like to use women as a sort of warhorse for their arguments against the image of Islamic oppression. One of the leaders of the Italian Shi'ite community says:

More women than men enter the Shi'a. I don't know why. Obviously the message is fascinating and attracts women, probably because we have a central figure, Fatima, whom we often talk about. I realize that it must be hard for women to become a Sunnite Muslim through marrying an Arab, with their mentality: it's a shock. With us it's different, women are much freer.

His wife adds:

Perhaps Shi'ite women are no better than Sunnite women, but women in the Shi'ite world are treated as the Qur'an says, and the Qur'an says that women must be treated very well.[9] Even if they are then happy to point out that there are more women converted to Islam among Shi'ites because Iranian women, contrary to Arab women, do not stay at home: once they have put on the veil, they go out, talk in public, get involved in politics, etc.[10] They are veiled, but for that very reason they can do anything;

while in the Arab world women are locked up culturally, so it would be difficult for a
Western woman to become Sunnite.

The greater "cost" of conversion for women does not therefore seem to prevent the conversions themselves. There is often talk of a prevalence of female
conversions, at least in some countries (see van Nieuwkerk, this volume).
Yet, it is not certain that this corresponds with figures for other situations, or
that such figures can be generalized to all situations. Nevertheless, this prevalence has certainly become an important element of the Islamic ideological
construction on the subject.

Shifting Significances: Some Reflections

What is true for the convert is also true for the researcher: the meaning of
symbols is shifting and slippery. My initial intention was to describe the differences between the meanings that men and women converts give to the
hijab and the different use they make of them. But my analysis and observations have led me to a quite different position. Before dealing with that,
we need to advance a more general point. As a sociologist specialized in religions and cultural change, and not only or exclusively in Islam, I am more
and more convinced that we must de-Islamize (if I may use this expression)
the study of Islam and Muslims, especially, but not only, in Europe. Too often,
even in serious works and not only in journalistic vulgarizations, Islam is
considered a special, if not unique, case, both theoretically and empirically.
Islam is different. Muslims are different. This is the usual starting point. Is
this the case? I am not at all sure.

In the theoretical part of my book on converts I compare different theories of conversion, and empirical studies on conversions to different religions
(1998; see also different contributions in *Social Compass* 1999, and in this volume). There are obviously many differences, in both theories and empirical
observations, but they are much less related to observable "intrinsic" differences among religions than to individual cultural, social, and psychological
factors. In the push-and-pull (or supply-and-demand) process that conversion
is, demands are often similar. This is why some types of conversion, such as
the "relational type" that I have described, are very common and even conventional in their trajectories in many religions: an ideal type in the proper
Weberian sense. What is more often different is the role of the religious "supply," which may respond to different demands. In this sense Islam, as other

religions, is significant: but Islam does not only have *one* offer. Like other complex religious systems, it has many, depending on the context, the moment, and what the individual is seeking. The "supply," under the name of Islam itself, is wide and articulated. A person can convert to Christianity in search of mysticism or a "total institution" (such as monasteries or religious orders).[11] The same can be said for Islam, which can offer, for instance, a sort of sacralization of political engagement in a spiritual community, or, on the contrary, a response to a highly individual spiritual and mystical thirst. Both these trajectories can frequently be observed among converts to Islam.

If we consider gender issues related to religion, there are far fewer specific *Islamic* issues than public opinion, including most professional observers, thinks. In comparative studies, statements expressing the conventional wisdom on subjects such as "the condition of woman in Islam" lose much of their expected self-explanatory meaning. This fact is also true for conversions. I have extensively researched both Muslim converts and immigrants within the Islamic *champs religieux*, to use Bourdieu's expression. In these cases, too, Muslim positions are not that significantly different. The differences are internal to both groups, and to men and women in both groups, as much as *between* the two groups.

Let us take the most sensitive example. It is quite easy to find differences in personal attitudes and *feelings* about the *hijab* between men and women: simply because women *really* wear and experience it, probably. It is less easy to find such differences in what they say about it. In fact, the reasons used to justify the *hijab* are not that different: if a woman convert decides to wear the *hijab*, frequently the reason for it, the rationalization, will be supported by traditional theological arguments, elaborated and transmitted by a typically "male" theology—the level of stereotyping is high as well. Differences, then, already exist *among* men and among women, not only *between* them. To summarize my argument on this point in a short expression, *the gender issue does not seem to be necessarily gendered* in its motivations and justifications. The difference is located at the level of individual experience. Hence, it is not easy to distinguish male and female arguments on the *hijab*. For the same reasons, it is not easy to distinguish the positions of immigrants and converts, even if different "accents" can be found. Similarities are more easily observed when we need to legitimize the *hijab*: differences may emerge more often when it is a question of refusing it.

The same can be said for the positions of the first and second generations, the latter being more similar to converts (Allievi 2000). In both cases, the accent is more on choice than on tradition. Although there are differences in the figures, we find veiled and unveiled women in both categories. It is easier to find differences between Sufi and Sunni arguments on the *hijab*, but again we can find veiled and unveiled women in both, even if—probably—in a different percentage. I have underlined these aspects to show that both the dimension of continuity and that of change are important. The cultural dimension often "continues," while personal lives change.

This aspect leads me to the last point: the importance of what I call the "T" factor (T for "time"). Individuals change in their lives: they change attitudes, opinions, and behavior. This is equally true for those who have changed religion. This aspect raises a serious methodological problem. If we elaborate statistics and percentages (for instance, of *hijabi* or non-*hijabi* converts, but also of converts in general), we have to face a general problem that has more obvious consequences for our topic: we normally interview our informants only once. But they change their mind and behavior even in their postconversion life, and more than once: this is why in the literature on conversions, concepts such as the "conversion career" and others like it have been introduced (see Allievi 1998). This is true for the choice of wearing the *hijab*, but also for conversions themselves. People deconvert and also "revert," but we normally interview only the converts, and not the deconverts, for the simple reason that, unless it is by chance, we do not find them in the same places in which we are looking for converts.[12]

This aspect is important also for the shifting meaning of the *hijab*. Opinions about it change, both in men and women converts, for instance, at the initial stage, immediately after conversion, or many years after (see Hermansen, this volume). I know and frequently meet converts with whom I have remained in close contact: their opinions have changed a lot over the years. This can sometimes be measured through interviews, particularly through life stories. However, only self-confident and well-established converts are able to talk at ease, over a distance of time, about the changes in their attitudes and even beliefs, with a high level of self-criticism. Many others are not.

As regards our topic, there may be changes in both directions: from being veiled (initially) to being unveiled seems quite frequent. But we can also observe trajectories going in the opposite direction, when the conversion is not a "moment" (as in Saint Paul's ideal type of sudden conversion), but a step-by-step process, in which the "converting" persons progressively acquire familiarity with certain references and progressively "include" them in their personality-building process. Why these changes, these shifts?

There may be many factors at play. The main ones refer probably to the fact that the meaning of the *hijab* differs depending on the moment, the person, the situation, the context, and its importance in establishing the *haram/halal* frontier. From this point of view, the main functions of the *hijab* seem to be the following. First, it helps women to convert (*obliges* them, from a certain point of view), to keep to the new choice, to "enter" it in a radical way, like circumcision for men (which is far more "definitive"). Second, it helps them to be accepted by the new "significant others." This is particularly true for women who see immigrants and pray in mosques, attending the Friday prayer and other moments of gathering, such as Sunday meetings, etc. The problem here is the "plausibility structure" they refer to. This is even more important if they want to marry a Muslim man, in order to "complete" their "plausibility structure" as Muslim women.[13] For some women there is also the idea of integration and solidarity with "deprivileged" women, as we saw in the case of Nura. Third, it helps them to establish and maintain the *haram/halal* frontiers: which in themselves, in the Western context, are shifting, unclear, and not at all stable. This is true not only for converts, but also for some "reborn Muslims," particularly of the second generation, who recuperate the *hijab* explicitly or implicitly with this function. Some *ijtihad* elaborated in Europe and some "new Islamic theology"[14] play exactly this role of reestablishing the *haram/halal* frontier: and the *hijab* is one of their topics of discussion. It can also be used to maintain or establish this frontier: "I am a walking symbol," as stated so effectively by Aisha. This statement offers us a key to a better understanding of why the *hijab* is so often a polemical tool in debates on Islam in the European public space.

Conflicts need symbols, and the *hijab*, with its implications in different fields (cultural, social, political, juridical), and its polysemy, is the perfect symbol to use for conflict. For instance, it can be understood by its opponents as a symbol of the structurally "primitive" character of Islam in general, but also specifically of the oppression of women. Women have always been—and still are, as anthropologists and historians have shown on many occasions—the typical "object" of appropriation by various cultural, ethnic, or religious groups, and the typical *enjeu* in conflicts and clashes. On the other hand, it can be understood and used even more as an instrument of emancipation, as often happens among second generations. And, of course, it can have many other meanings. This is why in many European countries the *hijab* has become a public issue, at the macro level, and will continue to be an issue at the micro level, until we have become accustomed to it as something *normal:* something which will not happen in the near future.

Conclusion

In more than a dozen years of fieldwork among the Muslim communities of Europe, and of observations of reactions to the presence of Islam in the European public space, I have become more and more convinced that what Europeans reject about Islam is not its difference and Otherness (Islam as the paradigmatic example of "the absolute Other," the other more Other than is conceivable), but its similarity to things European: Islam, in a way, returns to Europe not what is "Other" in its history, but what is familiar to it. Islam is not different: it is not the contrary of what we are, it is "us"—one generation ago, or more. What we see in the mirror of Islam is not the portrait of something that is unknown to Europe: it is Europe (a part of it, and of its cultural legacy)—perhaps a little younger than now (and not even in all cases—sometimes it is very contemporary). As Claude Lévi-Strauss (1955) stated: "I know very well the reasons for the uneasiness I feel in front of Islam: I find in it the universe I come from; Islam is the West of the East."

This is true for some "hot" topics concerning the links between religion and politics; but it is also true for many gender-related issues, the *hijab* included. We have to admit that many women converts find Islam interesting: not in spite of its "Otherness," but precisely *because of* its "Otherness" (or what the mainstream culture defines as Otherness, but is not perceived as such by the individuals attracted by it). Islam is something that is not alien to their mentality, but, on the contrary, familiar to it. The problem is, as Yvonne Haddad declared during the workshop in which the papers of this volume were discussed, that it is easier to say: "It is my religion, it is my duty as a woman in this religion, it is the will of God," in order to justify a preference, than to say: "It is my choice, I want to be a woman in the 'traditional' way—having different roles for men and women, for instance." Some women do not feel strong enough to counter the current cultural debate on the role of women in the West, and on the female models of mass communication. They need a "plausibility structure" to sustain their alternative position. They cannot find it anywhere in their own culture. But Islam offers just such a position.

Notes

1. It must be stressed that the RAMP project is considered the most advanced point of comparative research on the subject of pluralism, to such an extent that it also involved researchers from the more well-known EVS project (European Values Systems), which was then to become WVS (World Values Systems). On these

are based, for example, the well-known theories of Inglehart on the "silent revolution" and the progressive individualization of Western societies, criticized by many, above all from a methodological point of view, for their incapacity to really grasp the dimension of religious pluralism outside the Christian context. For further work on these subjects, see Allievi (2003b).

2. On the role of the media, see my chapter in Part III of Maréchal, Allievi, Dassetto, and Nielsen (2003), a comparative research work written at the request of the European Commission.

3. I have developed the distinction between relational and rational conversions in a detailed model of trajectories to Islam in my book *Les convertis à l'islam. Les nouveaux musulmans d'Europe* (Allievi 1998).

4. It must be acknowledged that Sufism is the aspect of Islam that attracts Westerners most, even non-Muslims: books on Sufism can be found on the shelves of many bookshops, and particularly in New Age environments, where we can find references to Sufi music, Sufi healing, etc.

5. A three-year research project (Allievi 1998), conducted between 1994 and 1997, with forty-six in-depth interviews (many with persons that I met on more than one occasion, and in different places: home, mosque, etc.) and periods of participant-observation during moments of Islamic sociability. These moments included meetings, conferences, and congresses, and involved both immigrants and converts, and specific meetings of converts, the *hadras* of Sufi groups, etc. Some periods of observation lasted up to two or three days. The number of converts contacted, and to whom I spoke personally, I cannot give, but they were in the hundreds. Those with whom I explicitly talked about conversion

issues, in face-to-face discussions between a researcher identified as such and a subject accepting to be "researched," with field notes being taken, came to another one hundred or more. Roughly one-third of them were women. Contacts and interrelations with converts continued after the end of the research, and are still continuing, with systematic meetings and occasional structured interviews.

6. The Biblical and Qur'anic example of Adam, who gives names to all the animals, thus giving them a meaning and a function, is in this sense more than clear.

7. Even if it is an ancient problem and not only Islamic: "'Why,' wondered Plutarch, 'do we cover our heads to adore the divinity?' The answer is simple: to separate ourselves from the profane person . . . and to live only in the sacred world" (van Gennep 1909).

8. Remember apropos that it is the man who is obliged to convert, in order to marry a Muslim woman, while a woman is only, so to speak, "warmly advised," or possibly there is an obligation connected with the couple's relationship, on the request of the Muslim partner, but in any case not a legal duty, or an obligation of the *sunna*.

9. There follows a list of the classic arguments, we might say the *vulgata* on the subject, basically similar for Shi'ites and Sunnites. We give this exposition without any comment, even though much could be said, both regarding the ideological construction and the deliberate confusion between the ideal plane and that of reality. "There are many rules for women to be protected and respected. Women have many rights. In the Shi'ite world women nearly always manage to have these, in the Sunnite world no, because being prevalently Arab, it is based on pre-Islamic rules which men have no intention of renouncing, because it is handy for a

man to have women to serve him. There are many negative things that are imputed to Islam, but they are not true. They are things instead that the Arabs have brought down over the centuries, and which they have not managed to free themselves of through Islam. Whereas in the Shi'ite world this does not happen, because women enjoy great protection. Also in marriage. The advantages for women are so many that probably, seeing how Islam is considered in the West, they will not be believed. It is not true that the woman becomes a slave of the man. It is true that before marriage, in her father's house she is under his protection, but after she has married there are a thousand rules. The woman does not even have the obligation to do work in the house if she does not want to do so. She does not even have to breastfeed her children if she does not want to, because in Islam they belong to the father, they carry his name. If a woman brings a dowry this dowry cannot be touched. If she works after getting married the husband still has to keep her, the money she earns all belongs to her. Of course she puts it into the house, she helps the family, but not because she is obliged to do it. If she so wishes, she can put her money away.

There are a great number of rules that protect the woman and therefore if a girl knows the Shi'ite world, it is easier for her to choose this path because she knows that she will be protected more."

10. Similar instances of this Shi'ite "pride" are given in Roald, this volume.

11. It will be enough to refer here to the well-known typologies elaborated by Max Weber, concerning asceticism and mysticism and their internal differences, to understand how different and articulated what we usually call the religious offer may be, as if it were only one.

12. I have personally met some of them: but, I should say, randomly.

13. Which, by definition, in Islam, includes the fact of being married. Theologically, this is true also for men, by the way: *al-zawaj nisf al-iman*, i.e., marriage, is half of faith; but, socially, this is "less" true for them.

14. Of which Tariq Ramadan is the most well-known expression. See, among others, Ramadan 1999. I have underlined some significant elements of this attempt in a long foreword to the Italian edition of the book.

References

Allievi, St. 1998. *Les convertis à l'islam. Les nouveaux musulmans d'Europe.* Paris: L'Harmattan.

———. 2000. *Nouveaux protagonistes de l'islam européen. Naissance d'une culture euro-islamique? Le rôle des convertis.* Working Papers No. 18. Florence: European University Institute.

———. 2002. *Musulmani d'occidente. Tendenze dell'islam europeo.* Rome: Carocci.

———. 2003a. *Islam italiano. Viaggio nella seconda religione del paese.* Turin: Einaudi.

———. 2003b. "Il pluralismo introvabile. I problemi della ricerca comparativa." In *Un singolare pluralismo. Indagine sul pluralismo morale e religioso degli italiani,* ed. F. Garelli, G. Guizzardi, and E. Pace, pp. 249–295. Bologna: Il Mulino.

Berger, P. 1969. *A Rumor of Angels: Modern Society and the Rediscovery of the Sacred.* New York: Doubleday.

Dassetto, F., ed. 1996. *Facettes de l'islam belge.* Louvain-la-Neuve: Academia-Bruylant.

Durkheim, E. 1912. *Les formes élémentaires de la vie religieuse.* Paris: Alcan.

Hine, V. 1970. "Bridge Burners: Commitment and Participation in a Religious Movement." *Sociological Analysis* 31: 61–66.

James, W. 1902. *The Varieties of Religious Experience.* London: Collins.

Levi, P. 1986. *I sommersi e i salvati.* Torino: Einaudi.

Lévi-Strauss, C. 1955. *Tristes Tropiques.* Paris: Plon.

Maréchal, B., S. Allievi, F. Dassetto, and J. Nielsen, eds. 2003. *Muslims in the Enlarged Europe: Religion and Society.* Leiden and Boston: Brill.

Ramadan, T. 1999. *To Be a European Muslim.* Leicester: Islamic Foundation.

Social Compass 1999. *Conversions à l'Islam en Europe (Conversions to Islam in Europe)* 46 (3). Monographic issue.

Straßburger, G. 2000. "Fundamentalism versus Human Rights: Headscarf Discourses in an Established-Outsider Figuration in France." In *Paroles d'Islam— Individus, Sociétés et Discours dans l'Islam européen contemporain/Islamic Words— Individuals, Societies and Discourse in Contemporary European Islam,* ed. F. Dassetto, pp. 125–144. Paris: Maisonneuve & Larose.

van Gennep, A. 1909. *Les rites de passage.* Paris: Nourry.

Weber, M. 1922. *Gesammelte Aufsatze zur Religionssoziologie.* Tubingen: Mohr. Italian translation, *Sociologia delle religioni.* Torino: Utet, 1976.

PART THREE. TRAJECTORIES AND PARADIGMS

CHAPTER 6

Female Conversion to Islam

The Sufi Paradigm

Haifaa Jawad

Conversion to Islam is increasingly attracting attention worldwide. It is said that Islam is the fastest-growing religion in the contemporary world, and that despite the negative image and bad publicity about the faith, the number of people converting to Islam is on the increase.[1] There is no reliable figure as to the number of converts worldwide, or at the national level in individual Western countries, primarily because censuses in most Western countries do not ask about religious affiliation. In Britain, where this issue was brought up in the last census, that of 2001, the question was confined to religious background only; the issue of religious conversion was left out. Moreover, most mosques and Islamic centers all over Britain (and by extension Europe and America) do not issue certificates of conversion, nor do they record the number of persons who convert to Islam, let alone their age group or social, economic, or educational backgrounds—an issue that makes the attempt at estimating approximate numbers too haphazard. Having said that, however, one can certainly affirm that the religion is claiming some followers, especially in the Western world. To take one simple example, which could be used as a gauge to indicate the number of people who are attracted to Islam: in 2002, the Muath Welfare Trust, a community center catering to the needs of the Muslim community in Birmingham, England, ran a "New Muslims" project. The leader of the project reported twenty-four converts. Seventeen among them were white women and the rest, seven, were men. One man was of African Caribbean origin; the other six were white.[2]

In the past, the dominant group embracing Islam was composed of those of either African Caribbean or African American background, whereas recently a string of white people have become Muslim. In the UK, some of these white people come from affluent backgrounds, such as, for example: Joe Ahmed-Dobson, the son of former cabinet minister Frank Dobson; Mathew Wilkinson, a former head boy of Eton; Nicholas Brandt, son of an investment banker; Jonathan Birt, son of the former director-general of the British Broadcasting

Corporation (BBC), John Birt; and the son and daughter of Lord Justice Scott, who investigated the arms to Iraq deal.

Despite the stereotypes that portray Muslim women as oppressed and mistreated, it has been noted that more women are converting to Islam than men. For example, in Britain, women converts outnumber men by two to one (*British Muslims Monthly Survey* 2002), while in the United States they apparently outnumber them by four to one (Wadud 2003, 275). The majority of the women are said to be white, young, and unmarried. The director of the Florida chapter of the Council on American-Islamic Relations states: "In the past there were more African-Americans coming into Islam, now I am seeing an influx of white, Caucasian females."[3] In Britain, it is interesting to note that some of these women, such as the daughter of Lord Justice Scott, Jemima Goldsmith, and the former TV presenter Kristiane Backer, come from middle-class backgrounds. The number may not be so significant, but the fact of conversion itself, especially among the elite, is revealing—to some, utterly incomprehensible—given the extremely negative image of Islam in the West and the consequent tensions and difficulties generated by conversion to this religion.

In this chapter I will deal with the issue of how Sufism, or Islamic mysticism, underpins or permeates the general Islamic principles that have found acceptance or attraction among Westerners, especially women. My approach in this context is theological rather than sociological, looking at how Sufism has informed the overall Islamic principles, thus making them ever more appealing to certain sectors within Western society. The key theme to be explored here is the ways in which Sufism—or the Sufi perspective on Islam—has contributed to the process by which Islam is made not just into an interesting approach to life, but into an acceptable, and, for some, an irresistible way of life. This phenomenon is all the more important given the increasingly grim picture of Islam that prevails in our times. But before dealing with the main theme, we need to put the subject into perspective and look at the phenomenon of conversion to Islam in a wider context.

Conversion to Islam

It must be stressed that there is no such word as conversion in the Arabic language; rather, the emphasis is on the idea of becoming a Muslim, that is, "submitting" to God in the form prescribed by his final revelation. Hence, to understand conversion to Islam requires an understanding of the word

"Islam" itself. Islam denotes an act of submission and envisages not only "the acceptance of the outward forms of any one particular prophet's practice, not even that of the seal of the prophets, Muhammad. Rather, the word represents that pure worship of, and obedience to, the Divine that is exemplified in the lives of all those prophets, from Noah, through Abraham, Moses and Jesus, to the seal of the prophets, Muhammad" (Dutton 1999, 153). Hence, to accept Islam is in reality "to take on the ancient, Abrahamic, way of worship, albeit given the specific detailed requirements reflected in the outward practice of the seal of the prophets, Muhammad" (Dutton 1999, 153).

Furthermore, conversion, from the Islamic viewpoint, is also a remembrance and an affirmation of the primordial testimony to the Lordship of God, as the Qur'an says, "when your Lord brought forth from the children of Adam, from their loins, their seed, and made them testify of themselves. He said: 'Am I not your Lord?' They said, 'Yea, we testify!' That was lest you should say on the Day of Resurrection: of this we were unaware" (Qur'an 7: 172).[4] Accordingly, those who embrace Islam often refer to themselves as "reverts" rather than converts.

Becoming a Muslim entails public acceptance of the declaration of faith in front of at least two witnesses, this being the first pillar of Islam. Once this is publicly stated, it is assumed that the "new Muslim" would live according to Islamic rules and regulations dictated by God and the Prophet Muhammad. This involves: the performance of the ritual prayer five times a day, payment of the annual alms-tax of *zakat,* fasting the month of Ramadan, and performing the pilgrimage to Mecca at least once in a lifetime. In addition, the new Muslim is obliged to stop consuming alcohol and eating pork and non-*halal* meat, and abide by the prohibitions related to issues such as stealing and committing adultery and murder. Most new Muslims tend to take on Islamic names, although this is not obligatory (Dutton 1999, 153–156). Some of those who choose not to adopt a Muslim name indicate that they decline on the basis of maintaining their social acceptability and avoiding discrimination at work. In a personal conversation, David Wanies, former head of the Department of Religious Studies at Lancaster University, who himself is a convert, stated that some lecturers and teachers who prefer to keep their original names do so for pedagogical reasons.[5]

For women, becoming Muslim can also entail a radical change in their appearance. Islamic law instructs women to dress modestly, and this includes covering the hair. The *hijab* is no longer seen as an innocent mark of a woman intent on maintaining her cultural or religious identity, but as a threatening symbol of a pathologically anti-Western ideology. The following statement by a Muslim woman demonstrates what this can lead to: "People would shout, 'Go back to your own country.' I had someone spit at me once when I was standing at the bus stop at College."[6] Covering the head could also prove to be an obstacle toward upward social mobility in society, especially among educated Western women, and for that reason, some of them choose not to don the *hijab*. From personal experience, I know of at least two university lecturers who decided not to wear the *hijab*, and a third one is in the process of abandoning it. The latter informed me that her motives for taking off the *hijab* are twofold: social acceptability ("I have been treated like them," she said, meaning immigrants and refugees) and job security and promotion. In a private conversation with her she stated that recently she had lost an opportunity for a senior position in a particular university primarily because of her *hijab*.[7] The *hijab*, for convert women, brings not only outside rejection and hostility but also strong family opposition. This could jeopardize family ties, which are already under strain as a result of conversion. A typical response is this: "You chose your religion over us... people will discriminate against you. You are making yourself a third-rate citizen. You have basically painted a bull's-eye on you saying—'shoot me.'"[8] However, reactions within a family can vary: "My mum said—'if you are happy, I am happy'—but obviously she was not. My dad said it and he meant it, that was the difference between them."[9] Others cautiously accept it: "My mom loves me so much she [would] buy me scarves sometimes. My grandmother gave me a beautiful, velvet embroidered scarf. They will respect my prayer, but at the same time ask—'why are you so fanatical?'—"[10] The question that needs to be asked is: But why, then, are these women embracing Islam against all the odds?

First, a large number of Western women who convert to Islam do so on the basis of personal connections such as marriage with Muslim men. That said, however, recently and increasingly, they are embracing Islam primarily because of their convictions. In 2002, the Muath Welfare Trust in Birmingham reported that seventeen women converted to Islam, eight of them through marriages, while the rest, nine, came to Islam as the result of a personal search.[11] Taking a closer look at those convictions, the appeal of Islam to Western women can be attributed to a wide range of factors. One can begin with the familiar idea of Islam as a form of liberation theology offering an accessible language of protest for marginalized groups in society (Winter 2000, 100). For example, women who are in general excluded from public life struggle because of that to achieve happiness. Islam in this context can offer them a practical alternative: "I was looking for peace, I had a rough past. My teenage years were not great; I was bullied at school, people called me fat and ugly, and I was looking for something to make me happy. I tried to go to Church once a week but . . . I did not feel in place there. [Islam] gives you a purpose in your life. The Koran is like a guide to help you: when you read it, it makes you feel better." [12]

Second, arguably, the nature of the religion itself and its simplicity appeal strongly to the religious consciousness of people who are drawn to its emphasis on the simple message of monotheism, thereby attracting those who are "confused by Christo-logical and Trinitarian controversies" (Winter 2000, 100). As another convert seeks to explain: "Something vital seemed to be missing from my life and nothing would fill this vacuum. Being a Christian did not do anything for me, and I began to question the validity of only remembering God one day a week—Sundays! As with many other Christians too, I had become disillusioned with the hypocrisy of the church and was becoming increasingly unhappy with the concept of Trinity and the deification of Jesus." [13] Many Western women come from a tradition that is historically dominated by male clergies and characterized by a strong aversion to and fear of the feminine, a tradition in which the concept God qua Father (a supreme male figure) dominates the overall understanding of the Ultimate Reality; such women can discover in Islam, with its emphasis on totality and integration, an appealing alternative. Despite its patriarchal features, they find in Islam an equilibrium on the plane of the "heart," in its relationship with God. I shall return to this theme below. The following testimony by a female convert hints at the kind of equilibrium to which Islam gives access: "There was an inner void that was not completely satisfied with academic success or human relationships. I had spent my life longing for a truth in which heart would be compatible with mind, action with thought, intellect with emotion. I found that reality in Islam." [14]

Third, in view of current social trends fostering widespread moral uncertainty, those aspects of Islamic teaching relating to morality, modesty, security, the sense of belonging, the sense of identity, close family ties, care and community, and deference to the elderly, as well as traditional notions of respect for women, have proven to be very popular among Western women. We hear the voices of women who say: "I am now more confident, happy and satisfied. I have achieved the fulfillment I was looking for." [15] Commenting on the supposedly outmoded traditional respect for women, one convert states: "You seem to be really looked after. [Pious] Muslim men really respect you; they do everything for you. You are highly thought of and protected."[16] These sentiments are echoed by another woman who extols, in the capacity of Muslims to participate in more traditional family/community values, "a feeling of belonging to a family . . . when with Muslim friends. . . . closeness, love, kindness, caring: these are the benefits I have gained" (Haleem 2003, 94). Another convert goes further, considering current liberal social cultural trends as "false": "Islam made me feel the need to discipline my life in a positive way and to bring about the necessary modifications to bring my whole being into balance. To set myself free from the false standards of society" (Haleem 2003, 94).

Underpinning the above factors, and by extension the overall attraction to Islam, I would argue, is Sufism, or the spiritual values of the faith, which are the core or the essence of the religion of Islam. For Sufism is Islamic spirituality, even if Islamic spirituality is not confined to the phenomenon of Sufism. The spiritual values of the religion of Islam are brought into sharp focus by the Sufis and are implemented practically by them in various ways. But the Sufis do not claim that these values and the doctrines and practices emerging therefrom are anything other than those of quintessential Islam. Their "esotericism" is but the complement to the exotericism of the formal religion, and both alike are rooted in the sources of the Islamic revelation—the Qur'an and the Sunnah of the Prophet. To understand the inner, spiritual values of the revelation, one can turn to the Sufis, who have incorporated these values organically into a dynamic way of life. Inasmuch as most Sufis integrate these inner values with outer Shari'a practice, the result of their presence in Islamic society is a strengthening of the religion as a whole; the Sufis do not promote these inner values at the expense of the outer forms of Islam.

Sufism . . . became the framework within which all popular piety flowed together; its saints, dead and living, became the guarantors of the gentle and co-operative sides of social life. Guilds commonly came to have Sufi affiliations. Men's clubs claimed the patronage of Sufi saints. And the tombs of local saints became shrines which almost all factions united in revering. It is probable that without the subtle leaven of the Sufi orders, giving to Islam an inward personal thrust and to the Muslim community a sense of participation in a common spiritual venture quite apart from anyone's outward power, the mechanical arrangements of the Shari'a would not have maintained the loyalty essential to their effectiveness. (Hodgson 1974, 125)

Sufism, as Martin Lings says, "is necessary because it is to Islam what the heart is to the body. Like the bodily heart it must be secluded and protected

and must remain firm-fixed in the centre; but at the same time it cannot refuse to feed the arteries with life" (1975, 106–107; see also Nurbakhsh 1981;
Nicholson 1997; Eaton 1994).

If one wishes to appreciate the deeper motives for conversion to Islam,
one cannot afford to ignore this inner aspect of the religion, especially, as
will be seen below, in regard to women converts. The following quotation
illustrates this well:

*I knew that I yearned for more spiritual fulfillment in my life. But, as yet, nothing
had seemed acceptable or accessible to me. I had been brought up essentially a secular
humanist. Morals were emphasized, but never attributed to any spiritual or divine
being. As I met more Muslims, I was struck not only by their inner peace, but by the
strength of their faith. In retrospect, I realize that I was attracted to these peaceful
souls because I sensed my own lack of inner peace and conviction.*[17]

Women—in particular those belonging to the higher classes or the elite, who
have no social, economic, or racial motives for conversion—are, in my opinion, drawn to Islam by the spiritual values of Islam that Sufism has espoused,
even if this is not always made explicit. But before elaborating this claim,
it is necessary to give a brief summary of the role of Sufism as a vehicle for
conversion to Islam.

The Importance of Sufism as an Agent for Conversion to Islam

Historically, Sufism has played a major role in spreading Islam and recruiting
non-Muslims to the faith. It has been stated that the spread of Islam beyond
the frontiers of the Muslim states, and therefore the Islamization of such areas as Anatolia, Bosnia, Kashmir, Indonesia, India, and West Africa, should
be attributed in large part to the efforts of Sufi saints. This is the conclusion
reached by Thomas Arnold, in his classic and still unsurpassed study of the
spread of Islam, *The Preaching of Islam* (1935). Arnold shows that, far from
being "spread by the sword," as the common stereotype would have us believe, Islam was, in fact, spread by peaceful means: by the preaching of the
Sufis, on the one hand, and by the impact of traders, on the other. Often the
two went hand in hand, as traders were themselves often members of a Sufi
order, from the thirteenth century onward. The appeal of the Sufis continues
to this day, providing one of the main points of entry to Islam, especially for
contemporary Europeans and Americans (Dutton 1999, 163). Nasr describes
Sufism as "the flower of the tree of Islam . . . or the jewel in the crown of the

Islamic tradition" (1975, 49). Its emphasis on a universal supra-intellectual but very real *tawheed* (or science of God's unity), its focus on inner practices as a force for the transformation of individuals, its insistence on the detachment of the individual from the world rather than abandonment of it, its care for the welfare of the community, and its aim to bring about justice through injecting moral and ethical values into human lives have made it one of the most attractive forces within the religion of Islam, especially in Western society (Dutton 1999, 163; Lapidus 1988, 445–446).

In addition, its ability to fill the spiritual vacuum created by such ideologies as secularism, socialism, and modernism has made it particularly important as an avenue to converting to Islam. As a consequence, a considerable number of Westerners, including women, are attracted to Sufism and then to Islam. Currently there are many Sufi groups in Europe and America that are able to attract converts to Islam (Haddad and Lummis 1987, 22, 171). Moreover, there are centers in the West dedicated to the study of Sufism, chief among them being the Muhyiddin ibn Arabi Center in Oxford. The number of people who have adopted Sufism and then Islam both in Europe and the United States is considerable; they include "ordinary" people who sought inner peace, such as now-middle-aged people who lived through the "hippie" periods in the 1960s and '70s, those who were disillusioned with the Western material way of life and decided to embrace Islam to fulfill their spiritual needs. Also, a significant number of Western intellectuals found consolation in the wisdom of Sufism. These include the late French philosopher René Guénon—whose teachings on Sufism have become a model for Europeans interested in the spiritual dimension of Islam (Le Pape 2003, 232–234), such as the English mystic Martin Lings—and Swiss intellectuals Fritjof Schuon and Titus Burckhardt (Köse 1996, 20, 142–143). The same can be said regarding Nuh Keller of the Shadhiliyya order and his New Zealand wife, Umm Sahl, Tim Winter of Cambridge University, and James Morris of Exeter University.

The women (and men), especially from the elite, who have shown interest or entered into Islam did so by virtue of the fact that they were challenged by what one might call "the spiritual intellectuality" of the inner dimension of the religion. Having read literature on Sufi spirituality written both by practicing Muslims/Sufis and objective Western academics, they became aware of the link between the inner, universal spirit of the faith and its outer, particular form. While in the 1960s Sufism was part of the "hippie" movement, and divorced from its Islamic roots, in the 1990s, it was becoming known increasingly, and more accurately, as the form taken by Islamic mysticism.

Many intellectuals came to see such values as secular cleverness, wealth, relativism, and pragmatism in the light of Sufi ideals of wisdom, sacrifice, a sense of the absolute, and idealism. These characteristics ultimately lent a sense of balance and completeness, primarily through the power of integration proper to Sufism. Integration means *tawheed*, the verbal noun stemming from the verb *Wahhada*, literally, "to make one." Whereas theologically, this means declaring or affirming God's oneness, in Sufism, it comes to mean realizing oneness—the oneness of God, but also the oneness of being, and thus the necessity of "being one," or being "integrated" as a personality, in order to properly affirm and realize the oneness of God. Thus, *tawheed* is fully realized when God is worshiped by the "whole" human being: to be "whole" is to be "holy" (the words being etymologically related). This state of integration is ultimately antipodean to the dissipation and agitation that so many feel is generated by modern life: "For to be dissipated and compartmentalized, to be lost in the never ending play of mental images and concepts, or psychic tensions and forces, [means] to be removed from that state of wholeness which our inner state demands from us" (Nasr 1972, 43–44). Sufism strives toward the attainment of the state of purity and wholeness "not through negation of intelligence, as is often the case in the kind of piety fostered by certain modern religious movements, but through the integration of each element of one's being into its own proper centre" (Nasr 1972, 44). Accordingly, the spiritual method is crucial for the integration of the person. For it brings the dispersed elements in human beings back together and ensures that the outward-going tendency is controlled and reversed, so that the person can live inwardly with his/her emotions, reactions, and tendencies, aiming primarily at the center rather than the rim (Nasr 1975, 3–17), "for at the centre resides the One, the Pure and ineffable Being which is the source of all beatitude and goodness, whereas at the periphery is non-existence, which only appears to be real because of man's illusory perception and lack of discrimination" (Nasr 1972, 49).

Normative Sufism does not go outside the framework of the law to achieve such transformation in the human mind, body, and spirit, but seeks to base its practices on the injunctions of the Shari'a. Sufism integrates the outward *(zahir)* and the inward *(batin)* aspects of the faith and integrates male and female on the basis of the integration within God of *Jalal* (Majesty) and *Jamal* (Beauty), ultimately resulting in a totality on the metaphysical plane, which implies complementarity at the human level within and between man and woman. This is very much a part of the traditional Islamic conception of the nature of things. Therefore, when men lack beauty *(Jamal)* of soul, they tend to oppress those weaker than themselves through lack of compassion, thus disobeying God, in the process, through lack of wisdom and submission. When women lack strength *(Jalal)* of the soul, on the other hand, they are unable to assert their true strength, whereas Sufi women have always been able to bring forth their reserves of strength and remain impassibly independent. Sufi women throughout the ages have been an inspiration to other women and have taken on male disciples (Smith 1984; Nurbakhsh 1983; El-Sakkakini 1982). This affirms the necessity of the feminine/spiritual dimension as a balancing factor; for when men (and women) lose the balance between the two sides of their nature, then *ihsan*—that is, virtue or beauty of soul—loses its meaning. Where there is no perception of or conformity to beauty—*ihsan* in the deepest sense—there is no virtue, and where men (and women) have no virtue, society collapses into the kind of chauvinism and abuse that characterize male-female relations in so many parts of the Muslim world on the whole.

In addition to the appeal of the spiritual values of Sufism to many Westerners, the Sufi gender paradigm in this context is also of particular relevance. Sufism offers a particular notion of feminine equality and dignity. To understand this concept, it is important to consider the Sufi approach to the feminine principle within Islam. The capacity of Sufism to incorporate and encourage feminine activities within its sphere in both spiritual and social terms attests to the importance attributed by the Sufis to the feminine element in the Divine Nature itself. We shall examine each of these elements in turn.

Sufism and the Acceptance of Feminine Activities

Sufism continues to favor the development of feminine activities more than any other branch of Islam. The Qur'anic emphasis on the spiritual equality between the sexes: "For Muslim men and women, for believing men and women; for devout men and women; for men and women who are patient; for men and women who humble themselves; for men and women who give charity; for men and women who fast; for men and women who guard their chastity; for men and women who remember Allah much—for them all has God prepared forgiveness and a great reward" (Qur'an 33: 32). "And whoso doeth good works, whether male or female, and is a believer, such will enter paradise, and will not be wronged the dint of a date-stone" (Qur'an 4: 124–125). And its

constant reminder of the ability of women to fulfill their spiritual needs; the
respect of the Prophet for women in general and his ideal relationships with
his wives. His kindness and care for his daughters "excluded that feeling of de-
jection so often found in medieval Christian monasticism" (Schimmel 1975,
426; Jawad 1998, 11–14, 26). Despite the fact that one can find what could
possibly be seen as antifeminine sayings in the traditions and among some
early Sufis, "the Muslims scarcely reached the apogee of hatred displayed by
medieval Christian writers in their condemnation of the feminine elements"
(Schimmel 1975, 429). For example, Eve was never regarded as the cause of
the fall of Adam, nor was the possibility that women did not have souls ever
considered. On the contrary, the Prophet declared that "God has made dear to
me from your world women and fragrance, and the joy of my eyes is in prayer"
(Schimmel 1997, 21). Such principles from the Qur'an and the prophetic example gave rise in Sufism to a particularly rich tradition of female spirituality.
Hence, large numbers of women followed (and continue to follow to the present day) the spiritual path and in due time excelled in their virtues and piety.
Chief among them was Rabia al-Adawiyya, considered to be the first woman
saint in Islam (after the Prophet's wife, Khadija, and his daughter, Fatima). She
is credited with introducing the concept of unconditional love of God into
Sufism, thus transforming "sombre asceticism into genuine love mysticism"
(Schimmel 1997, 34). The following anecdote illustrates the notion of unconditional love: "[One day Rabia] ran through Basra with a bucket of water in
one hand and a burning torch in the other, and when asked about the reason
behind her actions, she replied: I want to pour water into hell and set paradise
on fire, so that these two veils disappear and nobody shall any longer worship
God out of a fear of hell or a hope of heaven, but solely for the sake of His eternal beauty" (Schimmel 1997, 34–35). Her devotion, and asceticism, and her
contribution to the development of Islamic mysticism earned her the respect
and affection of all the Sufi masters of her time (Al-Din Attar 1990, 39–51).

Rabia was not the only such woman of her times. Several other women at
the forefront of the Sufi tradition developed and articulated the Sufi way of
life. There were Maryam of Basra, Rabia of Syria, Fatima of Nishapur, to name
but a few; they attended Sufi meetings, consorted freely with Sufi masters,
sponsored Sufi activities, and organized circles in the pursuit of the mystical
path. Some of them who were advanced in learning and mystical knowledge
guided their husbands in religious and practical matters, and contributed to
the spiritual formation of future Sufi masters, educating great mystical thinkers such as Ibn Arabi, who was taught for two years by the great Sufi saint

Fatima of Cordova. His early encounter with her and other female mystics greatly influenced his positive attitude toward the feminine role in Sufism.

In general, these women played an important role in shaping the image of the ideal, pious Muslim woman, respected and venerated for her spiritual endeavors. These feminine activities continue to take place in modern times and can be found in some parts of the Muslim world, where Sufi women still teach and train souls who are longing for spiritual enlightenment, maintaining continuity with the early example of Rabia al-Adawiyya and her fellow Sufi women following the spiritual path (Schimmel 1975, 426–427, 430–435; Nasr 1980, 74; Nurbakhsh 1983). The example of Rabia and other pious Muslim women like her serves as an inspiration and a model to be emulated in Sufis' personal lives, especially at a time when there is widespread antispiritualism (Sherrard 1987), the desacralization of knowledge, the diminution of feminine spiritual values, and the distortion of feminine dignity. For an ailing society, inner renewal and purification are the first step toward a more general cure for society as a whole. In this context the following quotation is of importance:

The more I pondered, the greater emptiness I felt within. I was slowly beginning to reach a stage where my dissatisfaction with my status as a woman in this society, was really a reflection of my greater dissatisfaction with society itself. Everything seemed to be degenerating backwards, despite the claims ... of success and prosperity. I wanted to find that thing which was going to fill the vacuum in my life. [This was achieved when I was] drawn ... [to] Islam.[18]

Sufism and Feminine Social Values

The emphasis by Sufis upon upholding the feminine values pertaining to the family, whilst at the same time maintaining a dignity and strength as a worshiper before God, has a special appeal for women who choose to fulfill an orientation toward the family and community. This balancing of values is set against a time when feminine social values are diminishing and no longer esteemed, when, in fact, there are constant efforts to undermine them in society. Ideals and concepts pertaining to womanhood and the family are no longer regarded as sacred, but on the contrary, as stigmatizing and stereotyping, resulting in confusion and leading to a void in the life of millions of women who want to be fulfilled by the capacity to nurture and strengthened by an independence of faith, qualities often pejoratively associated with "traditional norms." Sufism, with its strong affirmation of the sacred role of womanhood in society, presents an attractive alternative to fill the vacuum for those women who desire to live their lives as mothers, wives, or daughters in a spiritual way. For example, Sufis (and Muslims in general) highly respect mothers; the exhortation in the Qur'an and by the Prophet to be respectful to mothers testifies to the honor bestowed upon the maternal role, especially in its spiritual aspect. "There are several well-known hadiths that either state or imply that motherhood spent in accordance with the Shariah is one of the expressions of the spiritual role of a female" (Chishti 1989, 204). One of the most detailed hadiths, which brings to life the spiritual reality of the travails of motherhood, was related by Anas, who had heard from Sallama, the nurse of the Prophet's son Ibrahim: "O Messenger of God, you have brought good tidings of all the good things to men, but not to women." He said: "Did your women friends put you up to asking me this question?" "Yes they did," she replied, and he said:

Does it not please any one of you that if she is pregnant by her husband, she receives the reward of one who fasts and prays for the sake of God? And when the labour pains come no-one in the heavens or the earth knows what is concealed in her womb to delight her? And when she delivers, not a mouthful of milk flows from her and not a suck does she give, but that she receives, for every mouthful and every suck the reward of one good deed. And if she is kept awake at night, she receives the reward of one who frees seventy slaves for the sake of God. (Schleifer 1997, 49)

The Qur'an and the Sunnah demand that mothers be venerated, and cared for, especially in old age; the famous hadith of the Prophet "heaven lies at the feet of mothers" provides much cause for reflection in the life of the pious Muslim, who then endeavors to ensure that mothers are always respected, treated kindly, and gracefully obeyed. The very fact that the word for womb in Arabic, *rahm*, derives from the word *rahma* (mercy), which itself stems from the divine attributes of Ar-Rahman (the Compassionate) and Ar-Rahim (the Merciful), signifies the tremendously rich and deep understanding in Islam of the creation process as deriving from the very unfolding of compassion and mercy, so that each and every dimension of motherhood precipitates and participates in that unfolding. For Sufis this symbol, and in fact spiritual reality, of the maternal facilitation of Divine Mercy was irresistible and is exemplified in many Hadith Qudsi (the very words of God spoken on the tongue of the Prophet), such as that reported by Ghazzali: "If my servant falls sick, I care for him as a loving mother tends her son." Also, the great mystic Rumi is

reported to have said: "[Since] a mother's tenderness derives from God, it is a
sacred duty and a worthy task to serve her" (Schimmel 1997, 89, 93). For the
believers who benefit from the Sufi exegesis of the metaphysical understanding of the creation process, it is no wonder that they hold their mothers in
awe and do their best to be good to them so that the blessings of God descend
upon them, for pious spiritual mothers possess *baraka* (the quality of the sacred) by virtue of their proximity to God.

The role of spiritual mothers originates with Maryam (Mary), the mother
of Jesus and the only woman after whom a chapter in the Qur'an is named. She
is considered the "Chosen amongst all women" and highly revered (among
Muslims) for her piety, purity, and submission. In this context, the following
hadith is of great importance: "Aisha [the wife of Muhammad] asked Fatima
[the daughter of Muhammad]: Did I see [you truly] when you leaned over the
Messenger of God and cried; then you leaned over him and you laughed? She
said: He informed me that he would die from his illness, so I cried; then he
informed me that I would precede the other members of his family in being
reunited with him, and he said, You are the chief lady *(sayyida)* of paradise,
with the exception of Mary the daughter of Imran" (Schleifer 1997, 63).

Amongst the women in the history of Islam, the first wife of the Prophet
Muhammad, Khadija, was the first to enter Islam, and she, while supporting
her husband in his mission as messenger of God, also looked after her children
and ensured that peace and tranquillity prevailed in her home, thus becoming
the "embodiment of devotion and noble qualities" (Smith 1984, xxx) for Muslims, especially Muslim women. Her daughter Fatima, mother of Hasan and
Hossein, is regarded as the fountainhead of female spirituality in Islam; her
extreme piety and devotion to her family elevated her to a high station. She
and her mother "stand at the beginning of Islamic piety and occupy a very distinguished rank" (Smith 1984, xxx). Aisha, the youngest wife of the Prophet,
is also highly honored and respected; she served her husband as devoted wife
and guided Muslims with her divine knowledge; her close relationship with
the Prophet made her an authentic source of knowledge about his personal
life and so ranks her amongst the most reliable sources in the tradition of hadith science (Smith 1984, xxx). Other wives of the Prophet followed suit in
their holiness and piety. They all set examples for Muslim women by expressing their spirituality through their roles as mothers, wives, or daughters.

Thus, from the Islamic spiritual, and therefore Sufi, perspective, the role
of women within the family is highly valued and considered to be sacred,
as they are viewed as no less than the unfolding of God's mercy. Feminine

qualities and the homage paid to womanhood and their social and family roles become vital for women who desire to live in and through God, although, because of the very fact that mercy is understood to have derived from the feminine attributes of God's Nature, the example of women who bore no children but dedicated their lives to God was also a source of reverence and inspiration, as we shall discuss below.

Sufism and the Feminine Element in Spiritual Life

Conscious of the positive aspects of womanhood, the Sufis more than others highlighted beautifully the role of women in spiritual life and thereby ensured that Sufism is permeated throughout with feminine traits. Within this context, the purely spiritual role of females is fully accepted and elevated to a high degree. They bestowed upon women (in equality with men) the title of saint and accepted a woman (Rabia) to be a leading figure in the early development of Islamic mysticism (Smith 1984, 2–3). Ibn Arabi, in particular, played a major role in explaining the importance of the feminine element as a component of the Divine Reality (Schimmel 1997, 105). His belief that the Divine Reality ultimately contains and transcends the polarity of the masculine and the feminine continues to exert influence on Sufis until the present day. He declared that "there is no spiritual quality pertaining to men without women having access to it also" and "men and women have their part in all degrees [of sanctity] including that of the function of [spiritual] pole [a designation attributed to the most formative and inspiring figure of any particular phase in the life of the religion]" (Chodkiewicz 1986, 126). For Ibn Arabi, woman reveals the mystery of the compassionate God, and the feminine aspect is the form in which God can best be contemplated. He stresses: "God cannot be seen apart from matter, and He is seen more perfectly in the human material than in any other, and more perfectly in woman than in man" (Schimmel 1997, 103). In doing so, he elevates the image of the feminine to a high degree and paves the way for other Sufis to follow suit. For example, in the eighteenth century, Wali Muhammad Akbarabadi, a commentator on Rumi, declared: "Know that God cannot be contemplated independently of a concrete being and that He is more perfectly seen in a human being than in any other, and more perfectly in woman than in man" (Austin 1984, 12).

Thus, from the spiritual perspective, women embody and express aspects of the Ultimate Reality, which comprises the masculine and the feminine principles, as prefigured in the ninety-nine names of God. These names "are traditionally classified according to Majesty (*Jalal*—the archetype of masculinity) and Beauty (*Jamal*—the archetype of femininity). God is conceived, for example, both as the 'wrathful'—an eminently masculine trait—and as the 'merciful'—identifiable as a feminine quality. Moreover, if God is referred to as a He, the essence of God is referred to as a She" (Shah-Kazemi 1996, 2). In their approach to Divine Reality, the Sufis have always stressed the feminine dimension of that Reality. As Murata explains, while the legalistic authorities emphasize the incomparability and distance of God, the Sufis insist on the comparability and nearness of God. Hence, for the dogmatic theologians, God is wrathful, distant, dominating, and powerful. His rules must be obeyed, otherwise there is only punishment and hellfire. In other words, God's attributes "are those of a strict and authoritarian father" (Murata 1992, 8–9). In contrast, the Sufis see God as gentle, kind, and near. They believe "that mercy, love, and gentleness are the overriding reality of existence and that these will win out in the end." For them, "God is not primarily a stern and forbidding father, but a warm and loving mother" (Murata 1992, 9). Accordingly, they argue that the God of the theologians is a God whom nobody would ever love, essentially because he is too distant and difficult to comprehend, while the God of the spiritual authorities is a God who is compassionate and loveable because his prime concern is the care of his creatures; as a result, his creatures love him in reciprocal terms. This loving, caring God can easily be understood and approached (Murata 1992, 8–9).

To conclude, the dogmatic theologians, while accepting the feminine characteristics of the Divine Reality, lay strong emphasis on the masculine dimension of that reality, reducing in the process the feminine aspect to second place. In contrast, the Sufis affirm the supremacy of the feminine dimension, primarily because the famous hadith of the Prophet—"God's mercy precedes His wrath" (implying that God's feminine characteristics take priority over his masculine qualities)—permeates their understanding and their approach to the Ultimate Reality (Murata 1992, 9).

These spiritual ideals related to femininity are not only derived from mystical interpretations, but comprise the very fabric of the authentic Islamic tradition; they are enshrined in the Arabic language, which powers Islamic theology, and are reflected in the intellectual and social manifestation of the overall Islamic heritage. These ideals

permeated the ethos of traditional Islam. They may not have been articulated or even respected by all, but they were nonetheless implicit in the cultural ideals that defined gender relationships in societies that remained true to integral Islam. Ideals which continue to influence those who are trying to live according to the inner spirit of the tradition and not just outward prescriptions. This spirit leads to women being venerated and not incarcerated, held in awe and not treated with contempt. (Shah-Kazemi 1996, 2)

Taking into consideration the above discussion, it is important to stress that Sufism, or Islamic mysticism, is a key factor in influencing and shaping the main Islamic principles that have found an acceptance among certain sectors of the population within Western society, thus presenting Islam as a credible alternative way of life for some, especially women.

Notes

1. The rate of conversion to Islam apparently surges at times when there are strong anti-Muslim feelings such as those following the Bosnian conflict, the Gulf War, and the Rushdie affair (Winter 2000, 108). After September 11, 2001, "the number of conversions has risen in the UK, US and across Europe. A Dutch Islamic center claims a tenfold increase, whilst a steady stream of converts are reported at the new Muslim project in Leicester" (*British Muslims Monthly Survey* 2002). Similar activity is evident in mosques in cities such as London, Manchester, and Glasgow in the UK. Yet these numbers have to be taken with caution. See also the introduction to this volume.

2. Personal interview, Muath Welfare center, Birmingham, England, September 2003.

3. http://www.thetruereligion.org/mum.htm.

4. Cited in Winter 2000, 95–96.

5. Personal conversation, Lancaster, England, October 1997.

6. http://www.thetruereligion.org/mum.htm.

7. Personal interview, Amsterdam, March 2003.

8. http://www.thetruereligion.org/yfm.htm.

9. http://www.thetruereligion.org/mum.htm.

10. http://www.thetruereligion.org/yfm.htm.

11. Personal interview, Birmingham, England, September 2003.

12. http://www.thetruereligion.org/mum.htm.

13. http://www.unn.ac.uk/societies/islamic/women/women3.htm.

14. http://www.usc.edu/dept/MSA/newmuslim/karima.html.

15. http://www.thetruereligion.org/mum.htm.

16. Ibid.

17. http://www.usc.edu/dept/MSA/newmuslim/karima.html.

18. http://www.unn.ac.uk/societies/islamic/women/women3.htm.

References

Al Din Attar, F. 1990. *Muslim Saints and Mystics.* London: Arkana.

Arnold, Thomas W. 1935. *The Preaching of Islam: A History of the Propagation of*

the Muslim Faith. London: Archibald and
Constable Co.

Austin, R. 1984. "The Feminine Dimensions in ibn Arabi's Thought." *Muhyiddin
ibn Arabi Society Journal* 24 (2): 5–14.

British Muslims Monthly Survey. 2002.
Vol. 10, no. 1.

Chishti, Khawar Khan. 1989. "Female
Spirituality in Islam." In *Islamic Spirituality,*
ed. S. H. Nasr, pp. 199–219. London: SCM
Press Ltd.

Chodkiewicz, M. 1986. *The Seal of the Saints.*
Paris: Gallimard.

Dutton, Y. 1999. "Conversion to Islam:
Quranic Paradigm." In *Religious Conversion:
Contemporary Practices and Controversies,*
ed. C. Lamb and M. Bryant, pp. 151–165.
London and New York: Cassell.

Eaton, G. 1994. *Islam and the Destiny of Man.*
Cambridge: Islamic Text Society.

El-Sakkakini, W. 1982. *First among Sufis:
The Life and Thought of Rabia al-Adawiyya,
the Woman Saint of Basra.* London: Octagon
Press.

Haddad, Y., and A. Lummis. 1987. *Islamic
Values in the United States.* Oxford: Oxford
University Press.

Haleem, H. 2003. "Experiences, Needs
and Potential of New Muslim Women in
Britain." In *Muslim Women in the United
Kingdom and Beyond: Experiences and Im-
ages,* ed. H. Jawad and T. Benn, pp. 91–105.
Leiden: Brill.

Hodgson, Marshall G. H. 1974. *The Venture
of Islam—Conscience and History in a World
of Civilisation.* Vol. 2, *The Expansion of Islam
in the Middle Periods.* Chicago and London:
University of Chicago Press.

Jawad, H. 1998. *The Rights of Women in
Islam: An Authentic Approach.* Hampshire
and London: Macmillan.

Köse, A. 1996. *Conversion to Islam: A Study
of Native British Converts.* London: Kegan
Paul.

Lapidus, Ira M. 1988. *A History of Islamic
Societies.* Cambridge: Cambridge University
Press.

Le Pape, Loic. 2003. "Communication
Strategies and Public Commitments: The
Example of a Sufi Order in Europe." In
*Muslim Networks and Transnational Com-
munities in and across Europe,* ed. Stefano
Allievi and Jorgen S. Nielsen. Leiden: Brill.

Lings, M. 1975. *What Is Sufism?* London:
George Allen and Unwin.

Murata, S. 1992. *The Tao of Islam.* New York:
State University of New York Press.

Nasr, S. H. 1972. *Sufi Essays.* London:
George Allen and Unwin.

———. 1975. *Islam and the Plight of Modern
Man.* London: Longman.

———. 1980. "The Male and Female in
the Islamic Perspective." In *Studies in Comparative Religion,* ed. William Stoddart,
pp. 67–75. Middlesex: Perennial Books.

Nicholson, Reynold A. 1997. *The Mystics of
Islam.* London: Routledge and Kegan Paul.

Nurbakhsh, J. 1981. *Sufism, Meaning,
Knowledge and Unity.* New York: Khaniqahi
Nimatullahi Publications.

———. 1983. *Sufi Women.* New York: Khaniqahi Nimatullahi Publications.

Schimmel, Annemarie. 1975. *The Mystical
Dimensions of Islam.* Chapel Hill: University
of North Carolina Press.

Schimmel, Annemarie. 1997. *My Soul is a
Woman, The Feminine in Islam.* New York:
Continuum.

Schleifer, Aliah. 1997. *Mary the Blessed
Virgin in Islam.* Fons Vita: USA.

Shah-Kazemi, Reza. 1996. "Women in Islam: A Reminder to the Tabeban." Dialogue, Al-Khoei Foundation, London, December.

Sherrard, Philip. 1987. *The Rape of Man and Nature: An Enquiry into the Origins and Consequences of Modern Science.* Ipswich, England: Golgonooza Press.

Smith, Margaret. 1984. *Rabia the Mystic and Her Fellow-Saints in Islam.* Cambridge: Cambridge University Press.

Wadud, A. 2003. "American Muslim Identity: Race and Ethnicity in Progressive Islam." In *Progressive Muslims, on Justice, Gender, and Pluralism,* ed. O. Safi, pp. 270–285. Oxford: One World Publications.

Winter, T. 2000. "Conversion as Nostalgia: Some Experiences of Islam." In *Previous Convictions, Conversion in the Present Day,* ed. M. Percy, pp. 93–111. London: Society for Promoting Christian Knowledge.

CHAPTER 7

African American Islam as an Expression of Converts' Religious Faith and Nationalist Dreams and Ambitions

Gwendolyn Zoharah Simmons

When we look at Islamic conversion amongst African Americans, it is important to contextualize this phenomenon within the history of African American religion, which has traditionally been a response to the group's peculiar history and particular circumstances in the United States of America. "From the very beginning," Charles Long writes,

> [Africans] were brought here in chains and this country has attempted to keep them in this condition in one way or another. Their presence here as human beings in the United States has always constituted a threat to the majority population. From the point of view of the majority population, [Africans] have been simply and purely legal persons, first as slaves defined in terms of property, and then after the abolition [of] slavery as chattel property, [and] as citizens who had to seek legal redress before they could use the common facilities of the country—water fountains, public accommodations, restaurants, schools, etc. (1997, 27)

It was in this situation that African Americans had to retain their humanity and their sanity. One of the main ways in which they did this was through the development of various religious institutions, invisible and visible. At the heart of this development of African American religious traditions has been the effort, at both the individual and collective levels through social action, rituals, or political militancy, to counter the twin insults of white racism and economic exploitation. As Manning Marable, a well-known political scientist and social activist, asserts, "the totality of the black religious experience cannot be understood outside of the development of white racism and capitalist exploitation" and the African American response to these twin evils (1981, 34).

Scholars from numerous disciplines have all affirmed the significance of religion in African American life and what many believe was its indispensable role in the survival of this group. For African Americans, says the noted black historian E. Franklin Frazier, religion has historically functioned as a "refuge in a hostile white world" (in Baer and Singer 1992, ix). People of

African ancestry in America shaped Euro-American Christianity, as well as
Judaism and Islam, to meet their own needs and to serve as social institutions
that they could call their own. Baer and Singer, anthropologists who have
studied African American religions, state: "African Americans have utilized
religion as a way of creating space in addressing the vagaries of racism and
class stratification" (Baer and Singer 1992, ix). W. E. B. DuBois, the first American scholar to give serious attention to the religious life of African Americans in his 1903 seminal work, *The Souls of Black Folks*, wrote that "churches
[I would add mosques and temples] constitute centers of social life for the
African American and serve as primary vehicles of communication and sites
for entertainment and amusement in the black community. They have traditionally served as mutual aid societies helping members to survive the crises
in their lives" (Baer and Singer 1992, ix).

As Baer and Singer further note, another role that African American religion has played is as a "form of self-expression and [individual] resistance to
white dominated society." Marable has observed that black religious institutions have also "served as rallying centers for political and economic reform"
(Baer and Singer 1992, x). From Nat Turner (who led the bloodiest slave revolt
in U.S. history) to Elijah Muhammad, to Malcolm X to Martin Luther King, Jr.,
religious leaders have been the leaders and visionaries in the black struggle
against white racism and its institutional manifestations. African Americans
have expressed their "protonational consciousness" primarily through religion, which has enabled them as a mass of oppressed people to cohere as a
people and work for the good of the group. Blacks found a voice, many and
variegated voices, which spoke not only of their spiritual quest and fulfillment but also of their earthly trials and their social yearnings. It has been
through this "interplay of worldly and otherworldly images and attributes
[that] African Americans [have] constructed their identity as a people" (Baer
and Singer 1992, xvii). Because it is within a religious context and only
within that context that blacks were able to have some form of autonomy
and agency, their religion has been political and their politics has had a religious bent.

Some scholars of African American religion, such as Gayraud Wilmore
(1983), claim that African American religions have a liberatory or even radical ethos at their core, which is much more pronounced at some times than
at others, depending on the circumstances confronting the group at any particular time in its history. "African American resistance of white domination
is part of the very essence of African American religious sensibility," say Baer

and Singer. Quoting Marable, these authors write, "Blackwater [a term coined by Marable to describe black religious sensibility, which he defines as a vital-izing essence] is the consciousness of oppression, [and] a cultural search for self-affirmation and authority" (1992, 40).

I think it is important to establish that African Americans' religious ex-pressions, be they Christian, Jewish, African Traditional, or Islamic, have most often had this two-pronged approach, as described above: the seeking of a religious/spiritual faith for the individual, to sustain the soul or spirit of the person through whatever trials and tribulations confronted her, as well as a group response to the racism and injustice facing the group. This is especially important when one talks about Islam in the African American experience, since many have suggested that the Moorish Science Temple, founded by Noble Drew Ali in 1913, and the Nation of Islam (NOI), begun by Fard Muhammad in 1930, cannot be called "religions" in the classical sense, but rather were/are cults and/or black nationalist protest organizations, de-veloped to advance the political cause of black people. The scholars quoted above, as well as my personal experience, convince me that the NOI, which is the primary focus of this paper, and other heterodox expressions of Islam are religious and in keeping with more orthodox African American religious expressions. They are *also* expressions, on the part of the converts, of a black nationalist sensibility that is a product of blacks' exclusion from mainstream American life.

Islam in America amongst African Americans

There is some consensus, reports Jane Smith, that there are at least 6 million Muslims now living permanently in the United States and that at least 40 percent of them are African American converts (1999, xii–xiii). These num-bers of African Americans include followers of W. D. Muhammad (the largest single African American Sunni Muslim organization, whose membership is estimated to be close to 2 million), members of other Sunni Muslim groups, and those who belong to "heterodox" groups that adhere to some other in-terpretation of Islam, such as the Nation of Islam, led by Louis Farrakhan, whose membership is said to range from 20,000 to 100,000, presently, and the Ansaru Allah group.

A barrage of recent scholarship has revealed that there is an old relation-ship between African Americans and Islam. Most historians now agree that there has been an Islamic presence in the United States from the earliest times.

Muslim evangelists who were merchants, conquerors, and scholars fanned out across West Africa several hundred years before Christians arrived. Many Africans were converted in the area between the Senegal and Gambia Rivers. This is the region from which huge numbers of Africans were captured, enslaved, and shipped west to the Americas. One of the excellent books on this enslavement of West African Muslims is Sylviane A. Diouf's *Servants of Allah: African Muslims Enslaved in the Americas* (1998). Diouf estimates that from 10 to 25 percent of all enslaved Africans shipped to the Americas from the seventeenth to the nineteenth centuries were Muslims. The best-selling autobiographical book *Roots*, and the TV documentary of the same name created from it, first brought to light, via Alex Haley's distant relative, Kunte Kinte, how pervasive Islam was amongst the enslaved Africans.

Most, if not all, of the memory of Islam died out amongst the captive Africans, who were stripped of their names, their languages, and their religions by the whites, who feared these brutalized strangers and their "heathen religions." Given the circumstances, Africans over time adapted Christianity to their needs, and this Africanized form of Christianity became the religion of the overwhelming majority of the captives.

Richard Brent Turner, in his *Islam in the African American Experience* (1997), has provided us with an excellent historical chronology of how Islam came back into the lives and consciousness of African Americans. He, among others, writes about the role of Edward Blyden in the resurrection of Islam amongst African Americans. In the late eighteenth century Edward Wilmot Blyden (1832–1912), known as the father of Pan Africanism, began promoting Islam as a nationalist alternative to Christianity. "His 1887 book, 'Christianity, Islam and the Negro Race,' argued that Islam's racial tolerance and doctrine of brotherhood made it a more appropriate religion for people of African descent than Christianity" (Muwakkil 2002, 15). Blyden was a West Indian candidate for the Presbyterian ministry who came to the United States in 1850 to study at Rutgers Theological College. He was denied admission because of his race (Turner 1997, 48). Also, the Fugitive Slave Act, which gave federal agencies unlimited powers to apprehend runaway slaves, was passed in 1850. The most frightening aspect of this law was that "free" blacks were often seized as runaway slaves. This act, says Turner, was a landmark in the development of black nationalism, because the panic, terror, and turmoil that it caused amongst "free" blacks made many of them seriously contemplate the idea of emigration to Africa (Turner 1997, 48). Blyden, who was amongst those seized with the fear of being enslaved, felt that he could not remain in the United States. Needing desperately to find a way to leave, Blyden threw in his lot with the American Colonization Society[1] in order to bring "Christianity and Civilization to the 'barbarous tribes' of Africa" (Turner 1997, 48). He arrived in Monrovia in January of 1851. Blyden was destined to become one of the pioneers of the nineteenth-century Pan African movement, along with Martin Delaney, Alexander Crummell, and Henry McNeal Turner, to name the most famous of his contemporaries. These men and others planned and discussed various "back to Africa" plans to solve the problems of racism and slavery (Turner 1997, 48).

In 1857, the Supreme Court's *Dred Scott* decision further dashed the hopes of African Americans that slavery could be resolved quickly or peacefully. This led to the flowering of black nationalism. Turner quotes Wilson J. Moses, who describes the period from 1850 to 1925 as the "Golden Age of Black Nationalism." Moses is quoted as writing:

Black nationalism attempts to unify politically all black peoples whether they are residents of African territories or descendants of those Africans who were dispersed by the slave trade. Black nationalism has sometimes, but not always, been concerned with the quest for a nation in the geographical sense. But often it has been nationalism only in the sense that it seeks to unite the entire black racial family, assuming the entire race has a collective destiny and message for humanity comparable to that of a nation. (1997, 49–50)

Turner maintains that Blyden's most important contribution to Pan Africanist discourse was his use of West African Islam as a paradigm for black cultural nationalism. Blyden visited numerous Muslim areas in Liberia and Sierra Leone in the 1860s and 1870s and was favorably impressed by the level of learning and unity among African Muslims. He also admired the social and political organization of these communities, which he attributed to Islam. Although he was a Christian minister, his experiences in West Africa led him to believe that there was no racial prejudice in Islam and that the religion's doctrine of brotherhood made it a more appropriate religion for people of African descent than Christianity. Blyden also saw the religion as a focal point for an internationalist perspective that would lead Africans in the Diaspora to think of themselves, in concert with the darker races of the world, as having an identity over and against Europeans and Americans. As Turner so rightly observes, African American Islam, when it would emerge in the twentieth century, would use this Pan African nationalism "to globalize their religious/political discourse" (Turner 1997, 52). Blyden and other black leaders of that time, says Turner, observed positive racial, cultural, and political separation among West African Muslims and used these characteristics in their Pan Africanist discourses as a paradigm for black community development (Turner 1997, 52–53).

According to Turner, Blyden had an almost mystical view of Africa and the need for Africans' return to power and authority over Africa. His mysticism drew heavily on the biblical verse "Ethiopia shall soon stretch forth her hand unto God." It included many of the themes that we will see come to full fruition in the Nation of Islam—albeit with some significant changes—under the leadership of the Honorable Elijah Muhammad, whose self-proclaimed title was "Messenger of Allah." These similar themes include: First, stopping the decline of Africa. In the NOI, it was the decline of the black race. Second, Africa's redemption will be accompanied by a decline in the West. In the NOI, it was the change in the status of blacks that would accompany the decline of whites. Third, God will make a new covenant with black people. Fourth, "lack of civilization in Africa" was one of the causes of African slavery in the Western hemisphere. Lastly, the redemption of the black race lies in the destruction of the connection between slavery and blackness. In the NOI, redemption would come from Allah, who would destroy the whites and their societies.

Blyden saw the unification of Africa leading to the establishment of a great civilization. Most important, for this discussion, are Blyden's views on race. Blyden believed that each race was an "organic type of being." Each was endowed with a specific type of personality and divine mission. He believed in "black genetic racial purity"—a form of racial superiority or supremacy. This, of course, foreshadowed the Nation of Islam's black racial superiority teachings by approximately eighty years. Turner sees a direct link to Blyden's black racial superiority teachings, and he also sees Blyden's model for African unification and black power as an "extremely potent model for Pan African racial separatism and supremacy that was later adopted and expanded by leaders of the Universal Negro Improvement Association (the UNIA) [Marcus Garvey's Back to Africa Movement], the Nation of Islam and other black Muslim groups" (Turner 1997, 54).

Several scholars of black religion categorize the Nation of Islam as a messianic national sect, which they see as one variant of African American nationalism. Such a sect combines religious belief with the ultimate objective of achieving some degree of political, social, cultural, and/or economic autonomy. These groups, say Baer and Singer, are generally founded by charismatic individuals regarded by their followers as "messiahs" or "messengers of God, if not God in human form, who will deliver blacks from the oppressive yoke of white dominance" (1992, 59). Central to the ideology of the messianic nationalist sect is the repudiation of "Negro" identity as an oppressive white creation and the substitution of a new ethnic identity predicated on a belief in the unique spiritual importance of black people. Baer and Singer list five basic features of these groups. They are:

1. *belief in a glorious black past and subsequent "fall" from grace;*
2. *vocal opposition to and criticism of American society and whites in general;*
3. *anticipation of divine retribution against the white oppressors;*
4. *assertion of black sovereignty through the development of various rituals and symbols, such as national flags, anthems, and dress, and a separatist economic base as well, plus, at least in some cases, an interest in territorial separation or emigrationism; and*
5. *chiliastic and messianic expectations of a new golden age for black people. (1992, 60)*

These groups constitute the most radical protest against and departure from the institutions and conventions of the larger society. While these groups can and have chosen different religious expressions, the ones best known in the United States are those that adopt an Islamic orientation. The two most famous are the Moorish Science Temple, founded by Noble Drew Ali (Timothy Drew) in Newark, New Jersey, around 1913, and the NOI, founded in the 1930s, first under the leadership of W. D. Fard and later that of Elijah Muhammad (Elijah Poole). The NOI was by far the largest and most successful of these movements. There are others: the Hanafis of Washington, D.C., and the Ansaru Allah Community of Brooklyn, to name two of the more well-known groups.

The NOI under Elijah Muhammad taught that black people had intentionally been kept ignorant of "their origins, history, true names, [and] religion" (Baer and Singer 1992, 120). He further taught that black people were the original inhabitants of the earth and divine by nature. And, he went on, the white race had only been created some six thousand years previously by a black scientist named Yakub, through a series of genetic experiments that bleached the original people of their color and their humanity. In NOI demonology, "whites are referred to as 'Yakub's grafted devils.'" [2]

Elijah Muhammad attacked whites in his many speeches and in his writings. He often demonstrated whites' shortcomings and used examples of these in his efforts to bolster African American pride and self-confidence. It was a successful strategy. C. Eric Lincoln, the noted African American sociologist, has written extensively on the movement, and he says that the NOI was "the most potent organized economic force in the black community" and that it was Mr. Muhammad and the charismatic teachings of Malcolm X that brought "a pronounced public awareness of a religion called Islam" to the surface for the first time in American history (Lincoln and Mamiya 1984, 163). Lincoln wrote:

Temples and mosques sprang up in a hundred cities where none had existed before. Suddenly there was a visible, exotic religious presence in the form of a hundred thousand Black Muslims—conspicuous in their frequent rallies and turnouts, and in their grocery stores and restaurants and bakeries and other small businesses. The clean-shaven young Muslims hawking their newspapers on the streets, celebrating their rituals in the prisons, debating their beliefs in the media gave to the religion of Islam a projection and a prominence undreamed of in Christian North America.... And it was frequently argued in the black community that the Black Muslims had done more to exemplify black pride and dignity, and foster group unity, than some of the more respectable middle-class organizations. (Lincoln and Mamiya 1984, 163)

Baer and Singer note that ideologically, messianic-nationalist sects provide the most vehement religious critique of racism emanating from the African American experience. As in the NOI, their religious discourse turns the majority discourse on its head. In the NOI, Fard and Muhammad transposed white racist interpretations of blacks as a cursed race into one in which they constitute the first and most select human beings. Whites conversely are depicted as "diabolic beings working in opposition to the will of God." Muhammad taught "Whites were 'blue-eyed devils' of low physical and moral stamina" (1992, 139).

Baer and Singer contend that messianic nationalism, as a distinct voice in African American religious life, emerged as a fairly explicit protest movement against racism and social stratification in American society. I would add that it was this feature of the NOI that attracted me and a number of my friends and associates in the civil rights and Black Power movements to membership in the group. Many who did not join nevertheless admired the group and were proud of its accomplishments and approved of its ideology. G. Llewellyn Watson's analysis of the NOI and the Ras-Tafarian movement in Jamaica certainly resonates with my memories of the NOI's attraction for me.

Yet at the same time, I know that this was not the case for many of the members, particularly the women in the group who were devoutly committed to the movement as a religion and believed fervently in its teachings. It seemed that more of the men whom I knew in the group were more politically motivated. Perhaps the main reason for the difference between my own motivation for joining and that of most of the women I met in the group stemmed from my own political motivations, which grew out of my nontraditional role as a civil rights movement veteran who had helped to launch the Black Power movement within my organization, SNCC (Student Non-Violent Coordinating Committee). Interestingly, while I went into the NOI because of its black-nationalist ethos and its economic "do for self" motto, I became very attracted to Islam as a religion after joining. I began to read the Qur'an, in addition to Mr. Muhammad's "Message to the Black Man" (1965) and "How to Eat to Live" (1967). I ate one meal a day as we were instructed to do, fasted at the appointed time,[3] and did my prayers assiduously.

G. Llewellyn Watson, in writing about the NOI and Ras-Tafarians, states:

Neither of these movements should be summarily dismissed as ephemeral religious cults. Religion per se is not their major attraction. Both are social protests which move on a semi-religious vehicle, with emphasis on social action geared to transforming their objective life situations. They are nationalistic and nationalism is political; their foci move from one plan to another—from one based on the quest for religious experience to one grounded in the struggle for readjusting the status systems of their respective societies to accord with an ideal concept of society. (1973, 199)

It is important to note, however, that not all of the scholars see the NOI as a political movement. E. U. Essien-Udom, who conducted extensive interviews with Muslims in preparation for his important work *Black Nationalism* (1962), is one of these. Essien-Udom maintains that while the Muslims' objectives of establishing a black homeland and their image of a postapocalyptic Black Nation were political in theory, in practice, the NOI was "apolitical, as well as non-revolutionary because it eschewed any clear-cut political program as well as direct involvement in local or national politics." Instead, says Essien-Udom, "Muslim chiliasm claimed that the oppressor would be destroyed by Allah or that whites by their own inequities would destroy themselves" (in Baer and Singer 1992, 142). Essien-Udom wrote that the "revolutionary possibilities of the movement were mitigated by the ideology of the Nation and by the Muslims' need for achievement and status." The most the Muslims may hope for, he wrote, was "work, watchfulness, and prayer" (Baer and Singer 1992, 143).

Baer and Singer do not agree with Essien-Udom and offer cogent rebuttals, which I will not go into in this chapter. Whether in actuality the movement was revolutionary or even radical is not what I want to turn my attention to at this point. However, it is important to end this section of the chapter with the fact that African Americans, converts and outsiders, viewed this movement both as Islamic and as the preeminent expression of black strivings for self-determination and empowerment. Claude Andrew Cleage III has written one of the recent scholarly biographies of Elijah Muhammad (1997). He writes that Elijah Muhammad played a seminal role in the evolution of black nationalism, *and* Islam as an alternative religion in the twentieth century. He was the most prominent icon of the quasi-Islamic and racial separatist movements that developed among African Americans following World War II. As Cleage notes, many African Americans converted to the Islam of the NOI because it addressed both eschatological *and* earthly concerns (1997, xii). Cleage maintains that the reason earlier versions of Islam, such as the Ahmadiyya Movement, did not attract the following that the NOI did was because they did not adequately address the material reality of the emerging ghettos, nor did they satisfy the psychological need African Americans had to have their basic humanity and their destiny as a people forcefully affirmed by religious doctrine. Cleage suggests that it would take a teaching of strong medicine to pry African Americans away from their Christianity, which had psychologically sustained them through the slavery and early Jim Crow years.

I remember vividly when I first heard the teachings of Muhammad via his number one spokesman Malcolm X. I heard it on a 78 rpm vinyl record while sitting in the small headquarters of the Laurel, Mississippi, Freedom Summer office where I was project director. I had already been in Mississippi for over six months. The Ku Klux Klan or their kind had burned our first headquarters, one much nicer than the current one, to the ground. It had been really hard to get anyone else in Laurel to rent to us for fear that he too would lose his property at the hands of racist arsonists. A black man sympathetic to our cause rented us a three-room shotgun-style clapboard house with a tin roof. It did have electricity and cold running water inside. We were glad to get it. Someone sent me the Malcolm X record and I put it on to listen one day when I was alone in the building. Listening to it was like receiving what I imagine electric shock therapy must feel like. It both terrified me and thrilled me at the same time. This man was saying something that I never expected to hear in my life. To me, he was telling the unvarnished truth to the white man, spitting it out in his face; he was making it plain and I loved it. It would be several years before I joined the movement, only after I had been through many more trials and tribulations in the civil rights movement and its birthing of its Black Power wing. It would be a long while before I was seized by a black-nationalist fervor that would eventually lead me into membership in the NOI.

The space of this chapter does not allow for me to go into a lengthy discussion of my conversion to and time in the NOI. But as I have stated above, I was drawn into it because of its black-nationalist message and the hope it held out to me of black people doing for themselves and separating from racist white America, which I believed, at the point I joined, was irredeemably racist and would never be able to integrate African Americans into U.S. society as full-fledged citizens of equal worth.

Why Conversion?

Converts found something unique in the NOI. In the early years most were poor, relocated Southerners who felt alienated in cold and impersonal cities like Detroit, Chicago, Cleveland, and other large metropolitan areas of the Midwest and later the East Coast. The Muslims' conception of morality added order and a sense of dignity to the lives of many African Americans who had consumed alcohol and tobacco, perhaps fornicated or committed adultery, and possibly even engaged in crime. Also important were the rituals and symbols of the group, which impressed upon the new convert a sense of pride and belonging. The new convert felt that she was a significant part of a larger entity destined for some great purpose, says Cleage. This was certainly the sense I received when talking to the Believers, especially the ones who had been in the movement for a long time. A few of them even remembered W. D. Fard. They truly believed the teachings and were confidently awaiting the day when destruction would come down upon the white world and black people would be elevated to their rightful position in the world.

The converts received a sense of moral authority, an intense notion of togetherness or nationalism, says Cleage. I agree with this assessment.

Even I, as a skeptic in their midst, could let myself escape to the NOI's utopian vision and pray that it was true. While I often disliked the leadership, I was very fond of the rank and file members (especially the women and the older men), who were so sincere and so dedicated. I knew that I had an alternative if this movement proved to be bogus, but I was very worried about these little people who were giving so much of their time and their resources for this dream, this hope of "heaven here on earth, free of the white man." Perhaps it was because they reminded me of the devout believers in the Baptist church that I grew up in. The longer I remained in the group, the more suspicious I became and the more concerned for the thousands of Believers, especially the ones I had come to know and love.

Cleage writes about the symbols of the NOI and their importance. These included: the Muslim Star and Crescent; Elijah Muhammad himself as a divinely commissioned potentate; the NOI National Flag, which was an important part of the members' identity, just as the flag of any national state is important to its citizens. I remember well the emotion that members associated with the flag, which was very akin to a form of patriotism. The background of the flag was red—color of the sun, which members were told emits "light and life." There was a five-pointed star-and-crescent moon, which was white on the flag. Believers were taught that the star represented the five senses, and the crescent moon represented the equilibrium of the earth's water. At each corner of the flag was a letter, F, J, E, and I, which stood for Freedom, Justice, Equality, which "I" own (Cleage 1997, 102). The flag was seen by many of the members as mystical and magical. Believers were taught that it had protective powers to shield them from harm; therefore all should wear a replica of it on their person and display it in their homes, and it was always flown at the meetings.

In 1940, a national anthem was added to the movement's symbols. This was sung at all meetings prior to prayer. Its words spoke of NOI members as a "superior, martial people" (Cleage 1997, 103). It played upon the racial pride of the people. One could see tears well up in many Believers' eyes, especially the women, when the anthem was sung.

Even the structure of the NOI made many converts feel assured in the knowledge that black people could organize and run institutions in an efficient and orderly fashion. There was much pride in this structure. "The structure was organized to give such an impression. The organizational hierarchy was that of a 'military theocracy' arranged along dictatorial lines. It was designed to give a sense of order and respect for stratified authority" (Cleage 1997, 103). There were reverence and pomp surrounding important officials in the group, which conferred a certain mystique upon the office and the officeholder (Cleage 1997, 103). As a person who came out of the ultrademocratic structure of SNCC (Student Non-Violent Coordinating Committee), with its antihierarchical and antiauthoritarian ethos, I, too, became enthralled at the beginning of my time in the movement with the pomp and ceremony.

This had the intended effect upon the convert, who had rarely if ever seen black people conducting themselves with such discipline and confident aloofness. If my experience is any indication, just seeing the presence of uniformed Black Muslim officials, replete with orderly military marches, salutes, and other mannerisms, served as an excellent recruitment device among young and impressionable African Americans. The Fruit of Islam (FOI), with its precision drilling, attractive uniforms, legendary discipline, and reputation for no nonsense, was another real inducement to young males to convert. Malcolm X recalls in his autobiography that the Messenger told him, during his first one-on-one meeting with him, to "Go after the young people" (Cleage 1997, 134). Of course, we all know that this is exactly what Malcolm did, with great success. He was just the man to do the job.

After the movement began to grow by leaps and bounds with Malcolm as national spokesperson, Mr. Muhammad went after the middle class with increasing success. His appeal to this group was "to come and help lift your race." Stop giving all your talents to white society, which in the end just uses your talents against you. This message, like the black-nationalist one, was very appealing to me.

I had dedicated the previous four years of my life to "race-upliftment" in the civil rights movement; at this point, I was ready to dedicate a large part of my life to this movement, or so I thought. Unlike the SNCC, however, there was really no place for a woman to exercise what I considered real leadership as it had been in SNCC.[4] As I was to learn later, my role as a woman in the NOI was to be "a symbol of purity and chastity" and to be obedient and submissive to male authority, and the hallmark of my existence was that of mother of many children and a dutiful wife and helper to my husband, to whom I should defer in all matters of importance.

Women in the Nation of Islam

I left the movement five years after I joined due to my disenchantment over a number of things, including the emphasis on money and the "forced" payment of dues, tithes, newspaper sales money, bake sales moneys, the receipts from the endless fund-raisers, which burdened the poor people in the organization mercilessly; the extravagant lifestyles of the "Royal" Muhammad Family; the structural and militaristic hierarchy, to which the Believers were forced to submit; the authoritarian and sometimes brutal nature of some of the leadership; the hinted-at and actual violent punishments meted out to the disobedient; and last, but certainly not least for me, the horrible second-ary status of women in the movement.

From my list of grievances above, you can see that there were many things that I had difficulty with in the NOI's practice. In this section of the essay, I will focus on one of the particularly irksome ones for me: the status of women in the NOI. I also want to look at how the NOI's teachings and prac-tices regarding women have influenced women's position in other black-na-tionalist formations of which I was a member and how they have continued to shape women's status in contemporary African American Sunni Muslim formations.

The majority of Believers in the NOI were male, but women were a signifi-cant group within the Muslim fold. Cleage writes:

Black womanhood and the images of purity, domesticity, and piety that the Believ-ers associated with it [were] a prominent part of [NOI] Muslim doctrine. The train-ing of women and girls who aspired to the Nation's standards of feminine grace and cultured refinement was a mainstay of the organization. . . . There were mandatory meetings for all the Believers on Wednesdays, Fridays and Sundays. Additionally fe-male Believers also participated in nursing classes on Tuesday nights and a "culture and civilization" course on Thursday nights. The MGT-GCC [Muslim Girls Train-ing and General Civilization Course],[5] the comprehensive women's program, taught gymnastics,[6] cooking, sewing, and household management as well as child rearing, and the "proper" approach to gender relations. (1997, 101)

The NOI women were known by their attire, their long dresses and turbans. On Sundays women had to wear their official uniforms, which were man-ufactured in the organization's garment factory. They were either white or cream-colored and were fairly expensive for a poor woman to afford. Yet they were a requirement. Women unable to afford the "official uniform" were of-ten harassed for not wearing one and belittled until they found some way to purchase one (Tate 1997).[7] NOI women were said to be placed on pedestals, jealously guarded, and segregated in public meetings. NOI women were not to shake hands with men, nor were they to mingle with nonrelated males.

As I have learned throughout my long experience in black-nationalist groups, religious and secular, when women are put on "pedestals," it usually means that they are being discriminated against. Cleage writes about the clearly secondary status of the women in the NOI as compared to the men, who conducted the services, decided how funds would be spent, and made the important decisions for individual Muslim families and the organization in general (1997, 102). The image of virtuous black womanhood presented to the public through Muslim displays of chivalry and propaganda often gave outsiders the impression that female Believers actually held a superior place in the temple. I found out that this was simply a mirage. The reality of NOI gender affairs and the power relations between the genders were anything but what they seemed. Cleage writes about how this pedestal upon which women had been placed was constructed by men and reports that women could be cast aside when a "female Believer needed a good smack in the face for challenging the will of her male counterpart" (1997, 102).

I never saw a woman hit by a man in the temple. But I was aware that corporal punishment was permitted. It seems, however, that physical punishment was used primarily on men, who either had to submit to whippings or be "put on punishment," which most often meant banishment from the community for a set period of time.

Elijah Muhammad taught that black women were both the mothers of civilization and "man's field to produce his nation." They were praised as the nurturers and the first teachers of the children. Modest attire and a pious, chaste demeanor were used to denote their respected place in the race. Men were to exercise power and control over women. Women were to be discouraged, even by coercion if necessary, from mixing with white men, behaving promiscuously, or committing adultery. Birth control was not permitted and abortion was prohibited for "religious reasons and to prevent the lowering of the African American birthrate" (Cleage 1997, 186).

Elijah Muhammad also taught that "men had more powerful brains than women" since men "were made to rule" (Cleage 1997, 186). He taught that the husband had to have something above and beyond the wife (be superior to her in some way—for example, financially or educationally) to ensure her comfort and psychological well-being. The Messenger's official view of women and their place in the NOI emphasized the theme of "*beauty, purity,* and *domesticity,* bound together by the vigilance and *domination of men*" (Cleage 1997, 186).

Muslims, especially women, were to marry within the group. Divorce was permitted but frowned upon. Members were punished severely for adultery, often being expelled. Modesty, thrift, and service were recommended as women's chief concern. Men were constantly reminded to protect black women (Lee 1996, 30). As one finds amongst many groups who believe that they are the chosen people, Muslim women and children were exalted for their role in continuing the race. Two priorities for the NOI were: first, training women to be good wives and mothers, and second, the education of the youth (Lee 1996, 31).

Elijah Muhammad believed that there was a birth control conspiracy in the country aimed at African Americans. Mr. Muhammad wrote the following about this conspiracy:

America desires to keep us a subjugated people. So she [the U.S.] therefore wants to stop our birth (as Pharaoh did). The birth control Law or Act of today is directed at the so-called Negroes and not at the American whites. They are seeking to destroy our race through our women. (In Lee 1996, 31)

Elijah Muhammad, like many conservative religious leaders, often blames women for the downfall of the group. He taught that while all blacks were susceptible to the devil's wiles, it was women who were his easiest target. Continuing further with this line of thinking, Mr. Muhammad taught that the serpent that tempted Eve in the Book of Genesis reappears in the Book of Revelations to tempt women again. According to the Messenger:

It is his [the devil's] first and last trick to deceive the people of God through the woman or with the woman. He is using his woman to tempt the black man. He [the white man] stands before the so-called Negro woman to deceive her by feigning love and love making with her. (Elijah Muhammad 1965, 127)

Mr. Muhammad often cited the difficulty he had recruiting women into the fold as evidence of women's resistance to the truth. At the time he wrote *Message to the Blackman* (1965), the ratio of men to women in the NOI was five to one.

Malcolm X imbibed and taught sexist views of women. Michael Eric Dyson has written several perceptive critiques about Malcolm's negative teachings on women, in spite of Malcolm's iconic status for most politically conscious African Americans. Dyson wrote:

Unfortunately, as was the case with most of his black nationalist compatriots and civil rights advocates, Malcolm cast black liberation in terms of masculine self-realization. Malcolm's zealous trumpeting of the social costs of black male cultural emasculation went hand in hand with his often aggressive, occasionally vicious, put-downs of black women. These slights of black women reflected the demonology of the Nation of Islam, which not only viewed racism as an ill from outside its group, but argued that women were a lethal source of deception and seduction from within. Hence Nation of Islam women were virtually desexualized through "modest" dress, kept under the close supervision of men, and relegated to the background while their men took center stage. Such beliefs reinforced the already inferior position of black women in black culture.... It is this aspect of Malcolm's public ministry that has been adopted by contemporary black urban youth, including rappers and filmmakers. Although Malcolm would near the end of his life renounce his sometimes-vitriolic denunciations of black women, his contemporary followers have not often followed suit. (1995, 10–11)

The Nation, like the rest of the Black Power movement, continued its subordination of women. NOI went against the grain of societal change that began in the 1970s and '80s, making no significant efforts to liberalize its doctrines or practices regarding the masculine hold on power in the movement. Quite amazingly, Cleage says he found no evidence of discontent amongst women in the movement. The Nation continued to be gender-stratified and obscenely hierarchical. Cleage says that this was the case in spite of the negligible influence of female Believers on the affairs of the NOI. His research uncovered disparaging treatment of women in some temples. According to a newsletter of the Newark temple, quoted by Cleage, a woman could be suspended for ninety days for voicing her opinion about matters outside her rightful sphere (1997, 242). He also reports cases, particularly in the South, where ministers laughed in the faces of women who complained of abuse at the hands of their Muslim husbands. He also learned that older women members informed the national headquarters in Chicago about beatings inflicted upon female members, but apparently to little avail. Cleage says that there were no reports of such beatings amongst New York Muslims. He reports that Muhammad was not against corporal punishment of followers, even women who did not know their place (1997, 242). The leaders were able to manipulate the movement's religious symbols in such a way as to subordinate gender, age, and personality conflicts to the racial socioeconomic and educational commonalities that bonded the members together. There was definitely a "quasi-national culture" and "consciousness" among converts that stressed absolute loyalty to Elijah Muhammad, as well as selfless service to the NOI (1997, 102).

Conclusion

Elijah Muhammad and his NOI were dedicated to equating blackness with power and initiative. He had a prolonged impact on black consciousness unlike any other individual or group. For the Believers as well as the thousands of nonmembers, Elijah Muhammad and the NOI stood for black self-help, cultural regeneration (or redefinition), and moral living. All the subsequent Black Power and black-nationalist movements, writings, and activities have been influenced by Elijah Muhammad and the NOI.

In the NOI as in the Black Power movement, black power most often did not extend to black women. The official policy of respecting and protecting black womanhood was meant to seem attractive to converts, but appearances were often misleading, as it masked gross gender inequalities and biases. Unfortunately, much of the misogyny and sexism of the group has carried over into the African American Sunni Islamic groups of today. I continue to be shocked and displeased at how, in most African American mosques with which I am acquainted, women are marginalized and forced to submit to male authority in their religious and personal lives. Erroneous interpretations of the Qur'an and selective usages of hadith that support gender segregation and subordination now justify such marginalization and subjugation.[8]

Notes

1. The American Colonization Society was established in 1816 by white Americans for the purpose of making a homeland for free black Americans. These white colonialists were viewed skeptically by African Americans, as they tended not to speak out against racism and slavery in America.

2. Salim Muwakkil notes that Richard Turner and other scholars who have assessed the NOI's teachings say that these teachings have to be understood in context. "Fard's race-based depictions of the Islamic message were made necessary by African Americans' peculiar racial history. The mythic ideal that placed blond, blue-eyed northern Europeans at the pinnacle of a racial hierarchy and black people at the nadir was the guiding principle in Western racial thinking.... Before Fard could restore his converts' knowledge of their 'true names, history, religion and

ethnicity,' he had to destroy that aspect of the white race's invincibility that made black inferiority and self-hatred possible on a deep psychological level" (2002).

3. NOI Muslims fasted during the period of the year that included Christmas and New Year's. This was our Ramadan. One can see the psychological motive in scheduling the Fast during the time when most Americans are spending for Christmas and preparing for their biggest meal of the year.

4. Of course, exercising leadership in SNCC as a woman was also beset with difficulties, but nothing like what I experienced in the NOI.

5. I must admit to being very annoyed that these two female institutions, MGT and GCC (Muslim Girls Training and General Civilization Course), referred to those taking the classes as "girls," given that many of the people in them were women

and not girls, women who were sometimes senior citizens.

6. What the author calls gymnastics was really just quasi-military-style drilling. Women were not taught martial arts, as were the men who made up the Fruit of Islam (FOI), the men's elite security forces, who could put fear and trembling into Believers and nonbelievers who ran afoul of the NOI. Some of the FOI also served as a "morality police" who kept the Believers, especially the Sisters, in line.

7. Sonsyrea talks about the humiliation showered upon one woman who could not afford to purchase an official uniform, and wore a homemade one instead, by the "Sister Captain," who wielded considerable power over the women under her command. I rarely wore the one official uniform that I owned, as I preferred long African print attire, which I always wore in those days. The Sister Captains resented me for this and the fact that I was permitted to get away with it. There were two reasons: In Atlanta where I joined, there was a real effort to recruit college-trained persons like myself and my partner. Plus the fact that we were civil rights veterans gave us a special status too. Secondly, I was the sister-in-law of a high-up official and no one would "mess" with someone who was related to someone high up in the hierarchy.

8. I have written about this earlier in two articles (2000 and 2003).

References

Baer, H. A., and M. Singer. 1992. *African American Religion in the Twentieth Century: Varieties of Protest and Accommodation.* Knoxville: University of Tennessee Press.

Cleage, C. A., III. 1997. *An Original Man: The Life and Times of Elijah Muhammad.* New York: St Martin's Press.

Diouf, S. A. 1998. *Servants of Allah: African Muslims Enslaved in the Americas.* New York: New York University Press.

Dyson, M. E. 1995. *Making Malcolm—The Myth & Meaning of Malcolm X.* New York and Oxford: Oxford University Press.

Elijah Muhammad. 1965. *Message to the Blackman in America.* Chicago: Muhammad Mosque of Islam, No. 2.

———. 1967. *How to Eat to Live.* Book 1. Reprint, Newport News, Va.: National Newport News and Commentator.

Essien-Udom, E. U. 1962. *Black Nationalism:*

A Search for Identity in America. Chicago: University of Chicago Press.

Lee, M. F. 1996. *The Nation of Islam—An American Millenarian Movement.* Syracuse, N.Y.: Syracuse University Press.

Lincoln, C. E., and L. M. Mamiya, eds. 1984. *Race, Religion and the Continuing America Dilemma.* New York: Hill and Wang.

Long, C. H. 1997. "Perspectives for a Study of African American Religion in the United States." In *African American Religion: Interpretative Essays in History and Culture,* ed. T. E. Fulop and A. J. Raboteau. New York and London: Routledge.

Marable, M. 1981. *Blackwater: Historical Studies in Race, Class Consciousness and Revolution.* Dayton, Ohio: Black Praxis.

Muwakkil, S. 2002. "The Forgotten History of Islam in America." *In These Times* 26 (21).

Simmons, G. Z. 2000. "Striving for Muslim Women's Rights—Before and Beyond Beijing: An African American Perspective." In *Windows of Faith,* ed. G. Webb, pp. 197–223. Syracuse, N.Y.: Syracuse University Press.

———. 2003. "Are We Up to the Challenge? The Need for a Radical Re-Ordering of the Islamic Discourse on Women." In *Progressive Muslims: On Justice, Gender and Pluralism,* ed. O. Safi, pp. 235–248. London: One World Press.

Smith, J. I. 1999. *Islam in America.* New York: Columbia University Press.

Tate, S. 1997. *Little X—Growing Up in the Nation of Islam.* San Francisco: Harper San Francisco.

Turner, R. B. 1997. *Islam in the African American Experience.* Bloomington and Indianapolis: Indiana University Press.

Watson, G. L. 1973. "Social Structure and Social Movements: The Black Muslims in the U.S.A. and the Rastafarians in Jamaica." In *British Journal of Sociology* 24: 188–204.

Wilmore, G. 1983. *Black Religion and Black Radicalism.* Maryknoll, N.Y.: Orbis.

CHAPTER 8

Feminism and Conversion
Comparing British, Dutch, and South African Life Stories

Margot Badran

A signal foundational text of Islamic feminism was written by a woman convert to Islam. The text is *Qur'an and Woman*. It was first published in 1992 and was republished in 1999. The author is Amina Wadud, an African American and a professor of Islamic theology who calls herself a scholar-activist.[1] Feminism and conversion to Islam, however, have remained virtually unlinked as subjects of analysis in both the scholarly and popular literature. Indeed, they have constituted rigidly separate categories of inquiry, almost as if they were antithetical.

The spread of conversions to Islam, especially in countries of the West, is a phenomenon of the late twentieth century continuing its rapid growth into the present century, with women constituting the largest numbers of these new Muslims. A concurrent phenomenon is the global rise of Islamic feminism, a discourse, grounded in the Qur'an, that articulates full gender equality and social justice across the public and private spheres, and activisms based upon this. Among Muslims it is the cutting-edge feminism, pushing inquiry and activism into new zones. Conversion to Islam and Islamic feminism address intersecting religious, societal, and cultural needs, and both raise hard questions. If the present numbers of women converts are large—and exceed the numbers of male converts worldwide—the numbers of Islamic feminists are small, but they are vocal and growing. The acceleration of Muslim conversions and the rise of Islamic feminism both occurred in the wake of the surfacing of political Islam and subsequent broader Islamic cultural revival. Conversions to Islam and Islamic feminism have also spread during a moment when the "new racism," or "cultural racism," and more specifically Islamophobia, are on the rise in the West.

The gender projects of Islamic feminism and political Islam are diametrically opposed. The implementation of the Qur'anic message of gender equality and social justice that Islamic feminism supports is challenged by political Islam, which promotes a patriarchal gender system upholding the hegemony of men over women that is anchored in male dominance in the family and extends into society. While large-scale conversion to Islam predominates in the West, political Islam originates in the old Muslim-majority societies of Africa and Asia, although its outreach is now global. The current "cultural racism" and Islamophobia have predominantly, but not exclusively, surfaced in the West. Islamic feminism arose and continues to spread simultaneously in both the West and in old established Muslim societies. Iran, for example, is an important pioneering site of the production of Islamic feminist discourse. Islamic feminism, with its calls for the implementation of gender equality and social justice, is anathema to the projects of patriarchal political Islam and of cultural racism/Islamophobia, wherever they may exist.

I come to the subject of conversion and feminism as a historian and gender studies scholar with a longtime focus on feminisms among Muslims and others in the Middle East, and a more recent concern with the production of Islamic feminism(s) globally. My contribution is based on oral histories and open-ended interviews with Muslim women converts, methods I used in my research on the rise of Muslim women's feminism in the Middle East more than three decades ago. Many of us pioneering in the new field of women's history in the late 1960s and the 1970s (in my case, the history of Egyptian women's feminism) sought oral accounts from women on their own lives, as women and their experience were largely missing in the written record and thus "hidden from history." Today, Muslim women converts and their accounts are not hidden; to the contrary, they are highly visible (van Nieuwkerk, this volume). What *is* still largely hidden are converts' feminist stories.

In this chapter I examine Muslim women converts' approaches to Islamic feminism fully aware that I am moving in uncharted waters. This exploratory look at Muslim women converts' engagements with feminism connects Muslim conversion literature with the literature on Islamic feminism. I undertake a comparative study moving beyond the usual practice of examining conversion within national or regional frameworks and the tendency to focus on conversion mainly in the West.[2] The subject of feminism and conversion is part of the story of the politics of new Muslim communities in the West, of new Muslim sociologies in the West, indeed of new Wests. It is enmeshed with identity politics and citizens' rights. It connects with the story of migration and concomitant cultural transfer and cultural re-creation. It is part of the story of the contemporary production of Islamic knowledge at different locations around the globe. It is integral to the story of building modern progressive democracies in the East and South. It is about refiguring new publics both in Western countries and in Muslim societies in the

East and South. I intend to suggest new directions and new ways of thinking about Muslim female conversion and about Islamic feminism in multiple contexts.

I investigate convert women's approaches to feminism through personal interviews and oral histories—which together constitute part of the life stories—of a select group of women. I deliberately privilege the voices of the women converts claiming that both tone and content are illuminating. I suggest that these women display approaches to issues of agency and authority, and gender-progressive readings of Islam, that are ascendant. I find that they are gesturing toward Islamic feminism and/or are in Islamic feminist space in different ways. I do not pretend that the women presented here are representative of the majority of converts at this moment in history, but see them as being in the vanguard of a coming "revolution" in gender justice as idea and practice in Islam. I am eager to chart early movement in that direction.[3]

My basic argument is simple: that in the nexus of living, believing, and (continual) learning, some Muslim women converts come to Islamic feminism. Analytically I distinguish three stages: the path to conversion, the moment of embrace, and postconversion experience. While the three may be seen as distinct, they also form a continuum, with the first two stages impacting postconversion experience. In the conversion process and postconversion experience I look at the relational and rational elements (Allievi 1998) and intertwined issues of agency and authority, finding in the complicated mix keys to understanding converts' moves to Islamic feminism.

I argue that the logical and lived contradictions that women encounter after conversion, along with unfulfilled promises, impel some new Muslims to return to the Qur'an for inspiration and answers and that this, along with other readings on women and Islam, pushes them toward Islamic feminism. It is not coincidental that for both convert women and Islamic feminists the Qur'an is the central text. In analyzing the women converts' approaches to Islam and gender, I work with the notion of a "prior text" (Wadud 1999) and what I choose to call a "missing prior text." Some convert women bring with them a "prior text of feminism" or progressive gender ideas. All convert women bring with them a "missing prior text" of Islam (a belief in, and all that goes into shaping everyday ideas and practices of born Muslims enculturated into, the religion). Convert women, I argue, often experience contradictions between the Islamic ideal and its practice more acutely, or in a more raw way, than many born Muslims, for whom these contradictions may have become "naturalized" over time. Converts have not inherited coping mechanisms, thus compelling some to work through these inconsistencies. Yet, I hasten to stress, there are born Muslims in old Muslim-majority societies in Africa and Asia who *have* felt the contradictions and injustices, as attested to by their feminist discourse and activism (Badran 1995; Badran and Cooke 1990, 2004). They have dared to question "naturalized" patriarchal discourses and acts and have subjected them to scrutiny within their own inherited systems, as have growing numbers of born Muslims living in the West (Barlas 2002).

It is crucial to observe the contexts in which convert women's Islamic feminism emerges. It will be observed in this chapter that the converts from the United Kingdom, the Netherlands, and South Africa *au fond* confront the same basic issue of the conflict between the Qur'anic ideals and Muslim practice that sustains patriarchal hegemony. But there are different ways this plays out. In new Muslim communities in the West, in the United Kingdom or the Netherlands, for example, Muslim women converts get caught up in issues of identity and identity politics vis-à-vis their larger societies. Their marriages to new Europeans, who most frequently are born Muslims, and their repositioning inside their own societies are complicating elements. There are no large, organized movements of Islamic feminism on the ground with which new Muslim women in the countries of Europe—in the United Kingdom or the Netherlands, for example—may associate. In South Africa, on the other hand, there is an organized, militant movement of Islamic feminism that not only can convert women join but into which they are welcomed.

I organize my chapter into the following sections: converts who tell stories; methodology, concepts, and definitions; agency activated/deactivated; authority asserted/suppressed; the nexus of living, believing, and learning (including information-seeking, self-help, and awareness, a Dutch story; developing consciousness, organizing converts, a British story; and double embrace, a South African story); and a final section, new Muslims for a new Islam.

Converts Who Tell Stories

My interest in converts and feminism goes back more than a decade, when I began to speculate that those coming newly to Islam without old cultural baggage might be less likely to get stalled in repetitive debates over terminology, cultural imperialism, and authenticity, as so often happens to those born into Islam in older Muslim societies. Perhaps, I thought, new Muslims would be able to tackle core issues and thus move the debates forward, rescuing discussion of Islam and feminism from the quagmire in which it so often gets stuck. My desire to investigate feminism among converts was unwittingly jump-started in South Africa in 2001 and 2002 while I was taking oral histories as part of my research on Islamic feminism. At one point I noticed that women converts were among the most articulate and committed exponents of Islamic feminism. The stories of three of them form part of this chapter. Earlier, at an international conference of Muslim women in Khartoum in 1996 organized by women affiliated with the Islamist regime in the Sudan, I met two British converts and discovered through private conversation how they combined a commitment to Islam and feminist sensibility. I met one of them again recently, and she in turn introduced me to another British woman, who I discovered only in the course of our meeting was not a convert but on the path to conversion. The stories of these two women also inform this chapter. While all of the above encounters were serendipitous, my meetings with Dutch women were planned. I took the opportunity, while in Leiden continuing my work on comparative Islamic feminisms at the Institute for the Study of Islam in the Modern World (ISIM), to talk with Dutch converts about Islam and feminism. I spontaneously met some converts at lectures and events and deliberately sought out other women reputed to be either feminists or feminist-friendly.[4]

I conducted conversations and took oral histories from nine women in 2002 and 2003. All the converts came to Islam between 1995 and 2000, except for one who embraced Islam in 1986. I recognized that the woman still on the conversion path might offer the fresh insights of one moving toward Islam and therefore have included her in this exploration. When I speak of the converts in this chapter, I refer to the group of eight, but when I speak of the women who gave oral histories and interviews, I refer to the group of nine. The converts I interviewed come from the Netherlands, South Africa, and the United Kingdom. Thus, they all belong to Muslim minority societies. However, South African Muslims constitute long-established communities, while Muslims in the Netherlands and the United Kingdom belong to communities of recent formation. South Africa experienced colonial rule that ended only recently, while the Netherlands and Britain were colonizers and each formed part of the colonial domination of South Africa. Among the group of women interviewed, two (from South Africa) call themselves "colored" (in South African terminology, meaning of mixed race), while the others are identified as "white."[5] Race-ing also enters into the conversion stories in the West, where

Muslims of immigrant origins are constructed as "black" or "brown," with this coding casting a long shadow. In the South African case, the one white and two "colored" women entered the larger Indian/Malay Muslim community, whereas the African converts, who are numerically predominant overall among Muslim converts, tend mainly (but not always) to become part of African Muslim communities.[6] Race thus plays out differently in the case of Muslim converts in South Africa.

The converts are all well educated, most having taken degrees from universities or other institutions of higher learning, while two are presently completing university degrees. Apart from the two who are still students, the women are all professionally employed, except for one who has in recent years turned to full-time activism. Seven of the eight convert women were previously Roman Catholics and one formerly Anglican, as is the woman on the conversion path, while two come from nonreligious backgrounds. One of the converts initially embraced Sunni Islam and then turned to Shi'i Islam. The others are Sunni Muslims.

The nine women represent two generations. Among the younger women (born in the 1970s) are the three South Africans and two Dutch women. The earlier generation (born in the 1950s and '60s) includes two Dutch women and two British women. Two of the four Dutch women and the two British women belong to the earlier generation, which came of age while second-wave feminist movements were under way in their countries. Two of the Dutch women came of age in the postfeminist era. The South Africans, who grew up under apartheid, were young women when Islamic feminism emerged after apartheid ended.

Methodology, Concepts, and Definitions

I had had discussions individually or in groups and meetings with five of the women prior to the arranged sessions. These sessions were a cross between oral history–telling and interviews. I had made it clear in the process of setting up each meeting and again at the start of each session that I wanted to probe the connection between conversion and feminism. The conversations were highly fluid, interactive, and open-ended. I encouraged women to share biographical information, to tell the story of their conversion, and to speak about feminism per se and specifically Islamic feminism from both general and personal perspectives. In this way conversations about conversion and feminism, which typically have been kept separate, now converged.[7] It was my intention to stimulate candid debate. During the sessions I would throw out questions and views as a way to actively contribute to the discussions myself. At some point in our conversations I would explicitly ask if my talking partner considered herself an Islamic feminist, a question I knew would yield far more than a yes or no answer. In my long years of research I have observed that a researcher's active participation in the give-and-take of discussion yields multiple and often unexpected insights and information, and constitutes a form of giving and not just taking.

It is important to clarify my conceptual framework and terminology. I refer to the phenomenon of taking on, or embracing, a new religion, in this case, Islam, as "conversion" and the individual as a "convert." I do so because these are the ordinary terms in English, remaining in wide use and also applicable across a spectrum of religions. As conversion and converts are specifically situated, we should be attentive to the variable nuancing of these terms. Many Muslims use the term "revert," instead of "convert," to capture the sense of a person returning or reverting to Islam (as the original "religious state" of being).[8] Van Nieuwkerk uses the term "dormant Muslims" to capture the sense of awakening or recognizing that one has been Muslim all along (this volume). Among the nine women I interviewed, the South Africans most firmly adhered to the term revert. In this contribution I generally use the term convert as generically descriptive. But I also use the term "new Muslim," in contradistinction to "born Muslim" (or old Muslim, original Muslim), especially when wishing to stress the sense of "coming to" and the notion of "newness" as opposed to inheriting the faith.[9] The term new Muslim has gained wide acceptance in Britain.[10]

I discovered in the course of my research that the term "Muslima" is widely used in the Netherlands by female Muslim converts and local scholars whether speaking in Dutch or English. The Arabic loanword "Muslima" marks at once gender and religion. In the United Kingdom the term "Muslima" is not ordinarily used in English speech. The term Muslim is gender-neutral in English, both in keeping with standard grammar and with a feminist practice of degendering terms previously gendered (actor for actress, Jew for Jewess, etc.).

It is useful to note how the terms "foreign" and "indigenous" are bound up in issues of belonging and identity.[11] That which is strange, odd, different, not of or belonging to, outside, etc., is foreign. In the modern political vocabulary foreign indicates a noncitizen and is widely used to signify a person or groups coming from outside a particular nation. Islam and Muslims are still widely

perceived in Europe and the rest of the West as foreign, or in need of "natu-
ralization." This thinking marks, or marks off, Muslim immigrants and their
descendants in Europe, thus foreignizing that which has become part of the
polity. Native European or Western converts are also foreignized to a degree
by their conversion to Islam. It is important to bear in mind, then, that the
terms Muslim and Muslima are thus not simply religious markers but mark
the foreign in countries of the West. Van Nieuwkerk, for example, observes:
"Islam is perceived as the ultimate Other in contrast to Dutch national identity" (this volume). In South Africa, where there are old established Muslim
communities, being or becoming Muslim is not "foreignizing." We need to be
attentive to how women converts announce and construct their identities in
Western societies and beyond the West.

The term feminism has elicited wide debate and controversy among Muslims inside and outside the West. The rise of feminism in the West, occurring as it did during the colonial moment, has left a lasting taint. The rise
of feminism in the "East" (a construct including countries of Asia and Africa), and specifically in old Muslim societies during the colonial moment
(and sometimes before), firmly grounded in Islamic modernist discourse
and militant nationalist anticolonial discourse, has not left its own mark.
Lack of knowledge of Muslim women's homegrown historical and contemporary feminisms reinforces stereotyping of Islam by others as well as self-
stereotyping practices. Westerners have typically held that Muslims cannot
possibly generate a feminism of their own, because the underlying principles of equality and the gender-just notions implicit to feminism are alien
(or anathema) to Islam, which is in essence a patriarchal religion. For them,
"feminism and Islam" is an oxymoron. Meanwhile, Muslims who are unable
or unwilling to unpack the term feminism, who perhaps suffer from a "fear
of feminism," and who overlook feminist history in Muslim societies make
this claim as well.

I use the generic word "feminism" as an analytical construct capturing the
basic understanding that all human beings are equal, that women have been
discriminated against on the basis of gender; a rejection of this; and moves
to put things right. The term feminism has been continually defined and
redefined since it was first coined in French in the late nineteenth century
and quickly spread to English, Arabic (by the 1920s), and other languages.
Muslim women have been part of the process of defining and activating feminism as an explicit term since the early twentieth century, and even earlier as
an "idea without a name" (Badran 1995; Badran and Cooke 2004).

We can distinguish two kinds of feminism that women in old Muslim societies have generated: secular feminism and Islamic feminism. Secular feminism emerged in late-nineteenth-century Egypt (a pioneering site) in the context of modernization, Islamic reformism, and nationalist struggle against colonialism. This feminism drew upon secular nationalist and Islamic modernist discourse, and included among its adherents Muslim and non-Muslim women as co-nationals. Secular feminists in Muslim societies demanded full equality in the public sphere, calling for access to education, work, and political participation as part of women's self-development and the empowering of the entire society in the decolonizing process. Within this feminist framework women accepted the notion of complementarity (now called "equity") in the private sphere, upholding the notion of male predominance, regarded as a benevolent predominance, in the family. They called upon men to fulfill their duties, protecting and providing in ways that upheld the rights and dignity of women. The secular mode of feminism, accepting complementarianism in the private sphere, predominated throughout most of the twentieth century.

Around the 1990s, some Muslim journalists, writers, and activists began to refer to a newly emergent form of feminism as "Islamic feminism." This represents a paradigm shift in Muslims' feminism from a feminism (secular feminism) in which Islamic modernism constituted one discursive element to a feminism (Islamic feminism) grounded exclusively, or primarily, in Islamic discourse taking the Qur'an as its central text. The fundamental methodological tools of Islamic feminism are *ijtihad*, an independent rational search for meanings in Islam's sacred texts (the Qur'an and Sunna, or the sayings and practices of the Prophet Muhammad), and more specifically, *tafsir*, interpretation of the Qur'an. Muslim women as exegetes draw upon core Qur'anic principles to articulate an unequivocal theory of equality of all human beings *(insan)*. This equality cannot be qualified by gender, race, or ethnicity and cannot be a "situated equality" operative only in the public sphere, but by definition transcends constructions of a public/private divide. Only equality is equality; equity is not equality. The new interpreters demonstrate that the Qur'an recognizes difference(s) of gender, race, etc., but does not invoke difference to promote inequality. Equality does not negate difference, but it does negate power differentials built on difference. Equality does not subscribe to the notion of ordained roles for genders or races. Within the framework of equality, humans make choices; they shape and reshape roles and functions. Islamic feminism includes a theoretical and activist dimension, the latter grounded and deriving from the former (Webb 2000). Islamic feminism is a global phenomenon; it is part of *global Islam* and of *global feminism.* Islamic feminism, I argue, will come to be considered as part of the polyvocal global articulation(s) of feminism and recognized for making its distinctive contributions to wider feminist debates and theoretical formulations. However, this is to get ahead of the story.

I want to be careful in drawing attention to the distinction between feminism, as an analytical term, and feminist as a term of identity. Many Muslims identify *with* feminism as an analytical construct and act upon this, but do not identify themselves *as* feminists. Early last century, when Muslim women began to formulate their feminism as a named construct (in Egypt, etc.), they also proudly wore the feminist label. By contrast, from the end of that same century, Muslims who are credited with creating foundational Islamic feminist texts have been reluctant to name their new interpretive work "Islamic feminism" and decline to name themselves "Islamic feminists." However, debates and positions are not static. More recently, some allow that their work may be seen as "Islamic feminism," but continue to resist the Islamic feminist label (Wadud 1999). Among both born Muslims and converts, women who feel it imperative (and this is especially true of converts) to publicly declare their Islamic identity shrink from publicly declaring a feminist identity, even though they may identify *with* feminism.

Gender-egalitarian readings of Islam as elaborated by progressive women interpreters are new, coupled with the insistence that equality and social justice be practiced or lived, and not simply saluted as ideas. Islamic feminism, articulating the highest ideals of Islam as refracted through multiple lenses, including the lens of gender, is unusual and unsettling. Patriarchal readings of Islam have a long history and have been so entrenched in classic *fiqh,* or jurisprudence, in *tafsir,* or interpretation, and other religious sciences that they have become "naturalized." Patriarchal readings of Islam still appear to most, it seems, as "Islam" itself.

Converts to Islam, as to other religions, tend (especially initially) to access or absorb the "mainstream," or conventional, version of the faith. Typically, converts embrace Islam while their knowledge of the religion is still in the early stages. Some oscillate between a commonsense notion of gender equality that must logically be part of Islam (if Islam is a religion of justice) and a system of inequality into which they are introduced. Van Nieuwkerk observed that while convert women "hold that the sexes are of equal value, they do not consider them of equal nature" and that they find the notion of "complementarity" congenial (this volume). Most of the Swedish converts Roald met found the Swedish state-endorsed notion of equal (gender) opportunity *(jamstalldhet)* in the public sphere compatible with their ideas of family-based gender equity.

I observed in my conversations with the converts I met that they were in Islamic feminist space or gesturing toward Islamic feminism. I detected that they held a strong sense of Qur'an-endorsed equality of Muslims and of all *insan* that was not qualified by biological or race difference, or any other kinds of difference. I did not see that they looked at biological difference between males and females as positing fixed, rigid roles for human beings. The converts with whom I spoke had strong commonsense "prior 'feminist' texts" and a commonsense, rational approach to Islam that left little room for inequality, gender or otherwise. Their readings of Islam often affirmed this, yet the corpus of (conventional) knowledge they were given, or were able to access, might also disrupt, or shake, their commonsense notions and their own interpretation. But out of turbulence can come new plateaus of understanding.

In a chapter on feminism and conversion it is helpful at the outset to clarify how the women interviewed deal with the issue of feminism and identity. Five identify themselves as feminists (two South Africans, two Dutch, and one Briton—the woman who is on the conversion path). The other four identify with feminism; that is, they live by it and express it, but prefer not to take on the label. While three of the women interviewed were feminists before they were Muslims (along with the woman on the conversion path), the entire group of nine now locate themselves within the circumference of Islamic feminism.

Agency Activated/Deactivated

In converting, women exercise agency, bravely and decisively, in going against the grain of their background, family, and culture and in opting for something strange and new. If the degree of agency is measured by resolve in the face of family and societal reactions to conversion, this agency is more intensified among the women in Europe. The difference in reactions to conversion may be explained by the traditional negative Western stereotypes of Islam and especially the stereotypes of "women in Islam." This has been exacerbated in recent history by the identification of Islam as a religion of poor "black" immigrants. Meanwhile, the contention of mainstream second-wave feminism in the West in the 1970s and 1980s that secularism and feminism must go hand in hand and that religion is irredeemably patriarchal has contributed to the shrill responses to Western women's conversions to Islam.

In South Africa there appears to be an absence of highly negative feelings toward Islam and toward women who choose to embrace the religion. The antiapartheid struggle and the current project of constructing the new South Africa must be among the explanatory factors. Strongly held ideas about equality and justice (for so long hijacked in South Africa) in this highly pluralistic society create a different public space and a different public ethic. Moreover, South Africa is a more religious society than most societies in the West; people are more "at home" with religion and certainly display less religiophobia. While the South African converts clearly exercised agency in opting for Islam, they did this in a less hostile social environment.

Convert women's strongest expression of agency typically occurs in the process of coming to Islam and at the moment of conversion. This is certainly the time when Muslims around them support their assertion of independent agency. Women as would-be converts are encouraged to exercise their rational judgment and free will in making the choice to opt for Islam. Thereafter, it appears in most cases (within the context of a patriarchally inflected Islam) that the agency or free will of the female convert is reduced, muted, subdued, or managed. The new Muslim is now encouraged to defer or submit to the inherited (patriarchal) tradition of religious thinking (as mediated through specific cultures) and as a wife to submit to the dictates of the patriarchal family. Marriage complicates further the question of agency and conversion. Seven out of the eight converts in this study are married. All but one adopted Islam *before* marriage, while two took the *shahada*, or affirmation of faith, and marriage vows at the same time. In five out of seven cases the women converted, not only before marrying, but also before meeting their future husbands, thus disrupting a common pattern, or widely presumed pattern, of a future husband ushering a woman toward conversion. The married converts all took care to explain that they adopted Islam on their own initiative.

In pursuing the discussion of agency, conversion, and marriage, I focus for a moment on women converts in European contexts. First I would like to draw attention to how immigrants and new citizens in European countries are thrust into a position of being expected to adjust or fit in. The challenge for them becomes how to maintain their identity and pride or self-respect— in short, their distinctiveness or difference—and remain an equal part of the larger whole. Second, when European women, say Dutch or British women, convert to Islam, they enter new and unfamiliar public space within their own society. Moreover, they enter a new space without leaving the old space and now must straddle the two while adjusting to life inside the new space. When the convert woman marries a Muslim, she is further repositioned within the framework of the Muslim patriarchal family, allegedly ordained by Islam. She is positioned as "needing tutelage," much as Muslims in general in the West, including her spouse, are seen as "needing tutelage" to be shaped into good citizens of their adopted countries.

The veil plays a role in the issue of agency. Seven of the eight converts I talked with wear the veil, adopting various modes of covering. (The one who does not cover is also, interestingly, the only one who did not change her name.) Some believe it is religiously incumbent upon them to veil (cover their head and wear loose, enveloping clothing). Others freely admitted that they do not believe that covering is, strictly speaking, necessary from a religious point of view. They explain that they cover in order to make a public declaration of their new identity; they want to announce themselves as Muslims and to be seen as Muslims. This is in part to identify *with* the Muslim community and in part to make a statement *to* the wider society. Some women converts explain that "covering" is also an answer back to society that they are *not* oppressed by wearing the veil. Through the public display of a religious marker Western convert women are not just identifying with a group, but they are also assertively putting religion back into public space.

In assuming distinctive public markers, these women positioned themselves *by choice* as "outsiders," very much as most immigrant Muslims in European societies are positioned *without choice* through physical characteristics associated with Muslims (racial profiling) and distinctive demeanor as "outsiders" (or "outside insiders"). The converts find it important to announce their new identity or "go public" to signal that Islam is more than simply a personal matter in the narrow, privatized way characteristic of religion in Western society.

The question of agency with respect to conversion and marriage, as well as the practice of veiling, plays out differently in the South African context. I have already noted the more positive general climate regarding Islam and Muslim converts in South Africa. Drawing upon my interviews and wider observation, it appears that in South Africa when a woman convert marries a Muslim she does not face strong negative reaction from society. South African women converts tend to marry compatriots with deep roots in the country, so the societal and marital tensions surrounding marriage with an immigrant or second-generation citizen are typically absent.

The veil as a form of head covering seems a far less charged issue in South Africa than in European societies. In part, this may be because the practice of head covering for women (and for men) is widespread in African society. A large variety of headgear forms part of the ordinary visual landscape in South Africa. However, when television presenter Khadija Magardie earlier, as a university student, took up the *chador*, covering from head to toe in an enveloping black cloth, following her switch from Sunni to Shi'i Islam, this did cause a stir, including among other Muslims. This might illustrate the "stretch point" that exists in any society when dress and mode of presentation exceed certain limits.

If agency is associated with daring and bravery, more was demanded of women converts in the West than in South Africa. But if agency is about making independent decisions and taking charge of one's life, all of the women display a strong sense of agency in opting for Islam and in confronting gender issues in Islam.

Authority Asserted/Suppressed

When one assumes agency does one assume authority? Does one reject an old authority and obey a new authority, and does one freely choose that new authority? Can one participate in the construction of a new authority?[12] A woman's self-agency is encouraged on the path to conversion and applauded at the time of conversion, as I have remarked. I also pointed out that, after conversion, the new Muslim becomes more "managed and monitored." Does the convert, in now experiencing diminished agency, simply bow before a new authority? Can she decide who and what that new authority is? Converts, and those who encourage conversion, stress the rationality of Islam and the notion that the religion is accessible to all without the need for mediators. Islam endorses *ijtihad*, individual investigation of sacred texts. Yet the independent intellectual exploration encouraged in women while getting to Islam often becomes discouraged upon arrival.

From my conversations I observed ways authority is connected with knowledge. When I asked Dutch convert Ceylan Pektas-Weber, president of a national converts' association called Al-Nisa, to define what constitutes authority, she spontaneously replied: "Knowledge is authority." Since apprehending Islam as a rational religion was important to the women on the conversion path, and remains important, they continue their search for knowledge, which typically began with reading the Qur'an as the ultimate authority.

In Islam there is no "theological" need for mediators (although they may be sought); *ijtihad* is a legitimate practice, God is the ultimate authority, and individuals may apprehend Islam through direct access to God's book, the Qur'an. Some women who started their journey to Islam reading the Qur'an for themselves continue their journey toward knowledge by carrying on with reading the Qur'an for themselves, even as they seek knowledge from "authorities" who know more. This need not preempt the women's independent ability to evaluate or to make judgments on their own. Some converts get overtaken, or temporarily deflected, by patriarchal authorities exerting their power and imposing their interpretations in the name of Islam. This occurs especially in the early postconversion period. Convert women's stands against patriarchal insertions into Islamic thinking and their experiences of patriarchal pressures in their everyday lives are the beginning of the move toward a more gender-just and socially just interpretation of Islam that is the project of Islamic feminism.

The Nexus among Living, Believing, and Learning: Gravitating toward Islamic Feminism

New Muslims may *learn* about the religion of Islam as an abstraction and *think* about it in idealized terms, but they *live* it (or strive to live up to it or live it to its fullest potential) in concrete, everyday ways and do so as embodied beings, in the case at hand, specifically as women. Converts' biographies and personal narratives provide a good way to explore the nexus between living and believing, on the one hand, and the production of Islamic feminism, on the other.

Allievi (1998) notes that converts (men and women) come to Islam through relational *or* rational paths. In the case of the women converts with whom I spoke, the relational and rational paths converge. It is a "deep convergence," I would argue, that makes these women "Islamic feminists." The convergence that was salient in their journey to Islam remains crucial in their lives as new Muslims, albeit not without tensions.[13]

The relational element is highly significant on the path to conversion. Muslim women converts are allured by what they observe and experience of "lived Islam" through Muslims with whom they come into contact: university friends, other circles of friends and associates, among whom not infrequently are future spouses. Camaraderie, sensitivity, kindness, generosity, caring, and concern for others, seen as Muslim qualities, are highly attractive to potential converts. Interestingly, love, once a central and defining idea of Christianity, but now often lost, seems to be found again in Islam.

The rational is likewise important during women's journeys to conversion, when Islam is presented as a rational religion. While Köse and Loewenthal (2000) report that "affectional motifs" are found more in women's conversion stories than in men's, in my smaller sample of "feminist converts" (and broader observation), I found the rational to be a strong element that converged with the relational. Most of the women I met spoke about reading the Qur'an and found it rational; they said that it "made sense." Some of the converts read feminist studies of Islamic religious sources and were persuaded by what they found. Some, in reading conservative interpretations of Islam, found them logically wanting. In general, for most converts, and this includes the women with whom I spoke, religious knowledge acquired through rational inquiry is limited prior to the moment of conversion. It is helpful in considering the rational to distinguish between cognitive and intuitive elements. At the moment of embrace the intuitive dimension of the rational predominates. The "feminist converts" I met share with other converts an epiphany, or moment of exaltation, when they "suddenly" come to Islam. Dutch university student of religion Inji Icli referred to the phenomenon as "a tight bud bursting into flower." Malika Ndlovu, who calls herself a revert, experienced "an inexplicable familiarity" and called it a "coming home," the precise phrase Mariette Bogaers used. Rahma Bavelaar said: "It just felt right. It was as simple as that." Pektas-Weber expressed it as "falling in love." For all of the converts I met, who display a strong amalgam of the intellectual and the practical, the moment of conversion was intensely intuitive and emotional. Perhaps the metaphor of falling in love and marrying works well to explain the larger process: the big step is taken because it feels right and the practical details are worked out later. Conversion for the women I met constituted an unconditional embrace.

I have spoken of the path to conversion and the moment of embrace as a prelude to the postconversion period, when converts begin to experience lives as new Muslims. At this moment most women converts splice themselves into conventional (Muslim) patterns, culturally "tried and true" in countries of origin and transplanted to new European locations, or in the case of South Africa they enter older, locally established Muslim communities. Women converts enter new spaces that, as Talal Asad puts it in another context, "make different kinds of knowledge, action and desire possible."[14]

Seeking Knowledge, Self-Help, and Awareness: Dutch Stories
In this and the following two subsections I give slices of women's postconversion stories. Not having been socialized into the religion, converts must

find their *own* way. I now turn to Dutch stories that in certain ways will find resonance with the experience of other European converts.

To those on the path to conversion, members of the community are key in the relational equation; after conversion, often soon followed by marriage, the Muslim families of converts demonstrate high expectations as they seek to initiate their new convert members, mentoring and monitoring their ways. The convert women, on their part, often cannot find adequate answers to their questions about Islam. Pektas-Weber relates a typical experience in seeking information from her in-laws:

I had many questions for them about Islam. They would tell me: "We do not ask ourselves those questions." Sometimes, I was told those questions were haram, forbidden, because you should not ask questions, you should just take Islam as it is. That is how they had learned in Turkey. But later they told me that they were very proud of me for asking these questions. They would say: "You are more conscious of our religion than we are." So they were willing but they did not have many answers.

The challenge for the converts is how to practice Islam and live as Muslims in the Netherlands. Women converts turned to each other in continuing their search for knowledge, and in the process provided mutual support and solidarity. The drive to deepen their knowledge after conversion forms an important part of the "feminist converts'" narratives. While doing so, they began to shape a new collective culture.

It was while seeking deeper knowledge of Islam that a group of converts established Al-Nisa in 1982.[15] It was a self-help organization born of the difficulties in finding information about their new religion. Al-Nisa would invite whomever they could find to speak on Islam, including their own members who were learning as they went along. When the organization soon afterward started a newsletter also called *Al-Nisa*, it followed a similar practice of searching for knowledge while producing it in the form of its own articles. The newsletter became a forum for raising questions and trying out answers. Drawing upon rudimentary knowledge, *Al-Nisa* published many articles on "dos and don'ts." As Bogaers explains: "When you are a new convert you are looking for rules, for how to be a good Muslim." Meanwhile, Al-Nisa began to create branches in other parts of the country. In this way convert women were building a "community within a community," and, more specifically, a women-only community. Bogaers (b. 1954) and Pektas-Weber (b. 1962), who converted, respectively, in 1986 and 1989, discovered and joined Al-Nisa in the course of their search for knowledge, and each went on to become president. Bogaers joined Al-Nisa at the end of the 1980s and soon after took over as president, serving until 1997. Pektas-Weber, who joined Al-Nisa in 1997 and led in founding the branch in Utrecht, took over the helm in 2002. Both women came to Islam with a "prior text" of feminism. Bogaers was a young woman during the ascendancy of second-wave feminism in the Netherlands, although not a part of the movement as such. Pektas-Weber, as the daughter of a militant feminist, was raised in an atmosphere of staunch gender equality and female independence. Both claim a feminist identity within Islam.

While they were producing their own materials for each other to read in the form of articles in their newsletter *Al-Nisa* and in the process of developing their own discourse, the two convert women meanwhile continued to look for "authorities" on Islam. In time, they discovered publications in English coming from such places as Saudi Arabia and the World Islamic Mission in South Africa. Bogaers recalls her encounter with conservative Islamic literature and her recognition of its heavy patriarchal dimension. She admits: "At first I tried to adapt, thinking this was the right way for me but deep inside it was not fulfilling. I felt this is not why I embraced Islam. I started to question more and more what I was reading and thinking [some of this] was crazy, especially things Mawdudi [the Pakistani religious scholar] was saying." She went on to find the work of the Moroccan feminist scholar Fatima Mernissi. "There was, *il-hamdullilah* [thanks be to God], a scholar, a woman, who knows what's going on in the Islamic world and who knows how these new Islamic waves are oppressing women. I liked her way of doing research, her way of writing, and her humor. She pulled me back to the point where I had come when I embraced Islam." [16]

Converts confront the question of "culture versus Islam." They come to Islam as a religion and when they begin living Islam they are faced with a culture—or better, cultures—of Islam. Pektas-Weber says: "The women [in Al-Nisa] always wanted to concentrate purely on Islam. Converts know the importance of separating Islam from other cultural things. From the first that was Al-Nisa's strength, because we knew there was freedom in the religion and pressure in the culture." There was patriarchal culture glossed as Muslim and there was an egalitarian Islam. Many converts succumb to the readings of patriarchal culture(s), most firmly entrenched in the context of the family. In the course of the pressures of daily life, many convert women seem to make their accommodations, not finding the time, sufficient will or impetus, or resources (within themselves or without) to push their quest for knowledge further. Others sustain a struggle for the realization of the equality they understand or presume is a principle of Islam. As Wadud puts it, speaking of the fullness of Islam: "We [converts] strive even harder for a personally recognized, existentially realized meaning of Islam: a full at-one-ment. I hungered for a greater understanding of Islam." [17]

Bogaers and Pektas-Weber each relate their own stories of feminism and conversion. Bogaers, with her training in social work and studies in psychology, tried to encourage Al-Nisa members to confront feminist issues, especially in the context of the family, where they experienced problems, but she met with strong resistance. In many ways Islam, for new Muslims, seemed to be a comfort zone that they did not want to disturb. Bogaers wanted to unpack the mesh of notions of "the family in Islam" and how the family actually functioned. "You only have to take one step into the Muslim family, into books, etc., and [see] that there is always the notion, implicit or explicit, that men are above women or women below men. This view is shared by women and men. It is very important to oppose this way of thinking and acting. It is not good for men and it is not good for women. I have trouble more and more with people saying, you have to behave like this as a good Muslim woman or Muslim man. It feels as if I have to live like a statue that is not real. It is suffocating. It is harmful because if you have to live an ideal it becomes very hard to really look inside yourself, what you feel, what you experience, your emotions." The imposition of the ideal types of a Muslim man and Muslim woman, she claims, places unrealistic demands on both women and men and is harmful to both.

Converts often acquiesce in conventional patriarchal, so-called Muslim family practices, accepting a subordinate position, often euphemistically called a complementary position. Bogaers observed that often "they forget their own backgrounds." She continues: "Some women start realizing this [that their acquiescence in patriarchal family practices is harmful to their mental and physical health and that the imposed practices are not Islamic] after years of trying to make things work and they never do work so they come to a point where they say it never works and that I put all my energy into changing him and now I better change myself or live my life. Sometimes this means divorce or the relationship gets better." Bogaers emphasizes in her lectures and writings that Islam is not "behind this [patriarchal system]." "The women who feel secure enough to start looking find it a relief to hear that what they thought was Islam is not Islam."

Bogaers stresses that feminist ideas (or ideology) and confronting personal and family issues are deeply connected. "They are intermingled. I [have] mentioned the strange fact [of] how educated women who have minds of their own, after becoming Muslim, seem to stop thinking. It [Islam] is supposed to clear your mind and give you a broad view but it happens that you get a narrow view." In the family context, religiously and ethnically mixed marriages are usually more difficult than monocultural marriages. But, Bogaers says to women: "We have an advantage in dealing with this problem. We have Islam. So Islam can be a problem and it can also be the solution. Most of the women I know made the big step to become a Muslim out of their hearts, out of deep conviction. So I tell them go back to your heart. What does your heart say and try to connect this with basic love and caring that Allah has for you. There is a big connection between the psychological and social side with the spiritual dimension." Bogaers left Al-Nisa in 1997 because of difficulties she encountered inside the organization and has since conducted her feminist work elsewhere. "At the moment my work in the Breda Women's Prison [where she mainly serves immigrant Muslim women] is the most direct arena in which to bring out Islam and my beliefs, attitudes, and developments inside Islam."

Pektas-Weber, who asserted before the crowds gathered at a Muslim festival in the spring of 2003 that she had gone from Dolle Mina to Dolle Zina, speaks of a different moment in Al-Nisa. ("Dolle Mina" literally means "Crazy Mina," the diminutive for Wilhelmina Drucker, an early feminist pioneer in the Netherlands, while "Dolle Zina" is a combination of two adjectives, "crazy" and "beautiful"; in Dutch this is an effective play on words.) The wider social and political context has shifted in recent years. Pektas-Weber points to the impact of 9/11.[18] In the immediate aftermath Al-Nisa women, like many other Muslims in European societies (and elsewhere) in the face of taunts and insults against Islam and Muslims, went on the defensive. They were not examining issues as much as fighting back. This period, however, functioned as a temporary retreat or regrouping and served as a moment of intense reflection. Pektas-Weber relates that, a year later, convert women and other Muslim women moved from the defensive to the offensive. She observes that now convert women do not feel impelled to "defend their choice of Islam anymore," but are confidently asserting pride in being Muslim women and at the same time daring to publicly recognize gender issues and fight for real-life improvements.[19]

While 9/11 eventually served as a stimulus for some women to deal with gender issues, forms of feminist thinking had already been percolating in parts of the convert culture. Pektas-Weber explains that in Al-Nisa "We are proud to stimulate women to think for themselves. This has been true of Al-Nisa from the start and is a kind of feminist way to see things." This (somewhat delayed) post-9/11 feminist upturn coincided with a drawing together of converts and born Muslims. "To prove they are proud of Islam they [old and new Muslims] have to prove they are free women." A "feminist unleashing" and the convergence of old and new Muslims have received less notice than the more negative outcomes of 9/11.

By now born Muslims constitute about 30 percent of Al-Nisa's membership. They are women mainly in their twenties and thirties who are second-generation Dutch citizens of Moroccan and Turkish origin. They, too, are trying to forge a new Islam and trying to distinguish between the Islamic religion and culture. "This is why women of non-Dutch origin," Pektas-Weber claims, "are finding their way to Al-Nisa. This is the connection. They are finding their way to Al-Nisa because they see the importance to research Islam as a religion without all the cultural baggage. That will set them free. They see this." Thus there is a growing nucleus of converts and born Muslims coming together in the shared space of Al-Nisa, trying to separate patriarchal culture from Islam. This is at once a critique by born Muslims of their cultures of origin and a joint effort by old and new Muslims to offer an alternative to the implantation of a patriarchal Islam in the Netherlands. Roald notes in the Swedish context that born-Muslim women and convert women together are producing an "Islamic *jamstalldet*" (equal opportunity). The proliferation of Islamic feminist publications in recent years and the vibrant global electronic Islamic feminist culture aid this process.

I now turn to a different story of the search for knowledge of Islam and the production of Islamic feminism. This is a story told by two younger-generation Dutch converts who are presently university students (both at the University of Leiden). They are studying Islam in an academic environment in a community of fellow students and friends that includes born Muslims as well as non-Muslims. The younger-generation or more recent converts here, and elsewhere, include women who appear to come to Islamic feminism with alacrity. Van Nieuwkerk expresses what I, too, have observed when she says: "I have the impression that emancipation in the sense of independence and equality is more strongly expressed by women who recently converted, whereas those who converted several years ago stressed their freedom to develop themselves in the way they choose" (this volume). Self-development, as I see it, is a different route to the same destination of Islamic feminism. Inji Icli (b. 1974) converted to Islam in 1995, and Rahma Bavelaar (b. 1979) converted to Islam in 1998. The "prior text of feminism" they bring with them is a diffused kind of the feminism that is part of the post-second-wave feminist culture in which they grew up. Bavelaar has been part of a progressive leftist culture of social activism, within which her notions of gender justice were located and nourished. Neither of these two young women calls herself a feminist, but both can readily be seen as identifying with a notion of feminism that is not at odds with their Islam, or maybe better put, that is integral to their Islam.

Icli, like women in Al-Nisa, grapples with the question of culture versus religion, but she pushes further. She confronts problems within Islamic religious discourse and ponders hermeneutic challenges. With a deep desire to understand, she engages in her own *ijtihad*, her own rational investigation of religious sources.

When I first converted I thought Islam and Islamic culture was all beautiful and great. But when you educate yourself you really see there are a lot of problems, especially regarding women. At first you say it is the culture. It is the easy way out. It is culture and Islam is nothing like that. But when you start to read the text [the Qur'an] more deeply I think you must acknowledge that there are some elements in there that give people ideas they can treat women like that [negatively]. It is the way they interpret it. There are traces of patriarchal culture within the Qur'an because it was sent to a patriarchal culture. It was sent to them in their language, their conception, their worldview. I know that it constituted progress for women back then but this progress is incomplete. We need to look at the text ourselves and reinterpret it.

Icli explains that she began to read about gender and Islam around two years ago because "I was really sick of the way that Islam is viewed by Westerners and sick of the way it is interpreted by men and the orthodox movements. You are not allowed to go out by yourself, to get different knowledge and these kinds of things. For me it is such a limited way [to understand] Islam. For me there is more freedom in Islam than what you find now." Icli has read Rifaat Hassan (who often comes to the Netherlands to give talks) and Mernissi, but not Wadud (though she had just bought her *Qur'an and Woman*) nor Barlas's new book *"Believing Women" in Islam: Unreading Patriarchal Interpretations of the Qur'an* (2002).

Bavelaar, like Icli, does not claim a feminist identity, although, like her, she is in a "feminist space." She explains: "I think rights for women and the position of women is part of the greater picture, part of Islam as a whole, and

I would not want to think of it as a separate goal but part of a greater goal." She speaks of growing up in a progressive atmosphere and of her activism in left-wing organizations and environmentalist groups as informing her life as a Muslim. She retains her progressive approach and confident resolve to "try to do things my own way." She admits: "Unlike many girls who grew up in Muslim families I can remain independent from interpretations that do not suit me and I constantly have to distance myself from Islamic movements that are all around."

In pondering a new Islamic feminist culture in the Netherlands, Bavelaar spoke of divisions within the Muslim community both across the lines of new and born Muslims, with their respective backgrounds, and across the generational divide. These divisions revolve around problems of Dutch culture and Moroccan, Turkish, and other non-native cultures living in shared space in the Netherlands. As a volunteer Bavelaar teaches in an Islamic "Sunday school" for young Somali immigrant girls in the Netherlands and observes that "gender issues are very much alive in the minds of these girls." For her own part, Bavelaar tries to instill a sense of independent thinking (coming to one's own conclusions about ideas and issues—for example, whether or not to veil). She stresses "rights over duties" in her teaching of Islam, consciously "as a way of restoring balance." Bavelaar's Muslim friends are mainly second-generation immigrants. She does not have many contacts with converts and has only vaguely heard of Al-Nisa. Bavelaar's enactment of Islamic feminism (she does not identify it explicitly as such) is in community work and instilling progressive ideas in young women within an Islamic framework.

The four women above give hints of two Islamic feminist cultures-in-the-making in the Netherlands. Until now, they have not appeared to converge. Icli relates how she tried to publish some pieces in Al-Nisa's newsletter, but they were rejected as being too difficult for the readers. This may be one sign of the development of parallel Islamic feminist cultures: one a popular Islamic feminist culture and the other an academic feminist culture, separated, probably, more by style and social groupings than by substance. Bavelaar, the youngest of the four women—and youngest in the entire group of converts whose stories form part of this chapter—says about the Dutch context:

I think we still have a long way to go. The community is still very divided. I think in the third or fourth generation big changes will occur. At the moment there is also a language barrier. It is an important factor [having a common language] for the first generation to be able to communicate with the second generation. The commu-

nication between generations in formulating a new Islam is still very recent. Second-generation women from families coming from villages [in their original countries] are asking questions converts are asking. Asking these same questions is creating the coming together. Dutch converts have a problem of language in the Islamic sense with their parents.

Developing Consciousness, Organizing Converts: A British Story
Batool Al Toma (b. 1955), a convert of Irish origin, is research and education officer at the Islamic Foundation at Leicester. As a schoolgirl she experienced doubts about the Roman Catholic Church, in which she had been raised. She sought rational answers to her questions within her natal religion, but the answers persistently eluded her. In the 1970s she completed her higher education at the University of Wales and began working as a civil servant in Dublin. It was there that by chance she was introduced to Islam by Muslim foreign students. Islam made sense to her as a rational religion. For a period of seven to eight years she undertook her own intellectual investigation of Islam. Unlike the Dutch women I met, Al Toma had no difficulty in finding books on Islam (there have been large numbers of books on Islam produced either in the United Kingdom or in Pakistan and India available on the market and in libraries). She relates that in her reading she "was very comfortable about how Islam presented women and saw women." That was until she encountered Mawdudi, who evoked in her a response similar to that of Bogaers. "I read *Purdah and the Status of Women in Islam* and was shocked and appalled by it. I decided this was not what Islam expected or projected at all. It had a very cultural bias that I found very irritating." Al Toma explained that the reading she had done up to that point made her confident in her own ability to judge the works of exposition and interpretation that she read. To her, Mawdudi's approach to gender did not make sense; it challenged the concept of Islam as a rational religion, consistent with its own principles.

Al Toma is the only one of the converts interviewed who displayed a familiarity with the history and actual experiences of women inside Muslim societies. When I first met Al Toma in Khartoum in 1996 at an international conference of Muslims organized by women associated with the Islamist regime in Sudan, she told me that Muslim women's accounts of their real-life experiences in the anthology of Arab feminist writing that I had coedited with Miriam Cooke (1990) had had a big impact on her. She was impressed when she saw how Muslim women spoke out about the difficulties they encountered as women, while at the same time they forged ahead with their lives, and how some of them formulated an alternative discourse in resistance to patriarchal oppression. When I met her again in London in 2003 she reiterated this, expressing admiration for women who could hold on to their dignity as they insisted upon receiving just treatment. "It was through reading that book [Opening the Gates] and when I began to read Mernissi and Taslima Nasreen [the well-known Bangladeshi feminist writer] and others that I began to see that all of these women were products of their background and that it was not that these women were trying to be confrontational and to knock Islam—as alleged on the outside—but that [it was] this background [that] was the bane of their lives." Al Toma would not be among those who found it easy to blame the victims.

Al Toma was a young woman when second-wave feminism was under way in Britain, although this did not form part of her own experience as a young woman in Ireland. She acknowledges, "I am very interested in the whole subject of feminism," but she does not call herself a feminist. "I could see as I grew into Islam that Muslim women were dominated and controlled by male patriarchal society. But I always had a feeling that this had built up over the years and was part of culture and tradition and [coming] from male interpretation of the sources of Islam." She confesses: "I accepted it in the beginning because I was under the impression that the attitude about women was part and parcel of the whole sense of piety you had to adopt when you came to Islam. I toed that line for a while until I began to realize that there was something not quite right and that it felt very contrived." At this point in her story she made an explicit connection with the reading she had done and the confidence it gave her to come to her own conclusions in her critique of the patriarchal thinking that had intruded into Islam. In her own words: "The more confident you become with yourself and [in] your reading of Islam [the more] you begin to see things in a totally different light from that which is expressed in normal circumstances." Al Toma's story is another ijtihadic narrative. Her story tells us that when a person comes to Islam through an intensely rational path that enables her to critically examine her own religious background, and she has sufficient confidence and strength, she will apply that same critical analysis to issues of gender within Islam. She will recognize the "authority" of her own intellectual conclusions.

Outgoing and after all these years still exuding the excitement about Islam that comes with a fresh encounter, Al Toma devotes herself to assisting new converts, women and men alike. Within the Islamic Foundation at Leicester, where she works, she created the New Muslim Project in 1993. She edits the association's newsletter, called *Meeting Point*. To address the ritual needs of new Muslims, Al Toma recently published *A Simple Guide to Prayer.*[20] Individuals may go through the formal conversion process in the offices at the Islamic Foundation, which also issues certificates of conversion. Such a document is clearly not a religious necessity, but a modern invention, helping the convert prove her or his new status as a Muslim in cases where this might be required. Such proof, for example, is important when making the *haj* to Mecca. Institutionalizing Islam in public space is a critical part of new Muslim life in contemporary Western societies, and in this Al Toma is playing a salient role. In the United Kingdom, this public space is civil society beyond the circumference of state or governmental public space.

When women (or men) come into contact with Al Toma during their search for Islam, she presents what can be recognized as an Islamic feminist approach, although she would not define it as such. She speaks of the full equality of *insan,* or of all human beings, which is a central principle of Islam. She offers a rational critique of patriarchal practices that are allegedly Islamic. The New Muslim Project is not a women-only site, but a place that brings together both genders. It is also a site where converts and those on the conversion path come together. Al Toma plays a sensitive and significant role in a new convert culture in dialogue with non-Muslims. She not only shares her egalitarian vision of Islam with others, but also understands how other discourses may have something to say.

Al Toma introduced me to Yvonne Ridley, a high-profile British journalist who now works freelance. Her search, following a common pattern, began and continues with the Qur'an, yet her path to the holy book is singular. Following the attacks on 9/11, she gained illegal entry into Afghanistan to cover events as a journalist from inside and ended up being captured. While undergoing interrogation in prison she was asked if she would like to become a Muslim, to which she replied that she could not make such a life-changing decision while in captivity. But she promised that upon her release and her return to London, she would read the Qur'an and study Islam.[21] When she was freed she made good on her pledge.

Thrust in an unusual way into contact with the Qur'an, Ridley approached the sacred text as an inquisitor. "I went through all the women's issues first," she explained, "because I wanted to know what is in this religion that makes men subjugate women." For her the unexpected happened: "The more I read the more I realized that far from subjugating women the Qur'an elevates women and makes this quite clear." Without mincing words, she said: "The women's liberation movement began in the pages of the Qur'an." "Some of the ideas promoted by the Taliban could not possibly have come from the Qur'an but from Saudi Arabia. Where is this that women cannot drive? Aisha led the battle of the camel. It is rubbish and a distortion of Islam. It is culture over faith in my opinion. I am still on the learning curve but this is my opinion. I want to satisfy myself in so many ways about Islam and when I feel confident—and hopefully will have taken my *shahada*—I want to tackle some of these Saudi clerics." [22] Again we discern common sense and a common pattern. Women read equality and justice in the Qur'an and conclude that patriarchal culture(s) intrude and steal the name of Islam.

Meanwhile, as she explained, Ridley began to bring her lifestyle more into conformity with ordained Islamic practice. For example, she adopted a more conservative mode of dress and avoided pork and alcohol. She describes a gradual process of alignment of her lifeways with the injunctions of Islam, similar to that Köse and Loewenthal (2000) have discussed in their analysis of British conversions. While she makes such modifications in her habitual practices, Ridley as a woman does not shrink from her highly public professional life as a journalist who speaks her mind.

Ridley is prominently linked with born-Muslim women from old Muslim societies, as well as born Muslims living in the West. While she by no means is distant from converts, she is not primarily speaking to and with them. Moreover, her community of Muslims is a global community. In her writing, speaking, and living, she moves around the world. Her story shows how it is possible to participate in the dynamics of Muslim society without being a Muslim, yet one who is avowedly on the conversion path.

Double Embrace: A South African Story

The South African stories are different in significant ways from the Dutch and British stories just encountered. Khadija Magardie (b. 1975), Malika Ndlovu (b. 1972), and Aisha Roberts (b. 1971) exemplify the double embrace of Islam and Islamic feminism. Among the younger generation of the women whose narratives inform this chapter, Magardie and Roberts came to Islam in 1994, and Ndlovu in 2000. Roberts was a feminist before she became a Muslim, and Magardie was raised with a strong sense of gender equality. For both, their Islam and Islamic feminism are highly interwoven at the level of ideas and practice. Ndlovu, who seems always to have been a "free-spirit feminist," expresses her gender-progressive Islam through her intense engagement with the arts.

The Dutch and British stories tell of the search for knowledge of Islam. The earlier generation of Dutch converts experienced difficulties finding materials, while the British woman of the same generation did not, but in both instances these converts came to Islamic feminist publications later in their search. The South African converts came into contact with a feminist Islam early on, and moreover, unlike the Dutch and British, they found a homegrown Islamic feminist discourse and an activist movement (Esack 1997; Tayob 1995). They entered Islam through the door of a postapartheid Islamic feminist activist culture. Through meetings, conferences, camps, courses, books, and articles these new Muslims did not so much have to search for Islam and Islamic feminism as both greeted them full force.

For Roberts and Magardie connections with the Muslim Youth Movement and particular persons within the movement were pivotal in their dual embrace of Islam and Islamic feminism. Roberts had been an antiapartheid activist and a feminist activist as a student at Rhodes University in the Eastern Cape. She had been on a spiritual and religious search when she discovered Islam through contacts with Muslim students. She tells how she picked up her early knowledge of Islam mainly "by osmosis." She became deeply attracted to the religion of Islam as satisfying her spiritually, but was candid in confessing that she was not without certain misgivings concerning how it was lived. "For me the difficult part was reconciling what was in the Qur'an, and the spirit of the Qur'an, with contemporary practice. I could not find justification for a lot of practices, like not allowing women into religious spaces."[23] She decided to convert, "taking on balance the good against the bad," presuming that "the more I got into it the more I would find other explanations and other ways of understanding." Following the common pattern, Roberts continued in the beginning to be mainly self-taught in Islam. Her unresolved questions about gender and Islam and her introduction to archconservative Tablighi circles after her move from the Eastern Cape to Johannesburg put a heavy strain on her commitment to Islam. Roberts's chance meeting with Shamima Shaikh and Na'eem Jeenah at Witswatersrand University, while the wife and husband activists at the center of the Muslim Youth Movement were distributing copies of the MYM paper Al-Qalam, took her life in a new direction by bringing her into the Islamic feminist movement. Shamima Shaikh was the head of the Gender Desk and editor of Al-Qalam and the "shining light" of Islamic feminism until her premature death in 1997. Shaikh and her Islamic feminism had a huge impact on Roberts, who confessed: "I don't know if I'd have stayed a Muslim if I had not met Shamima." It was Shaikh who introduced Roberts to Mernissi's work. "That opened my eyes to a totally different gender dynamic in Islam." She found Mernissi's work more accessible than Wadud's hermeneutic work, which she found difficult. Roberts continued her reading, which now included Islamic feminist works, and became active on the Gender Desk of the Muslim Youth Movement.

Magardie embraced Islam during her final year in school. Her purely academic interest in "discovering more about different religions" took her to Islam. She recalls being impressed by Islam as a religion committed to social justice, stressing that she encountered Islam at a very turbulent time in the history of South Africa. Malcolm X's autobiography and the writing of the African historian Ali Mazrui made a deep impression on her. She took the Islamic profession of faith "on the basis of what I liked," admitting that she still had much to learn about the religion. She affirms: "My real introduction to Islam began through the Muslim Youth Movement." She had come into contact with the MYM when she went to its offices (upstairs from the *da'wah* office, where she had gone to make her profession of faith) expressing her interest in writing for *Al-Qalam.* She relates: "It was really in the ranks of the MYM that I became more confident in myself and more confident Islamically because nobody really ever taught me." Through the MYM youth camps she learned about Islamic feminism. She mentions Mernissi and Fazlur Rahman, whose work has deeply influenced Islamic feminist discourse. After entering the University of Natal she continued her study of Islam and Islamic feminist works and also read general works on feminism by Simone de Beauvoir, Germain Greer, and others. Unlike many, who find conflict between general feminist works and Islam, Magardie says: "The more I started studying secular feminism the more I started finding parallels within Islamic circles where feminism was an issue."

While excitedly trying to work through feminist questions and finding confluences between secular feminism and Islamic feminism, and being active on the MYM Gender Desk with Shaikh, her life suddenly took a different turn when she met and married an Iranian cleric and turned to Shi'i Islam. She began to feel that the MYM was not sufficiently orthodox and now continued to study Islam under the tutelage of her husband. But, she recalls, "I neglected the whole women angle." In the meantime Magardie finished at the university and began to work for the South African Broadcasting Company, moving from Durban to Johannesburg. She recalls how proud she was, as a fresh, young professional, to be a Muslim, and a Shi'i Muslim, and that her affiliation gave her a strong sense of identity. She explains that she was told she must, as a Shi'i Muslim, follow a *marja,* a person trained in the Islamic sciences, who would guide her in religious interpretation. In this case Magardie's *marja* was her husband (to add another layer of deference). So she went from thinking to being guided. Eventually she had problems, feeling deprived of her own ability to think. It was gender issues that provoked the turnabout. "I think it was polygamy that started the whole problem." And she says she learned soon afterward about *muta*, or temporary marriage, in Shi'i Islam. She had difficulty locating these practices in the Islam she knew, or imagined. Around this time she came into contact with Iranian Shi'i Islamic feminists. She read Shahla Haeri's book, with its critical analysis of *muta*, and the work of Ziba Mir-Hosseini on marriage and divorce. She questioned the idea of having to go through a *marja* rather than straight to the religious texts on her own.

Continuing to weave together the different dimensions of her life, Magardie explains that her move to Johannesburg and job at a leading South African newspaper thrust her into a wider world:

Perhaps the Mail and Guardian *can be credited with broadening my horizons. As my horizons broadened I guess I just came to feel more and more put down in my own life and thinking this [where she was at that moment in her thinking about Islam] is not really Islam. This is not the Islam that made me get up at the break of dawn and read* fajr *and feel so happy . . . and loving to go to pray. One of the things that made me feel part of a community, because I had no Islamic family, was going to* tarawiah *[the evening prayer after breaking fast] during Ramadan. When I became a Shi'i they told me* tarawiah *was* haram *[forbidden].*

Magardie grappled more and more with the notions of *ijtihad* and her conviction that she could read the Qur'an for herself:

My understanding of the Qur'an—and I stand by it—was that it was not revealed to an elite. The Qur'an is simple. These people make it complicated. It used to frustrate me more and more. Strangely enough, I started drawing on my own inner experiences. Ironically, it was when Shamima had already died that I started saying this to myself. [After she turned to Shi'i Islam Magardie drifted away from the MYM.] It was one of those bitter ironies in life that you only start to think about what she was saying and appreciating the courage of her conviction now. Strangely enough, I returned to her ideas, to MYM ideas.

She returned to her earlier Muslim self. Gender and *ijtihad* brought her back to the place where she had been. She speaks of trying to work out for herself the issue of polygamy by going straight to the Qur'an on her own. "I started to say to myself the only salvation in Islam is *ijtihad*, because it keeps Islamic learning and debate alive." Narrating and reflecting on her narrative at the same time, Magardie says:

I guess I plot out that particular course to say that my particular conclusion is now that—Allah forgive me should I be wrong and arrogant enough to come to conclusions about his Holy Book without having studied enough—that I firmly believe and I am not turning my back on Islam and it is not even an itch but a pain that brings tears sometimes: that I have got to reconcile that in my heart I am a feminist. You know I have problems with that term. I am a feminist because in the course of my job I have seen the most unbelievable horrors perpetrated against women in the name of culture and religion, and even in the name of nothing.

Magardie affirms: "I am going to take from the Qur'an what I can agree with and what I don't understand I am going to try not to throw aside anymore, because I have done that for long enough, but I am going to try and find an answer because I do believe Islam is the right way."

Roberts and Magardie bring two prior texts to their Islam: a prior text of feminism and a prior text of antiapartheid activism, a proliberation activism with an intense sense of equality and justice irrespective of race, ethnicity, and gender. The narratives of both women reveal the immediacy of these prior texts. They bring the South African vocabulary of struggle with them when they speak of being "conscientized Muslims."

Malika Ndlovu's narrative of coming to Islam is, at the core, a story of "coming home" and experiencing "an inexplicable familiarity with the religion." It is about "finding a degree of peace and relief that I cannot explain." She strongly prefers the term "revert," with its connotations of "return." Again, like other women who newly embrace Islam, there are unanswered questions.

My mind, my intellect tries to figure it out and to come up with questions but now [as a Muslim] the questions are coming from a place of implicit faith, of implicit acceptance [such] that the mind boggles . . . I cannot understand how I came to peace with things I still do not have answers for intellectually. I don't have answers for things I mentally grapple with. It is often like a sea and I would imagine literally the head of a question mark bobbing up and down on the waves . . . a whole range of questions. And constantly a wave comes and washes over these questions. It is not at all that these questions are being suppressed because it is not at all that water holds things down. It is a living, dynamic way of being at peace without having all the answers in order to commit to a certain place.

Ndlovu embarked on a quest for knowledge, wanting to learn about lived Islam through experiences of women. She created Project Nisa (in August 2002), which began as a theater project, as her "first Islam-focused work on the arts." She sought stories from Muslim women about their experiences of polygamy and divorce. Women's experience was the starting point, not jurisprudence. "As an artist and as a young Muslim and a growing Muslim, I have a lot of questions. By the grace of Allah, being an artist is a way I can happily raise these questions, as opposed to participating in academic debate or [being part of] a political saga. I can collaborate with a mixed group of Muslim women and also with non-Muslims." Ndlovu quickly came to the idea of the Internet and how she could be part of electronic story-sharing. The idea mushroomed beyond her expectations. It connected her as a new Muslim with a global community, or "family." Other women, upon converting, have mentioned the lack of a Muslim family and the importance of finding one. "I did not grow up as part of a Muslim cultural community, so if I talk about being from a Muslim community I think global. I do not fit into any of these little boxes." She affirms: "Through Nisa a community can be built of people who want to share and grow and express their creativity in a place where they feel at peace and a part of as Muslims and as women."

Ndlovu integrates her strong sense of justice, of dignity, of freedom to grow in Islam with her self-consciously "Islamic multimedia art." Although she enacts Islamic feminism with other women, new and born Muslims alike, she is uneasy with the baggage that attaches to "feminism." She worries about the notion of "feminism" as an outside imposition and about its elitism alienating the majority of African women. While the term "feminist" and especially its use in labeling are not to her liking, she confirms: "There are feminist bones in my body that rattle about certain issues so that I am totally in alignment with the cause, so to say." And in her art she conveys that women create their own feminism, helping to dispel the tenacious myth that feminism is simply something out there.

The South African convert women are at home in their own country. They do not feel they have to announce their new identity in any defensive way. They come to Islam with liberatory ideas, and these are the ideas of the new South Africa for which people so desperately fought. They came straight into an Islamic feminist movement that is part and parcel of a vibrant progressive Islamic movement led by women and men together.

New Muslims for a New Islam

I begin my concluding thoughts with a return to Wadud. As a convert, Wadud "brings to her engagement with the religion," as Barlas observes, echoing Pektas-Weber's approach, "a spirit of critical inquiry that leads her to ask questions of it that people who are born Muslim often do not consider asking" (2003). Barlas continues about Wadud: "She came to Islam [as a student, taking the *shahada* on Thanksgiving Day 1972] by asking critical questions of it about the purpose of life and her own role in it. . . . in the Qur'an, she found a 'vision of the world,' and beyond, with meanings and possibilities for self that lead to certainty" (2003). Through her hermeneutic investigation Wadud articulated the Qur'anic message of gender equality and social justice, and a call for their implementation, at the core of Islamic feminism.

Wadud's story became part of the story of South African Islamic feminist activism in a most immediate sense when she visited the country for a conference in 1994. At the invitation of progressive Muslims, Wadud was invited to speak at Friday congregational prayer at the Claremont Main Street Mosque in Cape Town. She gave a pre-*khutba* (pre-sermon) talk on the power of mothering. On that occasion women of the congregation came down from their usual places in the loft to the main space and sat together to the right in rows parallel to those of the men. The event, which was immensely inspiring and uplifting to many, was seen by others as an assault on Islam. Threats of violence ensued, but in the end progressive Islam was victorious. Women have since given pre-*khutba* talks and women congregants have remained on the main floor of the mosque (Esack 1999; Tayob 1999).[24]

I would like to quote Wadud from her new preface to the new edition of her book *Qur'an and Woman*, which is relevant for convert women and to all who dare to engage in *ijtihad*.

As an African-American who was embraced by Islam over a quarter of a century ago, I have felt that Islam was a haven in these times of global crisis and chaos. I was unprepared for the schisms that have arisen between me and some members of the Muslim community. Since the publication of Qur'an and Woman, *the gender justice I aspire for is sometimes resisted by more conservative Muslims. I often feel that although I entered into a tradition whose holy prophet required Muslim males and females to seek knowledge until the grave, that as a woman, of African origin, and an American convert to Islam, I was not supposed to seek beyond what others hand down to me.*

She goes on to say:

The two names most consistently hurled at me are "Western" and "feminist." "Western" could mean that I can only be who I am: a daughter of the West, born and raised an American of African descent. It is reduced, however, to mean anti-Islam. "Feminist" is used in a similar reductionist manner. No reference is ever made to the definition of feminism as the radical notion that women are human beings. (1999)

Wadud's story bespeaks the circulations of Islamic feminism and the global intersections of activism. To what extent can her life story be a model for other convert women, wherever they may be placed or "positioned"?

The narratives of the British, Dutch, and South African women reviewed here offer keys and clues about links between conversion to Islam and Islamic feminism. I have tried to follow the clues, to see where they lead in the production of a new Islam that recuperates the gender-egalitarian principles permeating the Qur'an. The converts' narratives form a story of the flowing and ebbing of agency (I intentionally reverse the usual order of this phrase), of the consumption and production of knowledge, of knowledge and knowing as authority, edging, if often haltingly, toward the articulation and practice of Islamic feminism.

The juxtaposition of South African narratives with European narratives reveals the power of history, identity, politics, and positioning in the lives of converts and how they impact gender thinking. In the first two stages, the path to conversion and the moment of embrace, the narratives of the converts are similar.

It is after conversion that the stories split: the South African and European. The South African converts entered (if with some detours) a world of progressive Islam. They entered into a scene in which an Islamic feminist movement enacted by women and men together to eradicate patriarchal injustices was under way. This was/is a progressive movement within an old established Muslim community, a minority community which is at the same time a project of building a new South Africa.

The British and Dutch converts entered new Muslim minority communities whose members are still in the process of finding their place in a larger society as new citizens. Many of them are now of the second generation, struggling to accommodate to a society marked by "cultural racism" in an atmosphere that, of late, has become more hostile. Yet, as I've already observed, the heightened hostility in the wake of 9/11 propelled some convert women in the West to take charge and to celebrate and enact their strengths as Muslims. Meanwhile, as also noted, second-generation Dutch Muslims who absorbed their religion as a set of inherited cultural practices (modified by their new environments) are starting to seek deeper Islamic religious knowledge alongside Dutch converts. Together, old and new Muslim women are beginning to unravel the patriarchal threads entangled in the stories they have been told about Islam as they work out their own understandings of Qur'an-based gender equality and social justice. Together, they are standing up to the patriarchal projects of political Islam and virulent cultural racism/Islamophobia.[25]

Islamic feminism is both modernist and postmodernist, as it is at once local and global. Islamic feminism clearly is not something "out there," but rather "internal." It is a work in progress: it is being constructed and enacted, refined and redefined, by Muslims at multiple sites. My purpose has been to see how converts access and produce Islamic feminism. This production may come in the form of asking hard questions, looking for sound answers, or having the courage to live by the Islamic principles that Islamic feminism uncovers and reappropriates. The enactment of Islamic feminism is about fighting multiple injustices. Thinking women, as converts to Islam, will not be able to stand back.

Van Nieuwkerk met a Dutch convert wearing a chain on her neck, from which dangled an Allah ornament and a feminist symbol. I end this early chapter in the story of conversion and Islamic feminism by leaving readers with this telling image.

Notes

1. She offers a reflective narrative on her life in "On Belonging as a Muslim Woman" (Wadud 1995).

2. An example to the contrary is Rebekah Lee, who is examining African women's conversion to Islam in South Africa, specifically in and around Cape Town (2002).

3. It was through interviews and oral histories that I first discovered evidence of Islamic feminism quietly taking shape before it became a public discourse. Moreover, this happened quite by accident as I

was investigating contemporary Muslim women's definitions of feminism, having previously focused on earlier historical definitions extant in written records or in the historical memories of women (Badran 1993).

4. In this chapter I have drawn from the narratives of three South African women, four Dutch women, and two British women, one of whom is on the conversion path. The imbalance from the British side was a problem of logistics. (Since I completed this chapter, the woman on

the path to conversion has converted.
See Bayman 2004.)

5. Clearly, the term "white," and other terms connoting "race," are problematic, and indeed, this came up in one of the interviews, but pursuing this in detail is beyond the scope of my chapter.

6. I interviewed one African male convert from Christianity to Islam in Cape Town, from whom I learned about some of the ethnic complexities within wider South African Islam. On African women's conversion to Islam, see Lee 2002.

7. The standardization of the conversion narrative has been recognized, as Wohlrab-Sahr points out in her chapter and as van Nieuwkerk illustrates in her analysis of online conversion narratives. While analyses of these standard conversion narratives and their stock of tropes can be put to various uses, they have their limitations, as Wohlrab-Sahr remarks. Such narratives are not helpful in probing links between conversion and feminism. To the contrary they suggest the lack of a possible feminist dimension in "the conversion story."

8. On the notion of reversion see Kareema Quick, quoted in Lee 2002, 55.

9. For a discussion of the term "new Muslim," see Harfiyah Abdel Haleem 2003.

10. See, for example, the New Muslims Project, http://www.newmuslimsproject.net.

11. For theorizations of the foreign see Rebecca Saunders 2003.

12. For a highly detailed and complex analysis of authority in Islam, see Khaled Abou El Fadl 2001.

13. Tuula Sakaranaho speaks of the significance of the rational along with the relational for women in coming to Islam, but does not refer to "feminist converts" (2003).

14. See *Thinking about Secularism and Law in Egypt* (2001).

15. By way of comparison, in 1984 Swedish Muslims formed the Islamic Women's Association in Gothenburg. Both converts and born Muslims pioneered in this association, where they played helpful organizing roles (Roald 2003).

16. She refers to her discovery of Mernissi's *Women and Islam: An Historical and Theological Enquiry* (1991).

17. See Wadud (1995, 264). Speaking of the often unrecognized imbrication of culture and religion by born Muslims, Wadud says: "Whatever has passed for 'Islam' in their cultures (and sometimes it is a big 'whatever') is unquestionably accepted as the full meaning of Islam" (1995, 263–264).

18. See van Nieuwkerk (2004) on the intensification and spread of the cultural difference discourse.

19. Pnina Werbner, who studies the South Asian Muslim diaspora in Britain, writes in "The Predicament of Diaspora and Millennial Islam: In the Aftermath of September 11" (closer in time to the events of September 11), that "The tragedy is that the global crisis precipitated on September 11 will leave its own trace, a sediment of alienation and radical estrangement which will impact on the way people conceive of their identity and citizenship in their country of settlement" (2001). A feminist resolve arising among Muslim women in the West a year or more after the events of 9/11 has yet to receive attention, as well as the way the events led to an intensified bonding of born and convert Muslims.

20. See http://www.newmuslimsproject.net, and Batool Al Toma's Personal Profile there.

21. She has written about her captivity and release in her book *In the Hands of the Taliban* (London: Robson Books, 2001).

22. A recent statement on her journey to Islam issued on March 5, 2003, can be found at http://www.sistersinislam.net.

23. Köse found in his research on British converts that they were turning to Islam because "the articles of faith and practices support each other more." This idealized version of Islam seems widespread in the West, according to the conversion literature (1999, 303).

24. Author interview with Sadiyya Shaikh, who was present at the talk.

25. In December I was invited to Utrecht to give a presentation on Islamic feminism to a small group of Dutch convert women and born Muslim women of Turkish and Moroccan backgrounds. One of the most impressive things to me was the coming together of converts and born Muslims and how some shared common feminist concerns within an Islamic framework and some were intrigued but reluctant, but the fault line was not between "new" and "old" Muslims.

References

Abdel Haleem, H. 2003. "Experiences, Needs and Potential of New Muslim Women in Britain." In *Muslim Women in the United Kingdom and Beyond: Experiences and Images*, ed. H. Jawad and T. Benn, pp. 91–106. Leiden: Brill.

Abou El Fadl, Kh. 2001. *Speaking in God's Name: Islamic Law, Authority and Women*. Oxford: Oneworld.

Allievi, St. 1998. *Les convertis à l'islam. Les nouveaux musulmans d'Europe*. Paris: L'Harmattan.

Asad, T. 2001. *Thinking about Secularism and Law in Egypt*. Leiden: ISIM.

Badran, M. 1993. "Gender Activism: Feminists and Islamists in Egypt." In *Identity Politics and Women: Cultural Reassertions and Feminisms in International Perspective*, ed. V. Moghadam, pp. 202–227. Denver: Westview.

———. 1995. *Feminists, Islam, and Nation: Gender and the Making of Modern Egypt*. Princeton, N.J.: Princeton University Press.

Badran, M., and M. Cooke, eds. 1990. *Opening the Gates: A Century of Arab Feminist Writing*. London: Virago; Bloomington: Indiana University Press.

———. 2004. *Opening the Gates: An Arab Feminist Anthology*. New expanded edition. Bloomington: Indiana University Press.

Barlas, A. 2002. *"Believing Women" in Islam: Unreading Patriarchal Interpretations of the Qur'an*. Austin: University of Texas Press.

———. 2003. "Amina Wadud's Hermeneutics of the Qur'an: Women Rereading Sacred Texts." In *Contemporary Muslim Intellectuals and the Qur'an: Modernist and Post-modernist Approaches*, ed. S. Taji-Faruqi, pp. 97–124. New York: Oxford University Press.

Bayman, H. 2004. "Yvonne Ridley: From Captive to Convert." *BBC News Online*, September 21.

Esack, F. 1997. *Qur'an, Liberation and Pluralism*. Oxford: Oneworld.

———. 2000. *On Being a Muslim: Finding a Religious Path in the World Today*. Oxford: Oneworld.

Köse, A. 1996. *Conversion to Islam: A Study of Native British Converts*. London: Kegan Paul.

———. 1999. "The Journey from the Secular to the Sacred: Experiences of Native

British Converts to Islam." *Social Compass* 46 (3): 301–312.

Köse, A., and K. M. Loewenthal. 2000. "Conversion Motifs among British Converts to Islam." *International Journal for the Psychology of Religion* 10 (2): 101–110.

Lee, R. 2002. "Understanding African Women's Conversion to Islam: Cape Town in Perspective." *Annual Review of Islam in South Africa* 2 (December): 52–56.

Mernissi, F. 1991. *Women and Islam: An Historical and Theological Enquiry.* Oxford: Basil Blackwell.

New Muslims Project. http://www .newmuslimsproject.net.

Ramadan, T. 1999. *To Be a European Muslim.* Leicester: Islamic Foundation.

Ridley, Y. 2001. *In the Hands of the Taliban.* London: Robson Books.

Roald, A. S. 2001. *Women and Islam: The Western Experience.* London: Routledge.

———. 2003. "The Mecca of Gender Equality." In *Muslim Women in the United Kingdom and Beyond,* ed. H. Jawad and T. Benn, pp. 65–91. Leiden: Brill.

Sakaranaho, Tuula. 2003. "Les rhetoriques de la continuute: les femmes, l'Islam and

l'heritage catholique en Irlande." *Social Compass* 50 (1): 71–84.

Saunders, R., ed. 2003. *The Concept of the Foreign: An Interdisciplinary Dialogue.* New York: Lexington Books.

Tayob, A. 1995. *Islamic Resurgence in South Africa: The Muslim Youth Movement.* Cape Town: University of Cape Town Press.

———. 1999. *Islam in South Africa: Mosques, Imams, and Sermons.* Gainesville: University Press of Florida.

van Nieuwkerk, K. 2004. "Veils and Wooden Clogs Do Not Go Together." *Ethnos* 2 (2004): 229–246.

Wadud, A. 1995. "On Belonging as a Muslim Woman." In *My Soul Is a Witness: African-American Women's Spirituality,* ed. G. Wade-Gayles, pp. 253–265. Boston: Beacon Press.

———. 1999. *Qur'an and Woman: Rereading the Sacred Text from a Woman's Perspective.* New York: Oxford University Press.

Werbner, P. 2001. "The Predicament of Diaspora and Millennial Islam: In the Aftermath of September 11." Social Science Research Council Web site, http://www.ssrc.org/sept11/essays.

PART FOUR. TRANSMISSION AND IDENTITY

CHAPTER 9

How Deborah Became Aisha

The Conversion Process and the Creation of Female Muslim Identity

Nicole Bourque

Until recently, most of the psychological and sociological research on conversion has been concerned with identifying: (1) what type of person might be predisposed toward religious conversion (Allison 1969; Batson and Ventis 1982; Christiansen 1963; Deutsch 1975; Gillespie 1991; James 1962; Lofland and Stark 1965; Meadow and Kahoe 1984; Salzman 1953; Ullman 1989); or (2) why someone converts (Allison 1969; Snow and Phillips 1980; Starbuck 1911). However, as Karin van Nieuwkerk indicates in the introduction to this volume, researchers are now recognizing that conversion is an ongoing process and are focusing their attention on the stages that converts go through (see, for example, Rambo 1993; Köse 1996; Poston 1992; Sultán 1999; Roald, this volume). These works recognize that there are various types of converts, many routes to conversion, and different types of Islam to which an individual may convert. Three important issues, however, are neglected in most studies. First, a consideration of how conversion to Islam requires not only a change in the convert's religious identity, but also a renegotiation of social, gender, and national identities. Second, how these new identities are embodied through taking up new bodily practices. Third, the wider context in which these identities are re-created, including power relations, interactions with other Muslims, and learning how to be a Muslim in a largely non-Muslim society.

In this chapter, I will address these issues by looking at the process of conversion and the re-creation of religious, gender, and national identity in Glasgow, Scotland. The bulk of the research upon which this discussion is based involved participant-observation and interviews with a group of twenty-five female Sunni converts who attended a weekly Islamic education/discussion group for women. I have also included information from an interview with a male convert and his wife who were not attached to this group.[1]

I begin my discussion by looking at the conversion story of Aisha, the leader of the Islamic education/discussion group. Her case study illustrates the importance of considering the social context in which the conversion process takes place. Not only was Aisha's conversion affected by her interactions with other Muslims, Aisha herself and the meetings she leads have had an impact on other convert women. I then look more closely at the conversion process and the re-creation of identity amongst the women in the group. This will include a consideration of how a Scottish Muslim female identity is embodied through changing bodily practices, shaped and internalized through discourse, and affected by interactions with other Muslims and with wider Scottish society.

Meeting Aisha: Talking to the Converted

When I first met Aisha and she told me her conversion story, she had been a Muslim for twenty years. She was born as Deborah and was raised in a working-class part of Glasgow. One day, when she was seventeen, she went to a local corner store that was run by a Pakistani family. She saw a man kneeling and bowing. She told me that at that time, she knew nothing about Islam. She thought that he was doing exercises. She waited with her purchases until he was finished and then asked him what he was doing. He explained that he was praying to God. The fact that a person would stop selling goods in order to pray impressed her deeply. The man lent her several books on Islam, and she frequently returned to the shop to discuss them.

Aisha said that she found that Islam answered many questions that Christianity did not. She decided to convert, changed her name to Aisha, and married the man who had introduced her to Islam. Aisha's parents accepted her conversion. They said they could see that she had changed for the better. She no longer went out drinking and dancing, as other girls of her age did. She was also more respectful to her parents. Her husband's family, however, were against the marriage. They had wanted him to marry "a nice Pakistani girl." They did not believe that a "white" girl could be a good mother and faithful wife. They feared that she would lead him "away from the path of Islam."

At first, Aisha found relations with her in-laws very difficult. This was complicated by their inability to speak English. Aisha gradually learned Punjabi, adopted the Pakistani style of dress, wore the *hijab*, and learned Pakistani customs. She read about Islam under the guidance of her husband. If she had questions he could not answer, she would turn to the *imam* of their local mosque, who was born in Pakistan.[2] Thus, Aisha's understanding of Islam was and continues to be influenced by people and scholars that meet with the approval of the local Pakistani-dominated Muslim community.

The more Aisha learned about Islam, the more active she became in trying to bring others to Islam. She began to do *da'wah* (spreading the word of Islam) very shortly after her own conversion. Her mother, father, and one of her brothers became Muslims. When her in-laws saw that not only was she practicing Islam but also bringing others to the faith, they began to accept her. Her commitment to the main tenets of Islam even led her, through her husband, to encourage her in-laws to abandon some of their practices that were part of Pakistani custom but not found in the Qur'an or hadith. Today, they respect her knowledge of Islam and even come to her for advice.

Aisha's experiences with her in-laws and the problems she had learning about Islam led her to set up an Islamic education/discussion group for Muslim women. Though any Muslim woman was welcomed to attend, the meetings were primarily directed toward the needs of new Muslim women or Scottish non-Muslim women who were interested in learning about Islam. Aisha invited me to attend. The number of women who attended these meetings varied from week to week. After several months, I got to know twenty-five women (including Aisha) at various stages of the conversion process. This included women who were married to Muslim men and were curious about Islam, but were not converts when they started attending the meetings. They later converted during the course of my research.

These classes were held in Aisha's own home rather than at the mosque. This greatly affected the content and social dynamics of the meetings. Because the meetings were at Aisha's home, she was able to set the agenda without the direct influence of local Muslim leaders or organizations. In contrast to the didactic lessons organized by the mosque, Aisha's meetings were interactive: the women were encouraged to ask questions and debate issues.

The meetings would usually begin with readings from the Qur'an and hadith related to a certain topic of interest to the women. For example, during Ramadan, we talked about the importance of fasting and how to go about fasting. After the Qur'anic part of the meeting, the women would generally discuss day-to-day problems, such as conflicts with in-laws. At times, these "problems" would become the focal topic of the next week's Qur'anic meeting. Because of this, these meetings were very important in making Islam even more relevant to the women who attended. A woman who had a problem with her mother-in-law could come to the meeting, discuss the problem with other women, find out what the Qur'an and hadith had to say about the matter, and get practical advice about what to do when she got home.

The Conversion Process

Before I discuss how identity is created, I want to take a closer look at what other researchers have said about the conversion process. Though, as I mention in my introduction, a number of people are working in this field, I will focus my discussion on Köse's work on conversion to Islam in Britain (1994, 1996). I have two reasons for this: First, Köse is one of the few people to have published work on the conversion process in Britain; and second, I found his work very helpful in explaining what I was observing in Glasgow, since his findings largely agreed with mine.

According to Köse (1996), reciting the *shahada* (the declaration of faith) was only one stage in a much longer and more gradual process of becoming Muslim. The process of conversion, in fact, starts long before one declares oneself as a Muslim. He noted that many of the converts he interviewed felt that their religion of origin and the values presented to them by their parents and society were irrelevant to their life. This disaffection did not lead to a "crisis of faith." Rather, they continued on with life as normal and entered a "spiritual moratorium" that lasted a number of years. At the end of this period, many of his informants either experienced cognitive concerns that led them to seek answers from other religions or experienced emotional problems or turmoil that led them to think that religion might lead them to answers. Because these people were not satisfied with their religion of origin, they did not experience a religious revival—that is, they did not become "born again." Rather, they sought answers elsewhere. At this stage, the presence of other Muslims tended to play a crucial role in the conversion process.

As I gathered conversion stories in Glasgow, I discovered that many—though not all—fit the pattern described by Köse (1996). Aisha, for example, was raised as a member of the Salvation Army. She felt that this belief system had some logical inconsistencies. These, however, were not an issue for her, as she found herself caught up in the concerns of a typical teenager. Her meeting with her future husband led her to question her previous beliefs. She admitted that she began to ask herself existential questions, such as "Why am I here?" and "What really happens after I die?" Aisha was attracted to Islam as a possible source of answers to these questions because she was impressed with the example set by the man who was to become her husband. After meetings and discussions with him she came to see that Islam answered questions that her previous Christian faith did not, and she decided to convert.[3]

For the majority of the women I talked with, affective ties with Muslims played an important role in their conversion to Islam. In fact, the majority of the women I talked to were married to Muslim men prior to conversion. All of these women stressed that they were not forced to convert by their husbands or in-laws. Rather, they claimed that because of their marriage they decided to learn about Islam and generally liked what they found. For example, Fatima, a more recent convert to Islam, said that the good example set by her Muslim husband and in-laws helped to counteract the negative media image of Islam.

Köse (1996) is careful to point out that people also convert because Islam has an intellectual appeal to them.[4] That is, it makes sense in terms of their own value systems and seems logical in comparison with alternative belief systems. The relationship between having affective ties with Muslims and the intellectual appeal of Islam can be complex. One woman I talked to first became interested in Islam when she had a Muslim boyfriend. The more she read about Islam, the more she realized that her boyfriend was not "a good Muslim." She noted that many of the older Pakistani people she met followed what she called "Pakistani village Islam," which owed more to Pakistani local customs than it did to the strict sayings of the Qur'an and hadith. In fact, she said that if she had met more of these people when she was becoming interested in Islam, she probably wouldn't have converted.

Köse (1996) notes that continued interaction with Muslims is very important in helping the converted remain converted. This can be seen in Aisha's case. As she learned more about Islam and had questions about it, her husband was on hand to guide her. Also, as she spent more and more time with her husband's family and other Muslims, she found that she received positive encouragement to "live as a Muslim." This process was also at work amongst the women who attended Aisha's meetings. Their conversions were received very positively by their husbands and in-laws. Interacting with other new Muslim women during Aisha's meetings also helped these women remain converted. Any problems that they had could be discussed with the group and practical solutions proposed.

I also found Köse's analysis useful because it stresses that the conversion process involved the gradual adoption of "Muslim" practices. Köse (1994, 1996) notes that many of the people he interviewed went through a "probation" period before declaring their faith. That is, they tried to practice some aspects of Islam before finally deciding to convert. Even after taking the *shahada*, most of his subjects only gradually came to take up all of the practices of Islam. He claims that they were more likely to take up the prohibitions first, such as avoiding pork and alcohol. Then they gradually adopted daily prayer or wearing the *hijab*. My own research supports this. Aisha claimed that she had been a Muslim for two years before she "felt strong enough in her faith to wear *hijab* in public." Many of the women I interviewed said that there was a difference between things that you could do on your own (such as not eating pork or praying every day) and things that you had to do in public (such as wearing your *hijab* at work). It was one thing to admit to yourself that you were a Muslim and to act accordingly in your private life, it was quite another to feel strong enough in your faith to present yourself as a Muslim to everyone else.

In spite of the fact that I found Köse's (1996) work helpful in explaining what I was seeing in Glasgow, I soon found that it had its limitations. His research is based on questionnaires and interviews with fifty male and twenty female informants and only scrapes the surface in discussing the changes that happen to a person who converts. For example, Köse helped make me aware of the importance of affective ties in the conversion process. However, his analysis looks at the presence or absence of affective ties and does not consider how this relates to the wider social context in which converts try to live as Muslims. Clearly, in the case of Aisha's group, meeting with other Muslim women had a profound effect on the converts.

Another area in which I feel Köse only scrapes the surface is his work on the degree to which Islamic observances are taken up by converts. This involves looking at measurable indicators of Islamic religiosity, such as frequency of prayer or observance of food taboos. As an anthropologist, I feel that the process of becoming a Muslim is not just about the adoption of certain quantifiable practices. It is also a process of learning how to see yourself as a Muslim, how to live as a Muslim, and how to present yourself to others as a Muslim. That is, Köse fails to deal with the process of how identity changes during the conversion process.

The key to understanding the conversion process is not simply to look at how certain individuals progress through the "stages" of conversion. We have to look at how progression through these stages involved the creation of a Muslim identity. In looking at this process, it is crucial to realize that this does not happen in a vacuum of self-discovery. A person does not become a Muslim in isolation.[5] Becoming and being a Muslim, particularly in the case of women, means interacting with other Muslims who may have different ideas of what Islam is and how it should be practiced. This means confronting media images of Islam. It also involves dealing with families, friends, and coworkers who have preconceived (and often media-fed) images of what Islam entails.

It is through this interaction with other Muslims and with wider British society that people begin to negotiate what being a Muslim means to them. This entails re-creating personal identity, creating a Muslim identity, and re-negotiating national and gender identity. I will look more closely at these processes in the sections to follow.

From Deborah to Aisha: Re-creating Religious and Gender Identity

All of the women I talked to recognized that conversion involved not just a change of religion, but a change in who they were. In spite of the fact that the conversion process begins before taking the *shahada*, it was this rite of passage that marked the start of a change in identity. Many of the women told me that after you take the *shahada*, you are forgiven for all of your previous sins. You start afresh, like a newborn baby. Many women described a feeling of euphoria after they committed to following Allah and recited the *shahada*. One woman described a feeling of peace; she said: "It is like you are born again and you can start all over again, free from sin." Most of the women who converted chose to take on a Muslim name to symbolize this new person that they had become.[6] The idea of starting life again clean of sin is important in terms of entering heaven, because on the Day of Judgment all your sins will be weighed against your good deeds. Many of the women commented on the fact that after taking the *shahada*, all your good deeds will get double the "reward" that a "born" Muslim would get for the same deeds. Thinking about your life in terms of the Day of Judgment marked a major shift in the way these women thought about their choices and actions. One woman said: "It is all down to the choices I make now. I can either choose to pray, or I can choose to watch *East Enders* [a popular soap opera]."

This view that life has changed as a result of conversion coexists in a somewhat contradictory manner with the commonly expressed idea that before conversion the women felt that they "were already Muslim." As one put it: "When I started reading the Qur'an, I realized that this is how I had always felt about things. So I knew that Islam was right." The women explained this feeling by referring to the belief that all people, angels, animals, and things are born Muslim. Aisha pointed out to me this is why Muslims have no form of baptism. When the sun rises and sets, it is obeying the will of Allah. Only humans have free choice. Those who are not Muslims have made choices that have taken them away from the path of Allah. When you take the *shahada* you are returning to Allah. For this reason, the women I talked with did not refer to themselves as converts, but as reverts.

Becoming a Muslim woman necessitates a renegotiation of your gender identity. You have to accept the role that Allah set out for women. This places you in a particular relationship to your husband, children, in-laws, and parents. Many women indicated that there were some aspects of the Islamic view of women that agreed with their own personal preconversion beliefs. A prime example of this is the positive value placed on motherhood. As Aisha put it, "In wider society, people say, 'Oh, you are just a housewife.' According to Islam, heaven lies at the feet of your mother. People have to respect their mothers. Being a housewife is an important role in society."

Women's rights under Islam were a common topic of discussion. As women learned more about their rights, this affected their relationships with their husbands. At one meeting, it was mentioned that under Islam, it was the husband's duty to provide for the family and that his wife's money remained hers to control. This came as a surprise to one recently married woman. She said that her husband sent all of his money to Pakistan, while her wages went to supporting the household. She said that her husband tried to justify this by saying it was his obligation to respect his parents and send money to them. Armed with this new knowledge about her rights as a Muslim wife, she went home to challenge her husband.

Many of the women said that being Muslim was something that affected their everyday life. That is, becoming Muslim is not just about taking on a new religious identity. It affects who you are as a person and how you live your life on an hour-to-hour and day-by-day basis. One woman, who was telling me about how Islam added structure to her life, said: "My day is divided by prayer, I know what to eat and what to avoid, I know how to wash, how to dress, and how to act towards my children and husband." It is not enough to think like a Muslim, you also have to act like one. The physical aspects of becoming a Muslim—changing your diet, your clothes, the way you wash; looking down when you pass men in the streets; and the actions of praying—all play an important role in the creation of a new identity. Effectively, your new religion becomes embodied, and your actions serve to reaffirm your identity as a Muslim woman.

In order to demonstrate the physical aspect of becoming Muslim, I will give several examples of some of the lessons and discussions that took place during Aisha's meetings. Even though a large part of the meetings was given over to discussing the Qur'an and hadith, we very often considered the practical aspects of living as a Muslim. In fact, many of the passages that we looked at in the Qur'an and hadith concerned issues such as dress, cleanliness, prayer, and fasting.

When a new convert arrived at one of the meetings, Aisha would always start with teaching her how to pray. Even women who had not converted were invited to join in the prayer. When I prayed with the women, I could not help but notice how standing side by side with these women made us feel part of the group. The actions of standing and bowing reminded me of our submission to Allah. During the meetings, we covered other aspects of living as a Muslim. The rules on purification were particularly important. Women were told how to wash before prayer and how to purify themselves after intercourse or menstruation. They even learned how to go to the bathroom: which foot to use to enter and leave the bathroom, which *du'a* (supplication) to say as they entered, and how to clean themselves without using toilet paper.

Appropriate dress for women and men was another popular topic. There were a number of debates on the *hijab*. A major problem some of the women faced was being told by their mothers-in-law that they were not dressed "properly" because they did not wear traditional Pakistani female attire. Hearing and discussing what the Qur'an and hadith said about dress helped women make decisions about what to wear.

Eating and fasting were also discussed during the meetings. Whereas most women were aware of which categories of food were *haram* and *halal*, they still talked about the practicalities of shopping: where could you get *halal* meat, which makes of gelatin you could buy, and what to do about providing *halal* school lunches. When we had a meeting to learn about fasting and Ramadan, one woman wanted to know how she could prepare food for her evening guests if she could not taste the food to check the seasoning. This led to a lively debate where various women described their strategy for coping with this: some women did not taste the food at all, others tasted the food on the tip of their tongue and then spat it out. I mention this example because it serves as a good illustration of the extent to which Muslim female identity is embodied. The woman who asked the question was not just concerned about being a good Muslim and doing her fast correctly, she also wanted to be a good Muslim wife and provide well-flavored food for her family and guests.

As with Köse's interviewees, not all of the women who attended Aisha's group carried out all of the practices mentioned above. In fact, some of the non-Muslim women said that even though they believed in the precepts of Islam, they could never become Muslim because it would be impossible to make all of these changes to their daily practices. Perhaps one of the reasons Aisha was so successful in *da'wah* was that she told these women that taking the *shahada* was a first step and that these practices could be adopted at their own pace: as their faith grew stronger, they would find it easier. Some of these women did eventually convert. They were encouraged by other women in the group who admitted to having similar misgivings about their ability to adopt all of these practices. For all of the women, even those who did not yet follow all of the practices of Islam, carrying them out played an important role in being a Muslim woman. Every time that a woman would pray, say a *du'a* before entering the bathroom, or provide a good meal for her family, she reaffirmed her decision to live as a Muslim woman. That is, a Muslim identity is embodied through daily bodily practices. These actions are also important in letting other people see that you are a Muslim. Many women would first take up practices that would be witnessed by other Muslims, such as prayer. Only later, when they felt stronger about their Muslim identity, would they take up practices that would identify them as Muslims to non-Muslims, such as wearing the *hijab* at work.

In addition to embodying Islam, the process of creating a Muslim identity involves reinterpreting the past. Discourse plays an important role in this reinterpretation. When women talked about their past, certain key themes and phrases were repeated. I have no doubt that these were learned by listening to or reading about other people's conversion stories. In their conversion stories, all of the women compared their current lifestyle to their past one. Many noted that before becoming Muslim their life had no direction. As a result of becoming Muslim, they now followed Allah's will and knew what their purpose was. Another common theme was that after their conversion, they had more respect for themselves as women. As one woman said:

Before, I used to wear short skirts and low-cut tops. I turned myself into a sex object just to please men. I always used to worry what I looked like. I always wanted to be prettier. Now I cover myself when I go out and men treat me with respect. I am not worried about what men think about my looks. I am worried about what Allah thinks. Of course, I still worry what my husband thinks. It is part of my duty to look good for him so that his eyes don't wander.

I have heard several variations of this quotation.

For the women I met, the classes that Aisha ran were an important forum for learning how to talk about their past, conversion/reversion, and future. As women talked about themselves, they began to relate to the experiences of other group members. I noticed that they used similar phrases and examples and began to rationalize their lives in terms of them. It was common to hear women say: "I had never thought about it like that before, but now that you mention it, that is exactly how I felt." For example, when I asked about women's rights under Islam or about wearing the *hijab*, I got very similar responses from the women. This indicated to me that they were all well versed in having to justify themselves to their family and other non-Muslims. Discussions during the women's meetings did not only help women learn about Islam. They also helped women learn how to talk about Islam. Talking within the group allowed women to concretize and order their thoughts and experiences. It also gave them a vocabulary to express their thoughts and problems and to re-create memories. Books and Web sites that focus on conversion stories and Muslim women's issues serve a similar purpose.[7] It is clear that in talking and thinking about yourself as a Muslim, contact with or reading about other Muslims plays a crucial role. In this next section, I will turn my attention to the wider context of how converts relate to the wider Muslim community.

Being a New Muslim in the Wider Muslim "Community"[8]

A very common topic of discussion at the meetings was women's relationships with other Muslims. Reverts to Islam refer to themselves, and are referred to, as "new Muslims," in contrast to "born Muslims." New Muslims are welcomed by other Muslims. Many commented that when they made it known to their Muslim friends or relatives that they had decided to revert, they were enthusiastically welcomed as "sisters." They were hugged and were offered presents such as a copy of the Qur'an, prayer mats, or head scarves.

All of the women I talked to said that they experienced a sense of belonging. This was especially noticed by women who had reverted after marriage to a Muslim man. This sense of belonging played an important role in keeping these women converted. Frequent interaction with other Muslims (new and born) helps shape the new Muslims' understanding of Islam. This includes learning how a good Muslim should act and react. At times, however, this help can lead to problems. A common topic of conversations during the women's meetings was the difficulties in distinguishing between Islam (what is laid out in the Qur'an and hadith) and Pakistani, Malaysian, or Arabic cultural practices.

All of the women noted that after their conversion, "born" Muslims were keen to pass on advice and criticism about how to dress and pray. Fatima complained that she noticed Malaysian women in her mosque dressing and praying in a different way from the Pakistani women. Nevertheless, she noted that the Pakistani women never criticized the Malaysian women. "It's like they are accepted for what they are because they are born Muslim, whereas what I do is open to criticism because I'm a new Muslim. Even if what I am doing is proper Islam and what the women want me to do is Pakistani custom."

This contrast between Islam and what I call Muslim customs figures in some conversion stories. Zenab was married to a wealthy businessman of Pakistani origins before she became Muslim. Her in-laws were opposed to the marriage, and Zenab had quite a negative attitude toward Islam because of the way she saw her husband's relatives acting. Nevertheless, she started to learn about Islam, because she knew that when she had children, they would have to be raised as Muslims. The more she read about Islam the more she realized that the practices she did not like were actually Pakistani customs. She found that she actually agreed with many of the teachings of Islam and so decided to convert. However, she did not tell her in-laws about the conversion, because she did not want them to think that she converted for their sake.

New Muslims who, unlike Aisha, decide not to let the dominant Pakistani group sway the way they practice Islam face criticism from the Muslim "community." During my investigations, I met a Scottish couple, Elisabeth and Paul, who had both converted to Islam. Even though Elisabeth knows Aisha, she does not attend her meetings. Elisabeth became Muslim two months before Aisha. She converted after learning about Islam from her husband, who had converted several years earlier. Elisabeth and her husband are both university-educated. They take a more questioning and critical approach to Islam than Aisha. Paul has traveled to many Muslim countries, speaks and reads Arabic, and has been studying Islam for twenty years. They feel that local Muslim organizations are "too Pakistani" in their interpretations and practices. They noted that this view of Islam is passed on to some new Muslims, such as Aisha, who are directed to read only "approved" books and translations.

Elisabeth and Paul criticize some interpretations and translations of the Qur'an and hadith that are commonly accepted locally, quoting the works of a variety of scholars that are not accepted by regional *imams*.[9] For example, Elisabeth does not wear the *hijab*, because the Qur'an does not say that women need to cover their heads. This controversial stance has caused friction between Elisabeth and other Muslim women. She was told to come back "properly dressed" when she tried to attend a women's meeting in the mosque without wearing the *hijab*.[10] At another meeting, there was an outcry when she suggested an alternative translation of a particular word in one verse of the Qur'an, which would change the meaning of the passage. She no longer attends these meetings and prefers to pray at home rather than go to the mosque.

The contrast between Aisha and Elisabeth highlights the necessity to understand the wider context in which women's meetings operate. Many of the women's meetings held in the mosques are very Pakistani-dominated. Aisha's meetings are among the few that cater to the needs of new Muslim women. While women are encouraged to ask challenging questions, there is no avoiding the fact that the woman who leads the group meetings and who plays a major role in shaping the development of newly converted women is herself very traditional in her views.

Can Haggis Be *Halal?* Becoming a Scottish Muslim

Scottish people who convert to Islam are placed in a problematic position. To some extent, they have "turned their back" on practices that are seen as typically Scottish/British, such as going to the pub after work and having bacon rolls for breakfast. Aisha, who speaks Punjabi and wears a shalwar chamese, described herself as "between cultures": "I feel neither fully British (I don't drink, dance, or celebrate Christmas), but nor am I Pakistani." In addition to redefining their religious and gender identity, new Muslims must also renegotiate their British and Scottish identity. Women do this in a variety of ways. Some feel caught between two worlds, like Aisha. Others emphasize their religious identity over all others: "I am a Muslim first, Scottish second, and British third." Some actively redefine their national identity: "I am a Scottish Muslim." That is, they feel that a Scottish national identity should include Muslims, a view the current Scottish parliament is working hard to encourage with its "One Scotland, Many Cultures" campaign. For people like Paul and Elisabeth, who have more or less cut themselves off from the wider Pakistani-dominated Muslim community, this is a popular option. Still others downplay the problem of renegotiating national identity by emphasizing the universal community of Muslims: "Islam transcends national and cultural boundaries, so my national identity is not an issue."

Becoming a British or a Scottish Muslim is not only about national identity. At a practical level it involves living amongst and interacting with other British and Scottish people, many of whom are not Muslim. As these women go about their daily lives, they have to seek Muslim solutions to problems that might arise. Christmas is a good example. Most of the Muslim women

I knew did not celebrate Christmas. These were women who were married to Muslim men and were raising their children as Muslims. However, one of the single Muslim women still celebrated Christmas with her family. She rationalized this by saying:

Christmas is about the birth of Isa [Jesus], who we recognize in Islam as a prophet. So, it is not against Islam to celebrate the birth of a prophet as long as you don't go in for the nonreligious stuff. Also, according to Islam, you are supposed to respect your parents. Going to see my parents at Christmas is a way of showing them respect. . . . My parents are very supportive. They even tried to get a halal turkey.[11]

During the women's meetings, national identity was rarely discussed. A more frequent topic of conversation was the reactions of non-Muslims to their conversion. All of the women felt strongly about the commonly held view that Islam is a religion that discriminates against women: "People see pictures of how the Taliban treat women in Afghanistan and think that all Muslim women are treated this way." A recently converted woman told me:

My parents were afraid that I was going to become a terrorist. My friends asked me how could I give up my freedom. I told them that in this country you can't sell a car without having a naked girl lying on the bonnet. How free and liberated is that?

When I asked women what bothered them the most about how they were perceived by the general public, they all mentioned the way people reacted to their wearing the *hijab:*

One man asked me if my husband forced me to wear the hijab! I told him I do it as a sign of devotion to Allah. Nuns can walk around with their hair covered as a sign of their devotion and no one complains. Why can't people accept that I wear hijab as a sign of devotion?!

Just as there were convergences in the women's conversion stories, there are similarities in the way in which these women talk about the rights of Muslim women. New converts learn how to explain Islam to their parents by listening to stories of how older converts managed to overcome the same problems.

Conclusion: The Process of Becoming Muslim after Taking the *Shahada*

Near the beginning of this chapter, I mentioned that most of the new Muslim women I talked to only began to wear the *hijab* a few years after taking the *shahada*. For these women, the process of becoming a Muslim was a long one that began with re-creating their religious and gender identity; re-remembering the past; learning how to verbalize their experiences; learning how to talk about Islam; and taking up new bodily practices. People need time to adjust to these changes and to feel comfortable with them. It is easiest to do this when surrounded by other Muslims who understand and support you in making these changes. It is only when these women feel confident about their faith and have learned to answer people's questions that they present themselves as Muslims to the wider public. Wearing the *hijab* when you go to work or the shops is not only a declaration to Allah, it is also a declaration to everyone that you want everyone to know you are a Muslim.

This chapter has tried to demonstrate that to understand why and how Scottish women become Muslim women we need to focus on the processes by which a new identity is created. This must take into account: (1) the ways in which identity is embodied; (2) the effects of social interaction with Muslims and wider British/Scottish society; (3) the wider power context in which these interactions operate; and (4) the importance of discourse in concretizing experiences and in re-creating biography.

In this chapter, I only refer to a small number of women. Nevertheless, the issues I raise could be used to study other groups of converts.[12] It would also be interesting to see comparisons with new Muslims in countries that are not dominated by Pakistani forms of Islam, such as France and the United States. Certainly, within this volume, Roald's account of converts in Scandinavia, where the Muslim institutions are not Pakistani-dominated, and Gwendolyn Zoharah Simmons's account of her conversion to the Nation of Islam in the United States provide a sharp contrast to the situation in Glasgow. These examples support my claim that the conversion process must be understood by looking at the wider social context in which converts live.

Notes

1. Since this is a very small sample that includes only one man and no non-Sunni Muslims, I make no claims that my findings are representative of Muslims in Glasgow.

2. The majority of Muslims in Glasgow are of Pakistani cultural origins.

3. Of course, my description of this conversion is based on Aisha's re-created memories of the events as they happened. It is difficult to say if events really happened in the way she describes. Nevertheless, it is important that she now perceives them as having happened in this way (see

my comments on discourse later on in this chapter).

4. Allievi (1998, 1999) also looks at relational (affective) and rational (intellectual) conversions.

5. This is particularly the case for people who have affective ties with Muslims before they convert. However, even people who convert for purely intellectual reasons will have some degree of interaction with other Muslims.

6. Even though most of the women took on a new name, not all of them used it in public after they first converted.

7. For an excellent discussion of discourse in online narratives of conversion stories, see van Nieuwkerk's chapter in this volume.

8. I feel I have to put the word community in quotation marks. People in Glasgow (Muslims and non-Muslims alike) talk about the Muslim community. In reality, however, there is little sense of this community. There is tension among the various mosques. The year I began doing my fieldwork, the mosques in Glasgow could not even decide on which day to start Ramadan. As a consequence, which of the two different start dates you observed depended on what mosque you belonged to. This is not uncommon in Britain. See, for example, Neilson 1987.

9. Some of their sources are non-Muslim Islamic scholars, who are uncritically rejected by the *imams*, due to the belief that Islam cannot be understood unless it is practiced and one has faith in Allah.

10. This meeting was run by Pakistani Muslim women.

11. See Roald (this volume) for a discussion of how Scandinavian converts incorporate Scandinavian ideals into an Islamic framework.

12. Köse (1996) suggests that the experiences of Shi'a and Sufi converts differ from those of Sunnis.

References

Allievi, S. 1998. *Les convertis à l'islam. Les nouveaux musulmans d'Europe.* Paris: L'Harmattan.

———. 1999. "Pour une sociologie des conversions: lorsque des Européens deviennent musulmans." *Social Compass* 46 (3): 283–300.

Allison, J. 1969. "Religious Conversion: Regression and Progression in Adolescent Experience." *Journal for the Scientific Study of Religion* 8 (2): 23–38.

Batson, C. D., and W. Ventis. 1982. *The Religious Experience.* Oxford: Oxford University Press.

Christensen, C. W. 1963. "Religious Conversion." *Archives of General Psychiatry* 9: 207–216.

Deutsch, A. 1975. "Observations on a Sidewalk Ashram." *Archives of General Psychiatry* 32: 166–175.

Gillespie, V. B. 1991. *The Dynamics of Religious Conversion.* Birmingham, Ala.: Religious Educational Press.

James, W. 1962. *The Varieties of Religious Experience.* London: Collins.

Köse, A. 1994. "Conversion to Islam: A Study of Native British Converts." Ph.D. diss., Department of Theology and Religious Studies, University of London.

———. 1996. *Conversion to Islam: A Study of Native British Converts.* London: Kegan Paul.

Lofland, J., and R. Stark. 1965. "Becoming a World Saver: A Theory of Conversion to a

Deviant Perspective." *American Sociological Review* 30 (December): 862–875.

Meadow, J. G., and R. Kahoe 1984. *Psychology of Religion*. London: Harper and Row.

Neilson, J. 1987. "Muslims in Britain: Searching for an Identity." *New Community* 8 (3): 384–394.

Poston, Larry. 1992. *Islamic Da'wah in the West: Muslim Missionary Activity and the Dynamics of Conversion to Islam*. Oxford: Oxford University Press.

Rambo, L. R. 1993. *Understanding Religious Conversion*. New Haven, Conn.: Yale University Press.

Salzman, L. 1953. "The Psychology of Religious and Ideological Conversion." *Psychiatry* 16 (May): 177–187.

Snow, D., and C. Phillips. 1980. "The Lofland-Stark Conversion Model: A Critical Reassessment." *Social Problems* 4: 430–447.

Starbuck, E. 1911. *The Psychology of Religion*. London: The Walter Scott.

Sultán, M. 1999. "Choosing Islam: A Study of Swedish Converts." *Social Compass* 46 (3): 325–337.

Ullman, C. 1989. *The Transformed Self: The Psychology of Religious Conversion*. London: Plenum.

CHAPTER 10

Keeping the Faith

Convert Muslim Mothers and the Transmission
of Female Muslim Identity in the West

Marcia Hermansen

This chapter is a study of Euro-American female converts to Islam in the United States who have raised daughters as Muslims since their conversion. Through a series of personal interviews conducted either in face-to-face meetings or over the telephone, I gathered data based on a loose protocol of questions. This study was intended to examine the experiences of convert mothers who attempted to raise daughters with Muslim identities. My theoretical analysis of the results frames their responses within identity issues—for example, how self-perceptions evolved during the individuals' life cycles against the background of external factors such as the development of a Muslim immigrant community in the United States, cultural change in American attitudes toward women's roles, and global political events.

My sample is a group of eleven Euro-American women who converted to Islam between 1967 and 1980 who reflected on their experiences raising nineteen of their twenty-one daughters (I excluded two daughters who are under fifteen years of age). In a certain sense all the mothers are "individual" converts, that is, women who claim to have chosen conversion of their own volition. Although some converted only after marriage to Muslim males, they asserted that they never felt pressured to make that decision. Seven of the women are married to other Euro-Americans, and I will subsequently refer to this combination as an "AA" marriage, and four others married immigrant Muslim males, which I will mark as an "AI" combination. In order to limit the variables in identity transmission, I did not interview African American convert mothers as part of this research.

The very fact that there is a new generation of Muslims born to the first cohort of convert women is a significant milestone. Allievi refers to the cohort of the convert mothers as "generation zero," since it is their children who will really be the first ones growing up as "American Muslims" (1998, 216).

Fifteen years ago I considered for the first time the types of American women who were choosing to convert to Islam (Hermansen 1991, 188–201). At that time, I concluded that the generational cohort of conversion (i.e., that of the 1960s,

'70s, '80s, etc.) played in role in the style of Islam that attracted and sustained these women's interest and commitment. I believe that the current research supports that conclusion. Since the current study selects women who have raised daughters to adulthood or at least adolescence, my age cohort are women who are at least in their late forties or early fifties, with some over sixty. These women are therefore "pioneers," converted before the largest impact of Muslim immigration and the conservative influence on the Muslim presence in the United States of organized Islamist movements, which began in the late 1970s.

In the 1970s, when many of the interviewees converted, there often were no large Muslim communities or institutions such as weekend schools or mosques, much less full-time Islamic schools, to sustain Muslim identity among children growing up in a largely Christian American culture. Some of that has now changed in the larger population centers. However, for many Euro-American Muslims the Islamic schools still may not be the answer for reasons to be discussed later.

This study is therefore a snapshot of a particular, fairly limited, and unusual group in its earliest phase of development. In another ten or fifteen years, another cohort of converted Euro-American women, who have raised daughters within a more institutionally supportive environment and with a more fully articulated conception of Islamic identity, can be studied.

I interviewed a preliminary survey of eleven women for this study, based on a loose protocol of questions assessing their family background, conversion narratives, the experiences they had in raising daughters, and the situations of these daughters currently. As a researcher, I have the advantage of over twenty years as a Muslim convert; therefore, I know the community and could rapidly network through acquaintances and snowball methodology to find interviewees. As a female Muslim, I have natural rapport with the women being interviewed, and I have visited most of the communities where these women live, so that I understand the social and physical settings.

At this point, I would like to indicate that there is a certain fluidity to the scene of emerging Muslim identities among the daughters' generation. After all, the eldest of the daughters are now approaching thirty, while the youngest that I consider are still in their teens. Much is still to be determined in terms of their choices of lifestyle and religious commitment in the future.

Composition of the Sample

I initially sorted the responses from the women I interviewed around the type of Muslim identity preferred by the mothers. Another significant variable was the combination of spouses: two American Muslims (AA) or an American Muslim wife and an immigrant Muslim husband (AI).

In terms of the preferred Muslim identity, my sample was composed of:

four Sufi mothers who lived communally—three of whom are disciples of Shaykh Nazim;[1]

two Sufi-oriented women living outside of communal settings, one of them a disciple of Shaykh Nazim;

two activist/conservative women (This category turned out to be difficult to define, and "conservatism" was not a characteristic claimed by the women themselves. I conclude that in this early cohort, Islamist identities had not yet made an impact, and therefore women that I might have expected to give this response answered "strong Muslim" or "practicing" rather than identifying with any specific movement or ideological orientation. At the same time, women I might have expected to answer "Sufi" or "liberal" often answered "committed" or "strong" Muslim);

three moderate, nonsectarian women.

Among my sample there were no women from sectarian groups such as Shi'a, Ismailis, or Ahmadis.

One example of this way of dividing the sample by Muslim identity is the study carried out by Gabriele Hofmann (1997) of German female converts to Islam. She grouped her interviewees according to four groups that are somewhat similar to my categories above: (1) Salafis; (2) independent freethinking; (3) Ahmadis; and (4) Sufis.[2]

Roald's study of Muslims in Sweden (2001), which focused mainly on immigrant Muslims and their perceptions on women's issues, isolated the following three factors that influence the style of Muslim ideology. First was length of residence in the West; second, the extent of immigrants' interaction with the non-Muslim community; and finally, the group to which they belonged: Salafi, independent, Hizb-e tahrir, etc. In considering my sample in terms of similar indexes, despite the different context, I initially surmised that the tightness of the age cohort studied would make factors such as the length of time being Muslim or the year of conversion less of a variable factor among these mothers. However, I take note that the two converts of the 1960s could be characterized as "activist Muslim" women who married immigrant student Muslims. I believe that this, although a preliminary conclusion, reflects both the situation of American culture at that time, before the major impact of the "spiritual seeking" movements of the 1970s, and the concurrent context of encounters with immigrant Muslims, primarily occurring on college campuses.

Islamic ideology seemed to be a less significant factor in identity and self-definition among the group of women I interviewed, except for the distinction between Sufi and non-Sufi Islam. In fact, the Sufi category varies within itself in terms of those in the Naqshbandi-Haqqani movement and those with more diffuse affiliations, and even within the Naqshbandi *tariqa* itself. As a differentiating factor in practice or Islamic identity transmission, the situation of being in a marriage between two American converts, as opposed to a marriage with an immigrant Muslim, seemed to be more influential in the identity development of the daughters.

The extent of interaction with the immigrant Muslim community seems to be an important factor as well, but normally it is those women married to immigrant Muslims who naturally have more extensive interaction both with the broader community and in their own homes and families.

Styles of Conversion and the Converted Life

All studies of convert Muslims in the West stress the common theme of gradual, reflection-based conversion rather than the sudden snapping of "self-surrender" (Poston 1992). This was also the case with the women I interviewed. All accepted Islam as a conscious choice after long periods of study and reflection. Five of the Sufi women (AA) converted at the same time as their American husbands; all of the four women married to immigrant Muslims converted after meeting their husbands, but for two of them it was a choice made independently before marriage. The third (AI) was not encouraged to convert before marriage but did have to agree to raise any children as Muslims. She and the fourth woman (AI) decided on their own to convert after some years of marriage, one shortly after the birth of her first child and the second while she was pregnant with a first child. One American woman converted on her own long before meeting her American husband, who had also become a Muslim on his own before meeting her. Another AA woman converted in college and after some time was introduced to her future husband, a Jewish American student who had already accepted Islam on his own, by foreign Muslim students on campus.

Travisano (1970) proposed two styles of adopting a new religion, conversion versus alternation (in Wohlrab-Sahr 1999, 351). He characterized

"conversion" as a radical change of worldview and identity that excludes former commitments. "Alternation," on the other hand, is an ongoing process
in which the past is accommodated, integrated, and negotiated in terms of
shaping the current identity. Wohlrab-Sahr develops these into the categories "syncretism" versus "combativeness" in terms of converts' styles of living within the natal society. She gives the example of converts in immigrant
marriages as preferring the "syncretistic" style. I think, however, that this is
more generational, as a younger cohort of Islamist women converts who generally marry immigrants can be very combative against "*kafir*" elements in
American society.[3] Also, a marriage of two American Muslims is unlikely to
produce a combative convert identity. In fact, I have never seen an instance
of this, although one woman (AA) I interviewed said that for some time after their initial conversion, she and her husband were very hard on other
Muslims who they didn't feel were "coming up to the mark," a fact she now
regrets.[4]

Another system of categories attempts to make a similar point by distinguishing between "verbal converts," who declare their new affiliation but
are not particularly activist, and "total converts," who become very active
in promoting their newfound identity (Allievi 1998, 74).[5] The role of some
total converts within this schema seems to me to be somewhat like what
one interviewee called the "born-again convert Muslims," who try to avoid
all things non-Muslim and have a more politicized view of culture and purity. These seem to be younger women than those interviewed in my sample.
In terms of Allievi's categories of motivations for conversion—political discourse, intellectual rationalizations, and mystical inclinations—the latter
two elements were the ones cited by the individuals in my sample (Allievi
2000, 167–177).[6]

Allievi observes that in today's marketplace of religious ideas, conversions to Islam are less socially costly than they once were (Allievi 1998, 78).[7] I
agree that alienation from American society or combative posturing did not
emerge in the narratives of the mothers I interviewed. For all of them, being
Muslim was a lifestyle choice, and they generally maintained good relations
with birth families and the surrounding American community. Although in
most cases their close friendships and associations changed, they still had or
made new non-Muslim friends, usually neighbors or coworkers. Among my
sample of women, however, conversion has entailed major shifts of identity
and shaped their entire life orientation in career, marriage choices, and child-
rearing philosophy and practice.

Relations with birth families were not ruptured but might initially be strained among the women, only to be resolved later in life. One mother, Marika (AA), explained:

My relations with my family have been distant, especially since becoming Muslim. We visit them [in another state] a couple of times a year. We used to send the kids there for a week or two when they were younger. Then, as young teenagers, they didn't want to go anymore because my father would argue with them about religion. They said unless we went together they didn't want to go, and when they came back it would be, "Grandpa said this or that." At sixteen or seventeen they were ready to go again; when they were younger and really shaky about answering about Islamic topics, they didn't want to go near their grandparents.[8]

In summary, it is difficult to completely bifurcate the styles of these women's converted lives according to "verbal"/"total" or "alternation"/"conversion" categories. From one perspective a choice of Muslim communal living could be seen as "total," yet interaction with birth families and the larger American society continues.

Historically and sociologically, the impact of migration of Muslims to the United States after the liberalization of the American immigration laws in the mid-1960s ultimately was to increase the accessibility of information about Islam. In the case of the Sufi-oriented Muslims, travel and contact with shaykhs or their disciples were an initiating element in their contact with Islam as part of a broader spiritual search. In the cases of women who married immigrants, their Muslim husbands came to the United States for study and ultimately decided to immigrate.

In the lives of the convert women whom I studied, Islamic activities or other elements of living a Muslim identity were striking. During one conversation we settled on the expression "doing Islam 24/7." In other words, career and lifestyle choices were completely dominated by Islam.[9] Seven of the eleven convert mothers currently have careers that evidence this commitment: teaching Islam, presenting workshops, editing for Muslim presses, or selling Islamic books. Two are housewives. Another does administrative work at a university but presents Muslim cultures through artistic workshops. The last tried teaching in an Islamic school, but found dealing with the male immigrant Muslim board too difficult and now teaches in a Christian private school. Three of the convert women have PhDs completed after marriage. Three others have master's degrees completed after marriage. Two have postgraduate teaching credentials. Only two did not finish at a university up to the bachelor's level.

In contrast to the mothers, only one of the convert American Muslim husbands is similarly involved in full-time Islamic work, and one of the immigrant husbands now devotes all his time to Islamic activities. At the same time, none of the daughters has chosen a full-time Islamic career, although it may be too early to draw a definitive conclusion regarding their career paths.

Islamic identity was not framed by these informants in terms of dualistic oppositions of pure/impure, Muslim/non-Muslim, or *halal/haram*. If anything, the interviewees stressed the need to allow their children aspects of American life that were "normal," such as TV, movies, and music, rather than dividing the world in a binary way. One mother, Qamar (AA), specifically resisted such limitations in child-raising:

I have a hard time being around people who are hard-line and conservative. I had other Muslim mothers calling me up and complaining, "How could you let my daughter play with a Barbie doll?" "How could you let my child sing 'Happy Birthday'?" "You're teaching your daughters to swim! Haram!" The search for Muslim community was problematic. People were judgmental and uptight. There was [a] time when my religious practice had more to do with my daily life than at present, it made me a very serious person and it made my kids miserable. I had to lighten up.

Community

Almost all respondents note the critical impact of community on child-raising, both in lending a sense of normality to the lifestyle, including religious practices of the family, and in providing a peer group that will not marginalize the child as being "different."

One style of Islamic practice is the small Sufi community. Here, many of the daughters were home-schooled and nurtured in an environment of a small number of families, many committed to a particular shaykh—one "loves the shaykh and takes allegiance *[bay'a]* to him." One such mother, Bilqis (AA), describes her search for Muslim community in the following way:

[Before conversion] my husband and I were reading a lot and tracing the footnotes in books such as Be Here Now.[10] *We saw the connection of the teachings we liked to people of the past who had been practicing Muslims. My husband and I lived in*

a small town but we drove to Boulder to try and connect with Muslims in mosques. Once we went to a Shi'a mosque, Iranian, after the revolution and found it displaying posters of dripping blood, so that wasn't our style. We wanted the spirituality. I attended a woman's Sufi retreat and encountered the salat *[Islamic prayer]. I came back and said: "This is what we want." We found Islam at that time to be something that could be "woven into the fabric of our lives." It was more accommodating to children than many other spiritual paths we were encountering. Also it did not require spending large sums of money for classes and seminars. In Santa Fe we connected with a number of families who were followers of the Naqshbandi shaykh Nazim. We started fasting [in] Ramadan and making the dhikr with them. We wanted to make allegiance* (bay'a) *to the shaykh and were told* shahada *came first and we were ready for that.*

A pattern common among the daughters from Sufi families who lived communally is their strong identification with traditional feminine roles as wives and mothers and early marriages. Marriages tend to be to the children of other Sufi families or to immigrant Muslim males involved in Sufism and may even be arranged by the shaykh. In cases of early marriage, the parents committed to an extended or joint family living situation in order to sustain the young couples. One mother, Jamila (AA), described her daughter's upbringing in this Sufi environment:

She had home schooling. Her training was like a village girl where she learned traditional ways of cooking and sewing. I saw she had an archetypal feminine transmission and a protected spiritual childhood. I wasn't planning that she would go to college and have a career, but she could have; after all, "heaven is at the feet of the mother,"[11] although the modern world may not support that. She [her daughter] always wanted to be like me, it was her soul, her identity.

The marriage of two Euro-Americans has the special challenge of finding a community in which to rear children with a Muslim identity. In marriages to immigrant Muslims, the extended family of the spouse often provided this community for earlier cohorts of convert women. In three of the four (AI) marriages, a parent of the husband had lived with the couple for a time while the children were growing up. In cases where the immigrant spouse had no family living nearby, a similar sense of needing Muslim families to constitute a play group or celebrate Muslim holidays together was felt by the mother.

Of course, many of these insights are basic to the sociology of the social construction of reality (Berger and Luckmann 1966). In order to sustain a particular worldview, one would want some reaffirmation of it and of identity from persons surrounding the child. One mother, Margaret (AI), spoke of her daughters' experience in trying to find community in college:

In university my daughters didn't click with the MSA [Muslim Student Association] crowd. Neither wears hijab *and they were given dirty looks attending the Friday prayers and made to feel uncomfortable by some of the cliquish and rigid Muslim students. They found the MSA speakers overly apologetic but they did participate in some other Muslim student activities like doing Mehendhi for Islam Awareness Week. They got their Islamic support at home, going to the Islamic center for prayers or Ramadan with the family.*

Another mother, Lorraine (AI), commented on her family's search for a compatible mosque community:

When you convert there is a big rush to welcome you, then they drop you like a hot potato. We went to several Islamic centers. I went through a period having issues with native clothes and culture—you know, should I wear a shalwar kamiz or Arab dress. Then I realized, this isn't really why I entered the religion, so I developed my own Islamic style. We liked one mosque that had a more progressive atmosphere, but over time the level of the programs there deteriorated and became the usual boring preaching.

Schooling and Peer Group

Educational experiences among the nineteen daughters were quite varied. Eight daughters principally attended public schools, one attended a private non-Muslim school, three were home-schooled, and three daughters, all from the same family, had a combination of all three forms, ending up attending high school at a private prep academy. Two sisters (AI) attended grades 7 and 8 in a strict Arab-run Islamic school, and then went on to Catholic all-girls' high school. One daughter (AI), who attended an urban public high school with a large contingent of some two hundred immigrant South Asian Muslim students, ended up marrying a young man of Indo-Pakistani background whom she met there.

The home-schooled children, all from (AA) communally living Sufi families, did not have access to an immigrant community or to weekend Islamic school. The children living in urban areas were often sent to weekend Islamic schools, and three AA mothers reported negative influences at the

Islamic weekend schools, which were too rigid. Fatima (AA), a single mother, explained one problem she encountered as follows:

For a while we went to weekend school at an Islamic center—another family gave us rides. One day the Arab teacher told the children: "If you disrespect your mother you will be suspended over the fires of Hell by a rope filled with sharp thorns and you won't be able to hold on and you will fall into the fire." The children were traumatized and they stopped going after that, so I had no ride, and anyway I was also turned off.

In the case of Margaret (AI), her husband had stated as a condition of marriage that he wanted any children raised Muslim. Five years after marriage Margaret accepted Islam out of her own interest and conviction. In fact, her husband didn't attend her *shahada* because he didn't want to seem like he was pressuring her. He himself became more observant only after a long time, and it seemed like his relatives also became more Islamicized through the 1980s. She describes how

one day, when my eldest daughter was three, my husband's cousin came over and said: "You need to teach her religion." Then she started Sunday school and Islamic preschool—once a week. She developed a Muslim circle of friends. My mother-in-law was living with the family then, and she also taught the children, so it happened naturally. I was not into pushing the children on religion, this is very risky at adolescence. They attended public school—there was no full-time Islamic school, and also the Islamic schools tend to be ghettoized. The children have close friends from public school, who were all non-Muslim. The home was the center of their Islamic identity.

For another mother, Linda (AI), and her husband, Islamic education at home was a high priority:

When all the children were young we would make them get up for fajr, *then we would study* hadith *together as a family. On weekends we would study Qur'an for thirty minutes or one hour. They [the children] all memorized at least two* juz"[12] *of the Qur'an, and they can read the Arabic letters and the sounds of the text.[13] They all went to Muslim Sunday school as well. Most of all we tried to be a good example.*

Some families maintained home schooling by the daughter's choice: "She made a conscious decision not to attend the local high school—it would have made it hard to cover [wear the *hijab*]" (Bilqis AA).

Alice (AA) and her husband tried integrating their daughter in an urban Sufi-influenced school and play group dominated by Euro-Americans after finding the immigrant Muslim weekend schools to be too rigid. In the Sufi environment, however, she found that because she and her husband were not initiates in that particular movement, they and their child did not achieve full acceptance. Lorraine (AI), both of whose daughters attended weekend mosque schools and for two years a full-time Islamic school dominated by Arab-Americans, found that their younger daughter, who is blond and blue-eyed, was sometimes treated as if she did not belong by the immigrant Muslim children. A sort of residual anti-Americanism arising from resentment of U.S. Middle East policy, and the stressing of distinctions between Islam and "*kafir*" culture at the school in order to reinforce Muslim identity, were not untypical of such institutions. Rayhana (AI), in reflecting on the Islamic component of her children's education, expressed some regrets:

My daughter went to the public school and a girls' Catholic high school. She also attended weekend Islamic school and madrasa every evening. All of the extra Islamic lessons were too much for the children—there was no time for TV, relaxing, or anything.

As I noted previously, the current ages of the daughters make some issues still fluid. Still, seven of the daughters who are college age have not chosen to attend college, a number that is somewhat high. The daughters who grew up in the communal situation were less likely to pursue higher education, and at least three took GEDs rather than completing regular high school. None of the daughters has pursued advanced Islamic Studies, although two are currently taking Arabic courses at college and two learned some Arabic while residing for five years in the Middle East and attending bilingual schools there. All of these daughters are AA; the AI daughters have not mastered Arabic, although they know enough of the script to sound out the Qur'an phonetically. One of the AI daughters learned Urdu, her father's mother tongue, from childhood friends and now interacts with an Urdu-speaking spouse and in-laws. Two of the others know conversational Urdu learned from relatives and a mother-in-law who lived with the family.

The mothers asserted that a key concept in raising daughters as Muslims is a sense of normality. This is achieved, as noted previously, by association with a Muslim, or at least a compatible, peer group, while at the same time avoiding excessive isolation from and condemnation of common features of American society. Fatima, single mother of a twenty-year-old daughter who is now only nominally Muslim, stated:

She had no Muslim peer group. At one time I consulted a famous child psychologist regarding her case. I had thought I understood the peer thing. He said: "You have no

*idea. They don't care what you think. Whatever their friends are doing, that's what
they want to do." Before growing up she had been "Miss Goody Two-Shoes." Then
she became a teenage monster. If her friends had been a group of hijabi girls, that
would have become her ideal. Children care most what their friends think. Among
the right crowd, "Who is the most modest," "Who wears the best hijab," could have
been her standard.*

Marriage Patterns

Of the eleven maternal marriages surveyed thus far, seven are between two
Americans (AA) and four between American females and immigrant males
(AI), three South Asians and one Arab. Nine of these eleven marriages were
not arranged. The two that might be considered "arranged" did not have parental involvement; rather, one immigrant Muslim matched an American
(non-Muslim at the time) woman with his brother, and in the other case,
Muslim students helped match two American Muslim converts at their university. Two of the women (AA Sufi) had been previously married to and divorced from non-Muslim men. One mother is now single, divorced from an
AA husband who left Islam. None of the women who married an immigrant
Muslim is a self-identified Sufi; all of the AA marriages have a Sufi element
shared by the partners.[14]

Among the nineteen daughters, nine are unmarried (three are teenagers).
Two daughters of (AA) and (AI) parents married non-Muslims who didn't
convert, one (AA) Naqshbandi married an immigrant Muslim (arranged
within the *tariqa*), one (AA) (Naqshbandi) married a Euro-American Muslim
who grew up in an (AA) American Muslim Naqshbandi family, one (AI) married a Euro-American Muslim who had converted on his own as a teenager,
two (one [AA] and one [AI]) married Americans who became Muslim in order to marry them and who now practice Islam, and one (AI) married a Muslim of South Asian background who grew up in America. Two daughters of
(AA) parents are currently divorced from American males who made token
conversions.

A trend among the daughters is marriage at a young age, as young as fifteen. This could be understood as part of the Muslim tradition of encouraging young couples to marry if they like each other. I note a difference based
on class, since the middle-class Muslim families with immigrant husbands
tend to stress education of the daughters to at least the college-degree level,

although in two cases the husbands met the girls while attending high school and waited for later marriage.

Several of the Sufi communal parents stressed marriage more than education, but not all agreed on this position. Attitudes toward the importance of maintaining virginity and the permissibility of gender mixing seemed to be a critical variable here. Qamar (AA) stated:

I'm not trying to control my daughters. I've pushed independence. Some people try to marry off their girls. I told them: "If you get pregnant I won't take care of your kids." They don't want to be used by men, and education is important to them. Al-hamdu l'illah, *my girls liked being in a group. We let them have guy friends. Half the human race is male, after all. They kept the proper etiquette and went out with a group.*

One mother, Rayhana (AI), whose daughter married a non-Muslim (AA) who said he would convert and later reneged, blamed the attitudes prevalent at her immigrant-dominated Islamic center at that time:

The [Muslim] community has to embrace the challenges it faces and open up and discuss things. No one was saying anything about the girls' marrying outside, so other young girls got the idea that they really "didn't get into much trouble." After all, there wasn't much scandal after they had been told all along that it was "so haram." No one was "honor killed" for out-marrying. Instead of talking about the problem, the parents just got tougher and tougher on their daughters. The community culture is unrealistic about boys and girls; we need to tell them what Islam says and why it makes sense socially and historically—and not just tell them "no."

Theorizing Female Muslim Identity in Mothers and Daughters

One place I found theory that was helpful in understanding gender in the lives of the convert mothers and their daughters is work on female participants in new religious movements (NRMs). Susan Palmer (1994), who studied women in the Hare Krishnas and Moonies, sees the choices made by female participants at least in part as a critique of secular gender roles. According to her analysis, women's conversion to unconventional religions could be interpreted as a response to "rolelessness resulting from dramatic upheavals in the structure of society," as well as a response to the devaluation of traditional women's roles in the modern West. Some of the women she studied were also seeking the magical or religious dimension missing in secular family relationships (Palmer 1994, xiii). Regarding the changes that have occurred in marriage dynamics in the modern West, Mary Ann Glendon observed: "Marriage has moved from a situation characterized by family selection of spouse to ... a veto by the child ... then to unfettered choice, and now to a situation where people may ... correct their original choice" (1985, 32).[15]

Overall, scholars who have attempted to analyze issues of sexuality in NRMs fall into two camps—those stressing the empowerment of women in unconventional groups versus those who view NRMs as a backlash against the feminist movement and a regression to patriarchal patterns (Palmer 1994, 6). The choice of Islam, while not exactly in the same category, perhaps, as joining an alternative religion or NRM, does offer a potentially radical reconfiguration of gender interactions. Islamic norms seem closest to what Palmer terms a "sex complementarity" philosophy of gender. While many converts to Islam accept this philosophy and enact it in their lives, there is a minority that negotiate gender in a way quite close to American norms, and in fact, modern Western culture and Muslim societies at the micro level each offer a continuum of gender philosophies and practices. That having been said, looking for a different approach to gender and the family as part of choosing Islam was not a specific motivating factor articulated by the women I interviewed. One woman (AA) indicated that her assumption of the female "role" was due to her husband's preference and not necessarily an Islamic norm.[16] In most cases the idea of a strong committed family life appeared to be important to the women and something they perceived as present in Islam.

The Sufi-oriented female converts characterized their reasons for converting primarily as a spiritual quest for meaning. The non-Sufis seemed to find Islamic theology more logical and convincing.[17] Still, gender practices were reconfigured in all cases. Several of the Sufi women, however, were not altogether comfortable with practices such as gender segregation. Qamar (AA), who wears the *hijab* but interacts with men, said:

I feel uncomfortable with a lot of the gender stuff in Islam. We don't have that stuff here [in America]. When people do that—gender segregating—they're trying to impose another cultural model. I advocate respect for both men and women. My daughters also think most of those things are ridiculous. They want to be natural with who they are as Americans. You have to be natural with your culture. At Sufi tariqa activities the men gather in one area and the women in another but it is natural. People acknowledge one another's existence.

According to Palmer's research, some new religious movements appeal to women more than others, and there is an elective affinity between specific choices and specific female interests: "Contributing to the argument that women select NRMs that serve their particular needs is evidence that different age sets are represented in different movements as are specific classes of women" (1994, 240).

It has been claimed that females in the West embrace Islam in disproportionately high numbers compared to males. I believe that this arises from the much stronger likelihood of born-Muslim males out-marrying and the limited mobility of born-Muslim women in choosing marriage partners. Therefore I propose that on this issue, only "individual" or "rational" converts should be compared, not those who convert in the context of marriage to a born Muslim, if the purpose is to assess factors motivating conversion aside from marriage and the relative numbers of converts according to gender. In addition, the "cost" of conversion to Euro-American males may be perceived as relatively higher, in socioeconomic terms.

Palmer's contention that women join unusual religious groups as part of experimental re-creation of self seems more applicable to the women in our sample attracted to Sufi movements, especially charismatic movements such as the Naqshbandis (1994, 239). Their communal lifestyle, in-marrying, and more visibly different practices and forms of dress position them closer to NRM adherents than women marrying immigrant Muslims and trying to integrate into a global, immigrant-dominated (in the American context) Muslim identity. For the mothers married to immigrants a whole other dynamic comes into play, which is negotiating a mixed marriage and moving between two different cultural worlds.[18]

Palmer concludes overall that such religious lifestyle choices reflect female empowerment strategies rather than oppression:

For this reason, the phenomenon of modern women choosing to inhabit the stylized roles in NRMs might be better understood not as a rejection of pluralism and contemporary experimentation..., nor as a lifelong choice to opt for traditional family values faced with gender uncertainty in the larger society..., but as the ancient and familiar search for powerful religious and social epiphanies available within the ritual passage. (Palmer 1994, 261)

Margaret (AI), reflecting on gender dynamics in raising daughters, said:

It's clear that there is culturally a differential treatment of boys and girls in our community. Boys have more liberty to go out and explore the world—it's part of becoming a man. I'm happy I didn't have both [sons and daughters] so I didn't face

that conflict. Islamically that shouldn't be an issue, both should have more experi-
ences of life. In the community, however, it's the girls who have to attend Islamic
schools. They are taught that careers for girls are more limited and they are not en-
couraged to excel.

Practice and Identity Compared across the Generations

One way of assessing the Islamic identity of mothers and daughters is through indexes of visibility such as veiling and using Islamic names. Taking a new Islamic name has been characterized by one scholar as "bridge burning" (Al-lievi 1998, 172). It seems on the basis of my interviews that women marrying immigrant Muslims were less likely to change their names; in this sample, three out of four did not. It is understandable that women married to fellow Euro-Americans may feel a greater need to assert their distinctive Muslim identity. In one case an American Muslim woman (AA) eventually stopped using her Muslim name and returned to her birth name.

As regards naming: six out of the eleven mothers use Muslim names, three of the four married to immigrants (AI) kept American names, and five of the seven married to Americans (AA) use Muslim names. One mother's name (Marika) was given at birth but sounds somewhat Muslim. For the daughters the picture is as follows: fifteen of the nineteen daughters have Muslim names and use them, including the three who have left Islam; one has a bicultural name; two (AI) sisters have American names; and one daughter (AI) uses her American name rather than her Muslim name (she used both contextually when growing up).

Comparing veiling among mothers and daughters, we see that eight out of the eleven convert mothers wear the *hijab.* Two of the three who do not wear it now each had worn it for a significant period of time (seven and twenty years). Among the daughters, fourteen out of the nineteen do not currently wear the *hijab.* Eleven from the AA families and three from the AI families do not wear it. Among the five daughters who do wear the *hijab* are three AA and two AI. Marika (AA) describes her Muslim identity as follows, in terms of both practice and interpretive orientation.

Muslim American, I'm Sunni and not a very good Muslim. Before we were striv-
ing, now we're just getting by. I do the Islamic practices, I pray and fast. I took off
the hijab, *which I had worn for twenty years when I started getting hot flashes.*
The scholars say that's not OK. It should only come off if you have no more sexual

desire. Even in the old days I used to tie the scarf behind my neck. Sufis are accepting of people as they come. I see Sufis practicing that acceptance. Others don't have that sense of generosity and kindness of heart. I would prefer to be sloppy in practice and outer form while trying to be perfect in the inner form.

A striking observation is that all but one of the married daughters are raising their children as Muslims. Two daughters who left Islam are younger and not yet married; a third who has left has a baby who likely will not be raised Muslim. The three daughters (AA) who have left Islam consider themselves agnostics, not following any other religion.[19] Nine of the nineteen daughters were identified by the mother as having less Muslim identity than she does; of those, five were still considered "adequately practicing" by the mother. Seven daughters were identified as having the same level of Islamic practice as their mothers. Alice (AA), the mother of a fifteen-year-old daughter who at present rejects Islam, said:

From the outside—I would have imagined myself encouraging her to get into her twenties and then decide, but I feel certain that Islam is the best, the capstone of religions. I know she still has it in her heart and she should follow that. I would be heartbroken if she married a non-Muslim, although I will always love her whatever she does. I feel it is not necessary for her to go on a spiritual journey. She doesn't need to go through the pain I went through.

Marika (AA), commenting on her children's Islamic identity, stated:

I see them making life choices that Islam is still a part of. They are outwardly less religious than I am but they have a strong core. Rahima's [her third daughter] identity is definitely Islamic, while her dress and demeanor are definitely American. None of them is doing all the Muslim things but all are doing at least some. They're making choices about who they are and what they are going to do. There's the path. I'm there with a broom trying to herd them along it from either side.

Transmitting Muslim Identity

The mothers discussed the need for a balance between maintaining controls and participation in normal childhood activities. Linda (AI) commented:

We had to put restrictions. They couldn't go to slumber parties. However, we taught them to swim when they were young. They had few Muslim friends in the neighborhood, but later my younger daughter did in high school. Girls tend to get infatuated with boys—it's hard to control that but you have to set limits. We planned a night out with other Muslim kids instead of the prom, and rather than going to the mall with non-Muslims we provided alternative activities. I went to the Muslim camps with them as a counselor. At the camp we had problems with issues of gender segregation. One year the boys refused to attend campfire if girls performed something. The next year we held separate camps for boys and girls and this was good for the girls, they didn't have to worry about makeup, being self-conscious, and so on.

Fatima (AA), now a single mother, whose twenty-year-old daughter identifies herself as Muslim but no longer practices, said:

The boys started asking her out (for a sandwich or something) in sixth grade, she was very attractive. They were nice boys from good families but I put restrictions on her because of our being Muslim. In junior high she stopped asking me—I should have realized something was going on, but I was relieved. In fact, she was sneaking out and got into a sleazy crowd, experimenting with drugs, and so on. Eventually she got into all kinds of trouble and was out of control completely. She had no Muslim friends.

At the Sufi dhikrs she asked troubling questions—she had to wear a scarf and saw and heard things she didn't understand. My philosophy had been, I'll teach her the external practice first and the inner meaning later. I wanted her to grow up Sufi. Now I feel I should have let her date, it's just everything to them at that age. Eventually she did go to the prom in a beautiful dress. I hope she makes it through college. I don't try to discuss Islam with her anymore.

Alice (AA), whose daughter, 15, rejects her Islamic identity, said:

Now a crisis is brewing. My daughter moaned: "I guess you're not going to let me go to the prom." A Muslim scholar friend said: "Let her. Don't make her turn away from you as well as Islam."

Margaret (AI), whose daughters are practicing and liberal, reminisced:

The girls could not date in high school or go to proms. I explained to them that it is "fleeting fun" and the difference between "love and passion." I made it up to them in other ways, like special outings.

Birth order seems to play an important role in how contentious these issues are for daughters. In all cases the only or elder daughter is perceived by the mother as being more independent-minded and potentially rebellious than her younger siblings. Maliha (AA), reflecting on why this might be the case, suggested:

For the elder child, the parents don't even know how to do it. You need the support of traditional community. In America you either have to keep her in isolation, which is crazy, or you have to guard her like a hawk.

It is important and probably inevitable that American daughters have choices about their Islamic identities. Margaret (AI) said: "Our daughters have the sense that they chose Islam; questioning is OK and they do question."

In transmitting Muslim identities to the daughters, the mothers' sources of support are crucial. Linda (AI), whose husband is a staunchly conservative immigrant Muslim, named her spouse as her main source.

My husband was my main source of support in raising my children as Muslims. I never took advice from my mother-in-law, who stayed with us part of the time—my husband used to mediate between us, and he usually took my side. He knew what to teach the kids about Islam and life. He was completely committed to the path of being Muslim.

Interestingly, two women whose daughters seem to be rejecting Islam were ones who had complaints about the role of their husbands. One of them, Rayhana (AI), the mother of a daughter who married a non-Muslim American, responded to the question about support as follows:

My main source of support was other Muslim friends who were like a family—we are still close after thirty years. A problem I felt was that most [born] Muslim mothers have stories to tell their kids—like if you drop food on the floor and it's still OK, you should eat it. I didn't have those stories so I felt I lacked authenticity. My husband had them but when was he around? Men are not there in those simple moments. I was like a sibling to my children in learning about Islam, my Arabic, my learning suras, was like them, in fact they were better than me.

The Sufi women living communally (AA) often noted their husbands as major helpers, very involved in the children's upbringing as Muslims. Other sources of support mentioned were the Muslim community, in the cases of those who experienced it as supportive and available, the Sufi shaykh and his teachings, and Allah. Marika (AA) commented on her efforts to create Muslim identity for her daughters:

You know, becoming Muslim is a lot like becoming an orphan. Our main problem is lack of community and lack of older people—to show you the way. It's a total cultural change—you lose your traditions when you convert. What do you tell your children for bedtime stories? Now we have all these wonderful things but then, I looked for Arab folktales. I had lived in Iran for six years as a child and I had cloth dolls from there the same size as my Barbies. I played with them together and they were all friends. I made my children Muslim cloth dolls. It was important for their identity that they had toys like that.

Generation and Gender

A distinction has been made by Harriet B. Nielsen between gender subjectivity and gender identity. Gender subjectivity is how others project a specific gender role onto the subject; gender identity is how the subject identifies, constructs, and imagines her gender role. In general, the moratorium period of youth/adolescence is considered to be the time for being the most self-reflective about gender identity (1993, 44).

The issue of shifting gender roles in Western cultures is an important backdrop for understanding the conversion experiences of the American women who become Muslim. In a sense, Islamic gender roles are an experiment for convert Muslim women. Their attraction to this difference may be understood as a personal spiritual choice that they find empowering, and this is consistent with Palmer's argument, as noted earlier.

On the one hand, these roles represent a form of cultural experimentation—in terms of adopting a new paradigm of gender, with new restrictions on sexuality, social relationships, and other forms of embodiment. At the same time, the relationships between the converted mothers and their daughters also occur within the context of generational shifts in dominant gender-role issues for American women, as explained by Nielsen (1993).

According to Nielsen the generation of women coming of age in the 1930s or '40s faced the beginnings of youth cultures and a loosening of sexual morality. Although they wanted to "live" before marriage, there were few social and cultural possibilities to break out of the mold and most married young. They transferred some of their thwarted ambitions to their daughters born in the 1940s and '50s—the generation of the mothers studied in this chapter—who had very different cultural and social possibilities. These women experienced gendered subjectivities with modernized versions of gender identity that encouraged, above all, achievement in education and career. In mainstream American culture, conflicts arose for many women in this cohort, for whom mothering was delayed or seen as a burden. In addition, the

late 1960s and early '70s were a time of great social upheaval and a loosening of restrictions on sexual experimentation. According to Nielsen, these
daughters inherited both their mothers' "updated" gender identity (how they
felt about gender) and their mothers' old-fashioned gender subjectivity (how
others and the society perceived them as women).

In terms of identity for younger females (the daughters) today, Nielsen
suggests that "it is more culturally manifold—and the construction of it is
more a personal project for the girl" (1993, 50–52). She can play with gender
in new ways, while she will have great demands on her in terms of quality of
performance and self-control. Fatima (AA), a single mother whose daughter
rebelled and now does not follow any Islamic norms, although she has not
formally rejected the religion,[20] stated:

*I had a strong sense of wanting her to have the [Muslim] identity, then a woman
friend in our Sufi tariqa said: "She'll grow up and do whatever she wants, because
she's American." I said: "Not my daughter." But if we went to any mosque or dhikr
the women were always in the back. She would ask me and I felt she couldn't understand why yet. Then later I told her: "Because men are animals and can't control
themselves." Before she stopped going to dhikrs at age ten she asked: "Why do the
women have to stay in the back? It's not fair." She said: "The Qur'an sounds like it's
written for men." The shaykh is male, so she couldn't fully identify with him either.
"It's a man's religion."*

Maliha (AA) resists traditional discourses on gender "roles," while affirming a progressive Islamic *ijtihad* regarding gender justice:

*Gender: throw out the roles! I go back to the Qur'anic verse that "humanity was first
created from a single soul, and then from her mate."[21] It starts with the womb, "rahm."
I personally lead a traditional woman's role because my husband wants that. My
daughters, like everyone else, live in a world where everybody works. The traditional
thing is unjust in that context because women end up doing twice the work. Roles and
assignments are not the way to work things out. In the next fifty years or so women
will not have to be so strident and men will recognize women's humanity. The movement for women's rights is in keeping with the sunna. The Prophet was absolutely
marvelous to women, both men and women should take him as their role model.*

I observe that the four women I interviewed who are in long-term AI
marriages seem to have held relatively conservative views about gender issues and "family values" before conversion and had already been critical
of the moral condition of American society. Overall, discourses on Muslim

motherhood played little role in the informants' self-presentation. Only one AA mother mentioned that "heaven is at the feet of mothers" and "Mary is the first in heaven."

Research on the influence of mothers on their daughters' attitudes to gender has determined that two factors are most important. One is the level of the mother's education and whether she is employed. The second is the style of parenting: authoritative (demands for mature behavior that also take the child's individuality into account, while seeking to induce an understanding of parental expectations and sanctions) versus authoritarian (high demands and uncompromising attitudes). Since educated mothers tend to hold more nontraditional attitudes toward gender roles, this will give more scope for daughters making independent choices (Carine and Janssens 1998, 173). This analysis seems fairly intuitive; perhaps the main relevance to our study is that so many convert mothers explicitly regard authoritarian models as ineffective. Several comments were made by mothers who blamed rules' not being sufficiently explained for their daughters' eventual major transgressions, such as marrying non-Muslims or rejecting Islamic norms. The need to set the example yourself and to be moderate was often cited. Jamila (AA) gave the following advice:

Go towards leniency, not strictness. Don't be too strict or caring about outer things like keeping children from watching TV or movies and leading a normal American life. Then they will run towards those things as the shaykh says: "Like fish trying to swallow the ocean." Love and enjoy them. Respect them.

Margaret (AI) recommended: "Don't turn them off by excessive pressure. They shouldn't feel they always have to be reading Qur'an or praying; movies and things like that are OK too."

Conclusions

The scope of this study was limited to Euro-American convert women living in the United States. Much work remains to be done on other subjects. For example, the experiences of African American women will be essential.[22] This limited sample suggests that Euro-American women who convert to Islam with a conscious commitment to the religion, whether they marry other Americans with similar commitments or religiously observant immigrant males, are raising their daughters with a Muslim identity that is strong. The evidence of this strength is the daughters' preference for Muslim marriage

Table 10.1. Biographical Summaries of Hermansen's Interviewees

Name	Age/year Conv	Age	Married	# Of D's	Age Of Daughters	Hijab	Type	Lifestyle
Alice	24/1977	51	A	1	15	N	mod/Sufi	urban
Linda	28/1967	64	I	2	33, 26	Y	Activist	urban
Margaret	31/1978	56	I	2	28, 23	Y	moderate	urban
Biqis	28/1976	54	A	1	29	Y	Sufi (N)	comm
Rayhana	18/1967	50	I	1	29	Y	Activist	urban
Fatima	33/1978	57	A	1	20	Y	Sufi (N)	urban
Jamila	25/1976	52	A	2	22, 19	Y	Sufi (N)	comm
Lorraine	34/1980	57	I	2	23, 20	N	moderate	urban
Maliha	33/1971	64	A	2	23, 21	Y	Sufi	rural
Marika	19/1975	46	A	6(4)	25, 23, 21, 18	N	Sufi	comm
Qamar	24/1976	52	A	3	25, 20, 18	Y	Sufi (N)	comm

partners and their raising children as Muslims. Factors in diffusing this identity are the absence of a surrounding and supportive Muslim community and a Muslim peer group as the child is growing up, especially in adolescence, and the absence of a committed Muslim father.

I note that the two women I interviewed who had converted in the 1960s and married immigrant males were quite different in outlook from those who converted in the 1970s. These two early women converts both came from small towns, and their style of being Muslim is both activist and conservative.

The later cohort of women are mostly those that had a strong element of interest in Sufism and spirituality (about seven out of nine) in their biographies. It remains to be seen if such interests will persist among future cohorts of converts, but my impression is that most spiritual movements, including American Sufism, that emerged during the counterculture period are now "graying," with membership not being replaced by younger recruits. This is not to say that conversion to Islam by Euro-Americans is declining. I suggest, rather, that Sufi-oriented conversions may be decreasing.

As I mentioned earlier, a fuller picture of the transmission of Islamic identity in families where the mothers are Western converts must be traced in future cohorts as well. Demographic shifts in the Muslim populations in the United States, changes in the attitudes of many Muslims toward a more conservative and politicized orientation, and the greater availability of Islamic centers and full-time education are all likely to have an important impact in the future that could influence the results I found among this early cohort of women converts.

Notes

1. Shaykh Nazim, a Naqshbandi Sufi from Cyprus, and his son-in-law, Shaykh Hisham Kabbani, are the heads of the Naqshbandi-Haqqani *tariqa*, a global Sufi movement that has attracted many Western converts to Islam.

2. Gabriele Hofmann talks about the role of the Naqshbandis in Germany. She quotes one researcher, Dornback, who said that in 1991 there were one to two hundred members of the movement. Hofmann estimates German membership at five hundred to a thousand by about 1995.

3. Marcia Hermansen, "Two-Way Acculturation" (1991), discusses later cohorts of convert women who adopt a more oppositional style.

4. Author interview with Maliha (AA).

5. Referring to Lofland and Stark 1965, 864.

6. In addition, Allievi proposes a distinction between "relational" conversions and "rational" ones that is useful, but seems to become blurred in many AI marriages.

7. Hermansen also comments on this shift in Western attitudes to conversion in "Roads to Mecca" (1999).

8. Here and throughout the rest of this chapter, I provide direct quotations in the voices of my interviewees to provide texture and evidence for the points made. The accompanying chart (p. 272) will help readers who wish to know more about the "convert" profile of the woman who made the statement.

9. Allievi comments on converts' careers and businesses in *Les convertis* (1998), 204–205.

10. *Be Here Now* (San Cristobal, N.Mex.: Lama Foundation, 1971) is a book by the American guru Baba Ram Das, aka Richard Alpert.

11. According to a tradition *(hadith)* of the Prophet Muhammad.

12. A *juz'* is one-thirtieth of the Qur'an. Memorization of one-thirtieth is quite a respectable achievement and is the amount required for certification from many of the formal imam training programs in the United States.

13. This is common in South Asian Muslim families, in which sounding out the Qur'an without full knowledge of Arabic grammar and syntax is standard practice. Linda's family had lived abroad for several years in the Arab world, so her children have a rudimentary knowledge, but no command, of Arabic. One daughter gravitated more to her father's heritage and learned Urdu quite well through her grandmother, later her high school friends from South Asia, and, currently, her in-laws.

14. Allievi comments on the tendency of the marriages between two European Muslims to be unions of Sufi Muslims (2000, 164). I do know of two divorced female American Sufis of this cohort who later in life married Sufi-oriented Muslim immigrants who were older widowers. I expect that most immigrant males in the

1970s who would have been Sufi-oriented would have contracted traditional arranged marriages within their own ethnic communities.

15. Quoted in Palmer 1994, 6.

16. Author interview with Maliha (AA).

17. Reflecting Allievi's categories of rational and mystical. See note 6.

18. Some aspects of this are discussed in Anway (1996, 11–128), although the women she discusses are from a later and more conservative cohort.

19. One is tempted to conclude that (AA) daughters are more likely to leave Islam. A larger sample would be needed to establish this, and anecdotal evidence suggests otherwise: one son of an (AI) family in my sample married a non-Muslim and no longer practices, and I have heard of two AI daughters from an activist family not included in this study who have left Islam.

20. Fatima states, for example, that her daughter would fill out "Muslim" on any form inquiring about religious identification.

21. Qur'an (4: 1). This is the sort of new reading that Muslim feminists make, and Maliha is aware of this. The word for soul in Arabic, *nafs*, is grammatically feminine, thus a reading of "her" mate is quite possible, although traditional commentaries saw Adam as the primal generator of humanity, rather than Eve.

22. Further variations could include studying mothers whose commitment to Islam is not as conscious and strong, or eventually studying a younger generation of other mothers whose ideological commitment to Muslim identity is more "combative." Also, the study of Muslim converts who already have children before conversion is important. In the cases I have heard of, these children reject Islam. For example, an eight-year-old daughter of parents who became Sufi Muslims eventually rejected Islam and went to live with her grandparents. Other important variations might include studying Christian women married to Muslims who agree to raise their daughters as Muslims, American women who marry Muslims and move to the Middle East, and American women who marry nonpracticing Muslims—and who either become religious Muslims themselves or do not. Other possible subjects of study are American Muslim men who marry immigrant Muslim women, and the sons of convert marriages.

References

Allievi, St. 1998. *Les convertis à l'islam. Les nouveaux musulmans d'Europe.* Paris: L'Harmattan.

———. 1999. "Pour une sociologie des conversions: lorsque des Europeens deviennent musulmans." *Social Compass* 46 (3): 283–300.

———. 2000. "Les Conversions à l'islam." In *Paroles d'islam,* ed. Felice Dassetto, pp. 157–182. Paris: Maisonneuve et Larose.

Anway, C. A. 1996. *Daughters of Another Path: Experiences of American Women Choosing Islam.* Lee's Summit, Mo.: Yawna Publications.

———. 1998. "American Women Choosing Islam." In *Muslims on the Americanization Path?,* ed. Y. Y. Haddad and J. L. Esposito, pp. 179–198. Atlanta: Scholars Press.

Bakhtiar, L. 1996. *Sufi Women of America: Angels in the Making.* Chicago: Kazi Publications.

Berger, P. L., and Th. Luckmann. 1966. *The Social Construction of Reality.* New York: Doubleday.

Carine, T. G. M., and J. M. A. M. Janssens. 1998. "Maternal Influence on Daughters' Gender Roles and Attitudes." *Sex Roles: A Journal of Research* 38 (3/4): 171–186.

Franks, M. 2001. *Women and Revivalism in the West: Choosing Fundamentalism in a Liberal Democracy.* New York: Palgrave.

Glendon, M. A. 1985. *The New Family and the New Property.* Toronto: Butterworth.

Hermansen, M. 1991. "Two-Way Acculturation: Muslim Women in America." In *Muslims of America,* ed. Y. Haddad, pp. 188–201. New York: Oxford University Press.

————. 1999. "Roads to Mecca: Conversion Narratives of European and Euro-American Muslims." *Muslim World* 89 (1): 56–89.

Hofmann, G. 1997. *Muslimin Werden: Frauen in Deutschland konvertieren zum Islam.* Frankfurt am Main: Universität Frankfurt.

Laughlin, M. L. 1999. "Eating Poison: A Tale of Women and Discipleship in a Naqshbandi Sufi Community." Master's thesis, University of Washington.

Lofland, J., and R. Stark. 1965. "Becoming a World Saver: A Theory of Conversion to a Deviant Perspective." *American Sociological Review* 30 (4): 862–875.

Mansson, A. 2002. *Becoming Muslim: Meanings of Conversion to Islam.* Lund, Sweden: Lund University.

Nielsen, H. B. 1993. "Whatever Happened to Gender? Female Subjectivity and Change in a Generational Context." In *Daughtering and Mothering: Female Subjectivity Reanalyzed,* ed. J. van Mens-Verhulst, K. Schreurs, and L. Woertman, pp. 44–53. London: Routledge.

Palmer, S. J. 1994. *Moon Sisters, Krishna Mothers, Rajneesh Lovers: Women's Roles in New Religions.* Syracuse, N.Y.: Syracuse University Press.

Poston, L. 1992. *Islamic Da'wah in the West: Muslim Missionary Activity and the Dynamics of Conversion to Islam.* New York: Oxford University Press.

Rambo, L. R. 1993. *Understanding Religious Conversion.* New Haven, Conn.: Yale University Press.

Roald, A. S. 2001. *Women in Islam: The Western Experience.* New York: Routledge.

Travisano, R. V. 1970. "Alternation and Conversion as Qualitatively Different Transformation." In *Social Psychology through Symbolic Interaction,* ed. G. P. Stone and H. A. Faberman, pp. 594–606. Waltham, Mass.: Ginn-Blaisdell.

Van Mens-Verhulst, J., K. Schreurs, and L. Woertman. 1993. *Daughtering and Mothering: Female Subjectivity Reanalyzed.* New York: Routledge.

Wohlrab-Sahr, M. 1999. "Conversion to Islam: Between Syncretism and Symbolic Battle." *Social Compass* 46 (3): 351–362.

Notes on Contributors

STEFANO ALLIEVI is a Professor in Sociology at the University of Padua. He specializes on migration issues and in the sociology of religion and cultural change, and has particularly focused his studies and research on the presence of Islam in and the religious pluralization of Europe. He has written numerous works on these topics, among them: *Muslim Networks and Transnational Communities in and across Europe* (edited with J. S. Nielsen) (Brill, 2003); *Muslims in the Enlarged Europe: Religion and Society* (edited with B. Maréchal, F. Dassetto, and J. S. Nielsen) (Brill, 2003). He is also the author of *Les convertis à l'islam. Les nouveaux musulmans d'Europe* (L'Harmattan, 1998).

MARGOT BADRAN is a Senior Fellow at the Center for Muslim-Christian Understanding at Georgetown University, is currently Edith Kreeger Wolf Distinguished Visiting Professor in the Department of Religion and Preceptor at the Institute for the Study of Islam in the Program of African Studies at Northwestern University. Her main publications include *Feminists, Islam, and Nation: Gender and the Making of Modern Egypt* (Princeton University Press, 1995); and, with M. Cooke, *Opening the Gates: A Century of Arab Feminist Writing* (Indiana University Press, 1990/2004).

NICOLE BOURQUE is Senior Lecturer in Social Anthropology, University of Glasgow. Her main research interests center on religious change and the role religion plays in everyday life. Her research has focused on religious rituals, festivals, and pilgrimage in Ecuador and Bolivia. Her recent research interest is religious conversion to Islam in Britain. She has published several articles on conversion, among them: "Doing Anthropology in Your Own Backyard: The Experience of Doing Fieldwork amongst Converts to Islam in Glasgow," in *Anthropology in Action* 4 (3): 47–51 (1998), and "Being British and Muslim: Dual Identity amongst New and Young Muslims," in *University Lectures in Islamic Studies*, ed. Alan Jones, pp. 2:1–18 (London: Altajir World of Islam Trust, 1998).

YVONNE YAZBECK HADDAD is a Professor of History of Islam and Christian-Muslim Relations at Georgetown University. She has studied contemporary Islam in its many aspects, ranging from the political to the legal, the sectarian to the pluralistic, while examining issues such as foreign policy, immigration, gender, and identity. She is the author of several books dealing with Muslim women, Islam in America, and Christian-Muslim relations. Her main publications include: *Islam, Gender and Social Change* (Oxford University Press, 1998); *Muslims on the Americanization Path?* (Oxford University Press, 2000); *Daughters of Abraham: Feminist Thought in Judaism, Christianity and Islam* (University Press of Florida, 2001); *Muslim Minorities in the West: Visible and Invisible* (Altamira Press, 2002); *Muslims in the West: From Sojourners to Citizens* (Oxford University Press, 2002).

MARCIA HERMANSEN is Professor of Theology at Loyola University in Chicago. She teaches courses in Islamic studies and world religions. She has written numerous articles in the field of Islamic thought, Islam and Muslims in South Asia, Muslims in America, and women in Islam. Among her publications are *The Conclusive Argument from God, a study and translation from the Arabic of Shah Wali Allah of Delhi's Hujjat Allah al Baligha* (Leiden: Brill, 1996); "Two-Way Acculturation: Muslim Women in America," in *The Muslims of America*, ed. Y. Haddad, pp. 188–201 (New York: Oxford University Press, 1991); and "Roads to Mecca: Conversion Narratives of European and Euro-American Muslims," in *Muslim World* 89 (1): 56–89.

WILLY JANSEN is an anthropologist and currently Professor of Women's Studies at the University of Nijmegen. Her research in Algeria on marginalized gender categories resulted in the book *Women without Men: Gender and Marginality in an Algerian Town* (Brill, 1987). She further published on such topics as gender identity, sexuality, Islam, Christian mission in the Middle East, and food rituals. Currently her main research topic concerns the history of women's education in the Middle East, with Jordan as a case study.

HAIFAA JAWAD is a Senior Lecturer in Middle Eastern and Islamic Studies at the Department of Theology, University of Birmingham. She has specialized in the sociopolitical study of Islam, modern Islamic thought, Islam and the West, Islamic spirituality, and women's issues in Islam. Currently she is working on *Islamic Feminism: Leadership Roles and Public Representation.* Her recent publications include: *The Middle East in the New World Order* (ed.)

(Macmillan, 1997); *The Rights of Women in Islam: An Authentic Approach* (Macmillan, 1998); *Muslim Women in the United Kingdom and Beyond: Experiences and Images* (coeditor with T. Benn) (Brill, 2003); and "Muslim Feminism: A Case Study of Amina Wadud's Quran and Woman," in *Journal of Islamic Studies* 42, no. 1 (Spring 2003).

KARIN VAN NIEUWKERK is a Lecturer in Social Anthropology at the University of Nijmegen and a Postdoctoral Fellow at ISIM (Institute of Islam in the Modern World), the Netherlands. Her main fields of interest are entertainment in Egypt, conversion to Islam, and Islam and migration. Her main publications include: *"A Trade like Any Other": Female Singers and Dancers in Egypt* (University of Texas Press, 1995); "On Religion, Gender, and Performing: Female Performance and Repentance in Egypt," in *Music and Gender: Perspectives from the Mediterranean*, ed. T. Magrini (University of Chicago Press, 2003); "Veils and Wooden Clogs Don't Go Together," *Ethnos Journal of Anthropology* 69 (2).

ANNE SOFIE ROALD is an Associate Professor at the School of International Migration and Ethnic Relations (IMER), Malmö University. She teaches religious studies as well as methodological and theoretical issues within social sciences. She has conducted fieldwork among Muslims in Jordan, Pakistan, Malaysia, the United Arab Emirates, Great Britain, and Scandinavia, where she has investigated Muslim responses to modernity. She has dealt with issues such as Islamization of knowledge; Islamic education; modern Islamic movements; Muslim communities in Europe; and Muslim minority communities, gender relations, and the role of converts in majority society. Her main publications include: *Tarbiya: Education and Politics in Islamic Movements in Jordan and Malaysia* (Almqvist & Wiksell International, 1994); *Women in Islam: The Western Experience* (Routledge, 2001); and *New Muslims in the European Context: The Experience of Scandinavian Converts* (Brill, forthcoming). She has written various articles, among them "The Mecca of Gender Equality: Muslim Women in Sweden," in *Muslim Women in the United Kingdom and Beyond: Experiences and Images*, ed. H. Jawad and T. Benn (Brill, 2003).

GWENDOLYN ZOHARAH SIMMONS is an Assistant Professor of Religion at the University of Florida. She received her M.A. and Ph.D. in Religious Studies from Temple University. Her primary academic focus in Islam is on Islamic law and its impact on Muslim women. She has conducted research in Jordan, Egypt, Palestine, and Syria on the Shari'ah's contemporary impact on women and the women's movements in those countries to change these laws. She currently teaches courses on Islam; women and Islam; African American religious traditions; and race, religion, and rebellion. Simmons has a thorough grounding in Sufism, having studied seventeen years with the contemporary Sufi mystic Shaykh M. R. Bawa Muhaiyadeen. In addition to her academic and spiritual studies she has a long history in the area of civil rights, human rights, and peace work. She has published several articles including: "Striving for Muslim Women's Rights—Before and beyond Beijing: An African American Perspective," in *Windows of Faith*, ed. G. Webb (Syracuse University Press, 2000); "Are We up to the Challenge? The Need for a Radical Re-Ordering of the Islamic Discourse on Women," in *Progressive Muslims: On Justice, Gender and Pluralism*, ed. O. Safi (One World Press, 2003).

MONIKA WOHLRAB-SAHR is a Professor of Sociology of Religion at the University of Leipzig. She was a visiting scholar at the University of California, Berkeley, and Chair of the Sociology of Religion Section in the German Sociological Association. Her fields of research include temporary work, conversion to Islam, and secularization and social transformation in East Germany. Her main publications include *Konversion zum Islam in Deutschland und den USA* (Campus Verlag, 1999) and "Conversion to Islam: Between Syncretism and Symbolic Battle," in *Social Compass* 46 (1999): 351–362. She is coeditor of the book series *Religion in der Gesellschaft*.

Index